SPALDING'S
World Tour

SPALDING'S
World Tour

———⟫●⟪———

THE EPIC ADVENTURE
THAT TOOK BASEBALL
AROUND THE GLOBE—
AND MADE IT AMERICA'S GAME

MARK LAMSTER

PUBLICAFFAIRS

New York

Credits: The photos and illustrations on pages xii, 6, 7, 15, 20, 32, 39, 130, 178,
179, 198, 218, 219, and 249 are courtesy of the National Baseball Hall of Fame
Library, Cooperstown, New York.
The photo on page 49 is courtesy the Photo Collection, Miriam and Ira D.
Wallach Division of Art, Prints and Photographs, The New York Public
Library, Astor, Lenox and Tilden Foundations.
The photo on page 123 is courtesy Robert Edward Auctions.
The figures on page 242 are courtesy MastroNet.com.
All other images are from the author's personal collection.

Printed in the United States of America.

PublicAffairs books are available at special discounts for bulk purchases in the
U.S. by corporations, institutions, and other organizations. For more
information, please contact the Special Markets Department at the Perseus
Books Group, 11 Cambridge Center, Cambridge, MA 02142,
call (617) 252-5298, or email special.markets@perseusbooks.com.

Library of Congress Cataloging-in-Publication Data
Lamster, Mark, 1969-
Spalding's world tour : the epic adventure that took baseball around
the globe-and made it America's game / Mark Lamster.
p. cm.
Includes bibliographical references and index.
ISBN-13: 978-1-58648-311-1 (hardcover : alk. paper)
ISBN-10: 1-58648-311-0 (hardcover : alk. paper) 1. Spalding, A. G. (Albert
Goodwill) 2. Baseball—United States—History—19th century. 3. Baseball—
United States—History—20th century. I. Title.
GV863.A1L26 2006
796.357092—dc22
2006003615

For Anna,
and for my grandfather,
Brandon "Bud" Stone, 1914–2005

"EVERYTHING IS POSSIBLE
TO HIM WHO DARES."

—*Albert G. Spalding*

❧ Contents ❧

MAP O

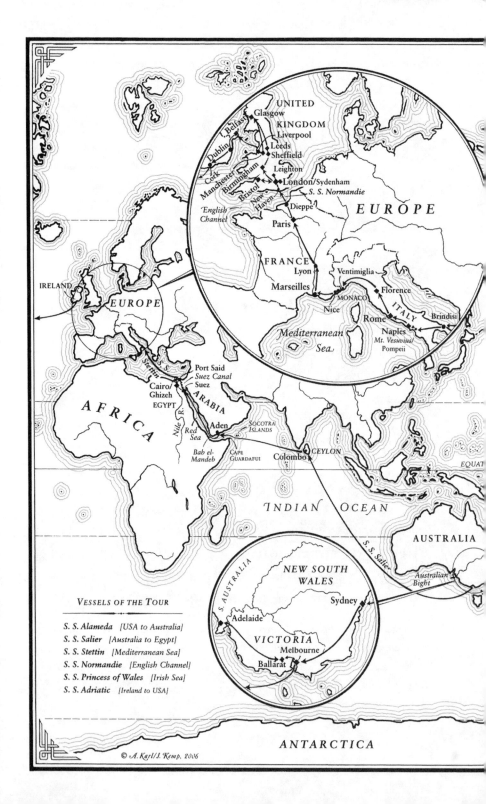

UNITED KINGDOM

Glasgow
Belfast
Dublin
Cork
Manchester
Birmingham
Bristol
Liverpool
Leeds
Sheffield
Leighton
London/Sydenham
S. S. Normandie
New Haven
Dieppe
English Channel
Paris

EUROPE

FRANCE
Lyon
Marseilles
Nice
MONACO
Ventimiglia
Florence
ITALY
Rome
Naples
Mt. Vesuvius/ Pompeii
Brindisi

Mediterranean Sea

IRELAND

EUROPE

S. S. Stettin

Port Said
Suez Canal
Suez
Cairo/ Ghizeh
EGYPT
ARABIA
Nile R.
Red Sea
Aden
Bab el- Mandeb
CAPE GUARDAFUI
SOCOTRA ISLANDS

AFRICA

Colombo
CEYLON
EQUAT

INDIAN OCEAN

AUSTRALIA
S. S. Salier
Australian Bight

NEW SOUTH WALES

S. AUSTRALIA
Adelaide
VICTORIA
Melbourne
Ballarat
Sydney

ANTARCTICA

VESSELS OF THE TOUR

S. S. Alameda   [USA to Australia]
S. S. Salier   [Australia to Egypt]
S. S. Stettin   [Mediterranean Sea]
S. S. Normandie   [English Channel]
S. S. Princess of Wales   [Irish Sea]
S. S. Adriatic   [Ireland to USA]

© A. Karl/J. Kemp. 2006

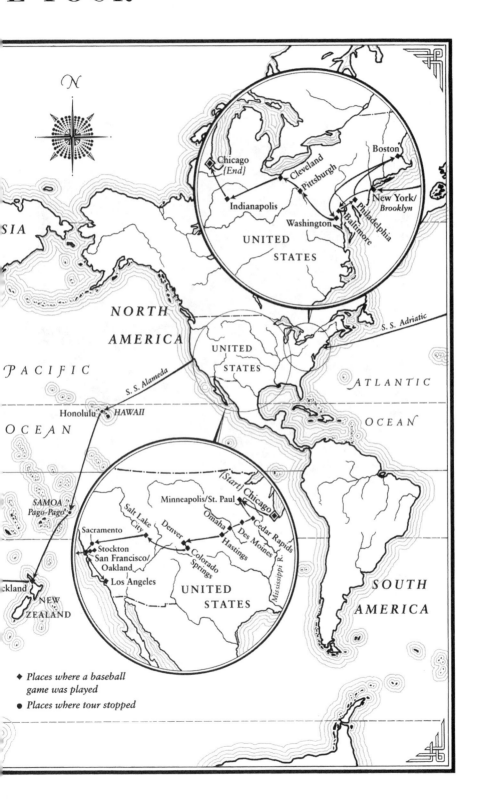

N

S.S. Adriatic

Boston
New York/
Brooklyn
Cleveland
Pittsburgh
Philadelphia
Chicago
[End]
Baltimore
Indianapolis
Washington
UNITED
STATES

NORTH
AMERICA
UNITED
STATES
ATLANTIC

PACIFIC
OCEAN

S.S. Alameda

Honolulu HAWAII
OCEAN

SAMOA
Pago-Pago

[Start] Chicago
Minneapolis/St. Paul
Cedar Rapids
Salt Lake City
Denver
Omaha
Des Moines
Sacramento
Stockton
Hastings
San Francisco/
Oakland
Colorado
Springs
Los Angeles
UNITED
STATES

ckland
NEW
ZEALAND

SOUTH
AMERICA

Mississippi R.

◆ Places where a baseball
   game was played
● Places where tour stopped

⇜ Prologue ⇝

A Galaxy of Stars

Shortly before seven o'clock on the evening of April 8, 1889, a jubilant gang of men stepped from the lobby of New York's posh Fifth Avenue Hotel and began a brisk walk uptown. Dressed in black tie and strapping to a man, they drew glances from all whom they passed, but cloaked by their good cheer and camaraderie they seemed oblivious to the attention. Leading the way, with his thick brush mustache neatly combed into place, was Albert Goodwill Spalding, at thirty-eight years of age already an American icon and master of the sporting-goods empire that still bears his name. Gathered around him were nineteen of America's greatest baseball stars. Together, they were on their way to Delmonico's, the city's most exclusive restaurant, just three short blocks up the avenue.

Two days earlier Spalding and his men had returned from an epic journey on which they had circumnavigated the globe. Their mission, endorsed by President Grover Cleveland, had been to bring baseball, America's budding national game, to the far reaches of the earth. In their six months abroad these hardball proselytizers had covered five continents and nearly thirty thousand miles. Now, finally, the intrepid group had made it back home, and on this night they would celebrate their adventure at a gala testimonial dinner, the first of many, to be attended by the cream of New York society.

It took just a few minutes for Spalding to guide the group to Delmonico's Twenty-sixth Street entrance, where they were immediately whisked to an anteroom adjoining the restaurant's second-floor ballroom. Everything had been precisely coordinated for their arrival. A gaggle of stewards were ready to take their coats, hats, and canes. Inside, three massive crystal chandeliers set the broad room aglow with gaslight, and a full orchestra played "Yankee Doodle" from a balcony festooned with flags and bunting. Red damask walls were animated by handsomely framed photographic portraits of the players on their journey: men in baseball uniforms riding through the streets of Ceylon in wobbly rickshaws, climbing about the great Sphinx in Egypt, standing in the Roman Coliseum, posing before a game in London for the Prince of Wales. Six long tables extended across the room, each with a towering centerpiece of freshly cut flowers surmounted by a three-foot-tall figure of a baseball player in action. (These *pièces montées*, a Delmonico's specialty, took four days to sculpt from a secret recipe of confectioner's sugar, egg yolks, and isinglass—a gelatin made of fish bladders). Waiting for the players to make their celebratory entrance were more than two hundred luminaries from the worlds of politics, finance, law, society, theater, art, literature, and sports. Placed neatly at each setting was a nine-page souvenir menu printed on heavy parchment paper and bound with red, white, and blue ribbons. The dinner, it informed, would be served "In Nine Innings," and each of these was illustrated with an engraving in brown ink that depicted landmarks from the many stops of the tour. On the cover, a globe floated delicately over a wispy bed of clouds.

When the doors were finally thrown open, the tourists were led in by John Montgomery Ward and Adrian "Cap" Anson, player-managers and future Hall of Famers who had shared top billing on the trip. Spalding followed, judiciously allowing the players to bask in the glory of a prolonged ovation before taking the place of honor on a dais that ran clear across the room.

What they saw, in the words of former National League president A. G. Mills, was a veritable "galaxy of stars" that included Mark Twain and Theodore Roosevelt (the young sportsman and power broker had lost a mayoral bid in 1886 but was seen as an up-and-comer and had been consulted on the guest list). In the years to come, these two men would face off on the subject of America's presence abroad, with Roosevelt spearheading America's expansionist foreign policy and Twain fighting against him as a founder of the Anti-Imperialist League. But on this night they were united in support of a trip that brought America's game, symbol of the nation's promise and modernity, to the world.

The subscription price for the exclusive dinner was ten dollars a plate—a serious tab at the time—and even this left the organizing committee nearly two thousand dollars in debt. (Two hundred and fifty extra menus were printed and sold as souvenirs at a dollar apiece to help defray the cost.) For the price, Charles Ranhofer, Delmonico's renowned chef de cuisine—the man who created Baked Alaska and Lobster Newberg—provided a cavalcade of dishes, each with some reference to the tourists' route. Between a soup of "Broth Ceylon" and a dessert of candies formed into giant "Pyramids" was a menu of oysters, red snapper, filet mignon, capon, plover, and sweetbreads "Italian style"—all fortified by a selection of fine wines, liquors, and Veuve Clicquot champagne.

The after-dinner speeches did not begin until well past ten o'clock, and opened with letters of regret and congratulation from the mayor and the governor, both of whom had been scheduled to appear. Instead, Chauncey Depew, president of the New York Central Railroad and gray eminence of New York politics, ably represented the state's power elite, though some may have considered him an odd choice to speak on behalf of a group of athletes. (He had famously quipped, "I get my exercise acting as a pallbearer to my friends who exercise.") But on this evening Depew struck precisely the right chord of jingoistic celebration: "When the American baseball team circled the globe, the effete monarchs of the East and the mighty powers of the West bowed their heads in humility and rose in acclaim." Next came Spalding, who was saluted with a prolonged ovation while the orchestra struck up "Hail to the Chief." "It does my heart good to see some Yanks again," he said, earning even more applause when he added, "I have the proud consciousness of having established our national game throughout the world and feel confident that many countries will adopt baseball as a game." Next came Twain, who delivered an extended soliloquy on his days on the Hawaiian Islands, which had been one of the the tourists' stops on their trip across the Pacific. Baseball, he told the assembled, was the "very symbol, the outward and visible expression of the drive, and push, and rush, and struggle of the raging, tearing, booming nineteenth century," and that Spalding and his men had "carried the American name to the outermost parts of the earth, and covered it with glory every time." Having charmed the audience, he closed with a toast: "I drink long life to the boys who plowed a new equator round the globe stealing bases on their bellies!"

The evening's festivities concluded with stage star DeWolf Hopper's inimitable dramatic reading of "Casey at the Bat," the formerly obscure comic ballad he had adopted as his own and had made famous during the previous season. By the time mighty Casey had taken his final, ill-fated blow, it was nearly 2 A.M.

For one glorious night, seen through a fog of champagne and adulation, Spalding's tour appeared to be an unqualified success. But careful, or at least more cynical, observers might have detected something slightly amiss in the story being ladled out along with Ranhofer's Ceylon Soup. The next morning, the editors of the *New York Times* saw fit to puncture the event's pompous air with a wryly sarcastic account of the proceedings: "Baseball heretofore has been regarded as an athletic game, in which muscle and a desire to dispute with the umpire have been potent factors," the paper chided, "but that is all a mistake. Baseball is an intellectual pursuit, which is indulged in only by gentleman of the highest mental calibre, and by those whose minds have undergone a singularly stringent training in the matter of intellectuality."

A little affectation was the least of it. Swept under Delmonico's handsome carpets was any mention of the tour's many feuds and acts of personal betrayal, and not a word was spoken of the bitter dispute, already thick in the air, that would soon plunge the sport into an ugly and corrosive war. The fact was that Albert Spalding's mission to conquer the world with bat and ball was not quite what it had appeared. But Spalding was not daunted. In the past he had always found it possible to mold reality to suit his vision. The truth was malleable, and he had always known just how to shape it. His motto, oft repeated, made that much clear: "Everything is possible to him who dares."

CHAPTER 1

BASEBALL'S BARNUM

As in the history of nations, so in that of all enterprises of magnitude, there arise from time to time men cast in heroic molds, the impress of whose acts upon the issues at hand is felt for many years.

–ALBERT G. SPALDING

IT WAS ANOTHER FAMOUS SON OF CHICAGO, THE ARCHITECT Daniel H. Burnham, who advised, "Make no little plans; they have no magic to stir men's blood." Albert G. Spalding surely would have agreed. Grand plans—historic, monumental, and unprecedented plans—were precisely what he had in mind when he welcomed select members of the Chicago sporting press into his private office on the afternoon of March 24, 1888. As the reporters filled the large, wood-paneled room, they found the young magnate standing before a tall window, casually reviewing the crowds bustling along Madison Street below. Perched on the broad desk in front of him, and strategically oriented so the reporters could not help but see it, was an overseas telegram Spalding had received earlier that morning. The dateline read Sydney, N.S.W., Australia, and the message consisted of but one word: *Kenwood*.

There was an awkward moment of silence in the room, only broken when *Sporting Times* reporter De Witt Ray blurted, "Sydney, New South Wales! Who do you know there?"

Spalding smiled coyly, but did not respond.

"Who is Kenwood?"

Still the smile, but nothing more.

Ray pressed on, and the magnate parried until he felt he had built ample tension in the room. "That name Kenwood means in October or November next I shall sail from San Francisco for Australia with the largest company of ballplayers that ever plowed saltwater."

Spalding had been parsing that sentence in his mind for much of the day, and when he finally uncorked it he was pleased with both his delivery and its dramatic effect. Taking twenty-odd baseball players—and a supporting cast nearly as large—halfway around the world was no small undertaking, and would come at considerable expense, facts Spalding was only too happy to make clear to his audience. The trip, he estimated, would cost "a minimum of thirty thousand dollars," a sum he would fund out of his own pocket. "I have such faith in the drawing attraction of the ball-playing we shall afford our Australian friends, that I prefer to assume the entire responsibility," he told the group. Two teams would make the journey: Spalding's own club, the Chicago White Stockings—they were the New York Yankees of their day, having won five championships in the 1880s—and a squad of stars, the "All-Americas," handpicked from the other National League teams. His plan was to depart from Chicago in October immediately after the World Series, barnstorm through the cities of the West playing exhibitions, and then steam across the Pacific to Australia, where the teams would introduce the game of baseball to their colonial brethren. With this mission accomplished, they would retrace their steps home.

Spalding's carefully orchestrated performance worked just as he had intended. The next day, papers across the country picked up a story featuring baseball's most daring executive and his grand plan to export the national game across the Pacific. The *New York Times* ran it on page 2: "American baseball players are to invade Australia." A *San Francisco Call* headline dubbed the trip "A Bold Venture." The *Omaha Herald*, noting the players would stop along the way for a game in Hawaii—then an independent nation ruled by an aboriginal king—slugged its story "Base Ball for Canibals [*sic*]." Of all the notices, none could have pleased

Spalding more than the passage he found in the *St. Paul Pioneer Press*: "That inimitable boomer, A. G. Spalding, has again come to the front with one of the greatest base ball moves in the history of the game. The famous base ball genius has been at work for several months on a plan to carry the game into foreign fields, make it known and popular at the furthest ends of the earth, and at the same time bring back a bountiful store of shekels."

He couldn't have said it better himself.

It was altogether fitting that the go-ahead to launch the tour arrived in code. *Kenwood.* Back in February, Spalding had agreed to use the word as a cipher with Leigh S. Lynch, the advance agent he had sent off to Australia to make arrangements for the trip. Cablegrams were prohibitively expensive at the time, and charged by the word; codes were used to keep things short and cheap. (Even Lynch's one-word missive cost Spalding fifteen dollars.) In the grand scheme of things, then, this bit of subterfuge was fairly innocuous—if anything, it merely suggested an extra bit of intrigue to the reporters gathered in Spalding's office—but it is telling of a broader truth about Albert Spalding: Deception was a part of his lifeblood, a way of thinking and acting and framing the world to meet his own ends and desires. His career, his most intimate personal relationships, his businesses, the sport he would champion, the great tour on which he was set to embark, all of Albert Spalding's successes—and they were legion—were built on deceptions, some of them small, others spectacularly elaborate. He was a master of misrepresentation in all of its forms, from the essentially harmless exaggerations that seemed a practical necessity in nineteenth-century business to outright and occasionally malicious fabrication. It is both the great irony of his life and a testimony to his mendacious genius that Spalding managed to make his own name virtually synonymous with transparency, square dealing, and rectitude. The sterling reputation he so assiduously manufactured would eventually lead members of California's Republican party to draft him as a candidate for the United States Senate. In death, his *New York Times* obituary described him as "a stickler for absolute honesty and cleanliness."

But of course the truth was more complicated. The appearance of honesty and cleanliness were ends for which Spalding always seemed willing to compromise his means. His own manipulations of truth would become so intermingled with reality that the two became impossibly confused—at times, even he seemed to believe his own fabrications. And these fabrications were not without consequence. Spalding's deceptions would dramatically alter baseball's history, and then shroud it in a false mythology that lives on to this day. His sporting-goods empire became so tentacular that a trust-busting government forced the divestiture of significant holdings after his death. His personal life was simply bizarre. The seemingly upright Republican senatorial candidate had married into a quasi-occult religious group that believed in reincarnation and was devoted to a charismatic if curious figure known as the "Purple Mother."

No event better defined the Spalding modus operandi than the great tour he had just announced. It would be, as he well knew, a grand production sure to capture the public imagination. But as with anything promised by Spalding, a closer look reveals an entirely different set of motivations and realities.

———

Albert Goodwill Spalding was born early on the morning of September 12, 1850, in rural Byron, Illinois, some seventy-five miles west of Chicago. His father, James, was tall and handsome, with hazel eyes, an Abe Lincoln beard—the future president was said to be a family friend—and an air of amicable authority. Harriet, his mother, was a broad and sturdy matron of thirty-four years. The Spaldings, who could trace their roots to an ancestor, Edward Spalding, who arrived in Jamestown in 1619, were a family of considerable standing in Byron. James, who was active in Republican politics, had acquired a large parcel of farmland prior to his marriage, and he and his wife lived a comfortable life on the rental income from this estate and several houses he had also purchased in the town center. James Spalding's primary interest in these antebellum years seemed to be his team of horses, a passion he tried to pass down to Albert, who was given a pony. (The boy, it turned out, was not much of an equestrian.) In 1854, Harriet gave birth to a daughter, Mary, and two years later another son, James Walter. By all accounts it was a happy family; the three siblings would remain close throughout their lives, even when distance separated them. But in 1858 James Sr. died, and soon thereafter the family's fortunes began to reverse. Harriet, it turned out, had few assets but her property, which she was reluctant to sell.

When Albert reached the age of twelve it was decided that he would be sent off to live with relatives in nearby Rockford, a boomtown where he might find a better education than was currently available in Byron's one-room schoolhouse. Harriet had ambition for her children, a hope that they might drink from the gushing fountain of American prosperity. The country's expansion into the West and great leap into the industrial age offered possibilities that, at the time, seemed almost limitless. Sleepy Byron would not do.

The decision to send Albert even so short a distance away was a difficult one for both mother and son. "Memories of the homesickness of that period haunt me like a nightmare to this hour," Spalding would write in *America's National Game,* the book that doubled as both a jingoistic history of baseball and his own autobiography. "The only solace I had, the only bright skies for me in those days of utter loneliness, were when I could go out to the commons to watch the other boys play Base Ball." But Albert, a blushing, stammering child, was too shy to approach the local boys and ask to join in their fun. "I think no mother, parted from her young, ever had a stronger yearning to see her beloved offspring than I had to break in to those crude games." For the moment, baseball would exist in Spalding's life only as a spectator sport.

Eventually Albert did manage to join one of those Rockford ball games. That time came on a typical afternoon, as he watched the unfolding action on the local diamond from his usual position on a rise beyond a drainage ditch in centerfield. There he sat, looking on in his self-imposed exclusion when a deep drive arced up over the field, its trajectory placing it on a course directly toward him. "Talk about special Providence!" he recalled. "That ball came for me straight as an arrow. Impulsively I sprang to my feet, reached for it with my right hand, held it for a moment, and then threw it home on an air-line to the catcher." So began one of the storied careers in the game's history. Baseball had come

Albert Spalding at age twelve. His baseball career began shortly thereafter.

to young Albert's rescue, offering salvation and refuge from an otherwise grim existence. The incident would become a standard part of the Spalding hagiography, a story with which countless boys could identify. Is it any wonder, then, that as an adult Albert Spalding would travel nearly any distance and go to any length to promote and protect the game of baseball?

While her son may not have realized it, the truth was that no mother, parted from her young, could have had a stronger yearning to see her

Harriet Spalding at age sixty. She accompanied her son
on his tour eight years later.

beloved offspring than Harriet Spalding. She would, in fact, relocate the entire family to Rockford after just one year of separation. But the time apart was particularly painful for her. Albert had always been her favorite; the two had a special bond even at this early stage in his adolescence. "I had a reputation of being a very indulgent mother," she would later write in a memoir he encouraged her to pen. "I had petted Albert very much." Looking back, it is not hard to understand just why she focused so intently on her precocious eldest child. Her life, to that point, had been a series of tragedies and hardships.

Harriet Spalding was born into a well-off family, the Goodwills, in upstate New York in 1816, but was orphaned at the age of ten after the death of her mother. In 1839, she married Austin Wright, a member of the family that had taken her in, and together the young couple moved west to Chicago in search of fortune. "We were not favorably impressed," she would recall. "We found the place low and marshy; many people were down with fevers, and some were suffering with ague." They moved on to bucolic Byron, with its "rivers as clear as a well-washed window, river banks high and dry, and the prairies covered with wild flowers." Harriet gave Austin a son, and by all rights the family's life was happy. But the bliss didn't last. Austin soon fell ill, and a country doctor treated him with a course of bleeding, killing him. Shortly thereafter, their two-year-old son died. There would be more heartbreak. Harriet became pregnant almost immediately after her second marriage, to James Spalding, in 1848. That child, a boy, would only survive for two months. By the time Albert was packed off to Rockford, Harriet Spalding had buried a mother, two husbands, and two sons.

If Harriet's early history is extreme in the relentlessness of its cruelty, it does provide a useful illustration of the difficulties of life in nineteenth-century America—particularly in the rural Midwest—and may in part explain the intense drive that she imparted to her eldest son. Life expectancy for men born in 1850 was just over thirty-eight years; for women it was forty. The infant mortality rate was greater than 20 percent. Medical training was rudimentary, and there was little benefit to be found in the patent treatments so many Americans depended upon. Even thirty years later, ads in the *Sporting News* for Spalding's very own baseball equipment regularly appeared nestled adjacent to those for such products as Dr. Owen's Patented Electro-Galvanic Body Belt, which "guaranteed" a cure for "all rheumatic complaints, Lumbago, General and Nervous Debility, Kidney Diseases, Trembling, Sexual Exhaustion, Wasting of the Body, Diseases caused from Indiscretion of Mouth or Married Life, in fact all diseases pertaining to the Womb or Genital Organs of male or female."

Albert understood the trials his mother had suffered, and when he began formulating the plan for his grand tour, he made sure that she would be a part of it. He owed her that much, at least. Harriet's friends were less enthusiastic, however, understandably concerned that, at the age of sixty-two, she might be too fragile for a long and potentially difficult journey, one with a group of rowdy ballplayers no less. "I suppose I looked pretty old to them even then to undertake a trip around the world," she wrote. But Albert was stalwart, and his confidence encouraged hers. He knew her strength. In the end, Harriet Spalding's fortitude would be a source of inspiration among her fellow tourists, many not even a third her age.

⸺••⸺

Back in Rockford, it was becoming abundantly clear that Albert, though a gifted student and a diligent worker, was cut out to be something greater than, in Harriet's words, a "desk man." But you wouldn't necessarily know it to look at him. As a teen, Albert was tall and gawky, with spindly arms and a flat chest—hardly the physique of an athlete. Yet his skill with a baseball was apparent from that very first throw from the boundaries of the Rockford outfield. At the age of fifteen, just three years after that fateful toss, Albert was playing for a local youth team, the Pioneers, and by his own account had already mastered the fine art of pitching. "Call it science, skill, luck, or whatever you please, I had at that time, when only fifteen years old, acquired the knack of pitching winning ball." In fact, he had just begun to discover the power deception could bestow when deployed with appropriate rigor.

With his thin frame and underdeveloped musculature, Spalding made for a gawky presence on the diamond. Pictures of him from this period show an awkward boy standing nearly a head taller than his peers. Though he could throw a ball harder than just about any of his peers, he understood that it would take more than pure heat to become successful in the long term, especially against those who were more physically mature. Baseball rules in those early days of the game's development favored the batter. A pitcher stood in a box (it would evolve into the mound and rubber slab we know today) with its front line 45 feet from home plate.

Pitches were thrown underhand with a straight arm and locked wrist—a style much like what is seen in today's fast-pitch softball. The strike zone was divided in two—batters could call for a high or low ball—though as many as nine balls were required for a walk. With overhand pitching precluded, Spalding learned to rely on guile as much as velocity to retire opponents: by subtly modulating the speed of his pitches, all located with pinpoint accuracy, he routinely left bigger, stronger men helpless at the plate. (By the time Spalding's tour departed on its great journey, the game had adopted rules much closer to their modern form, with overhand pitching and a conventional strike zone.)

In *America's National Game*, Spalding claimed that it was as a member of the Pioneers that he first exhibited the flare for self-promotional daring that would be his signature as a team owner and sporting-goods magnate. Rockford then possessed two baseball clubs: the Mercantiles, an amateur lot of adult tradesmen out for a little advanced recreation, and the Forest City's, a semi-pro team of recruited athletes whose living expenses were subsidized by the town fathers. These were the days before established professionalism—there was no major league baseball to speak of—and teams like the Forest City's represented the pinnacle of baseball play in the Midwest. Rockford was particularly ambitious about its team; the growing city saw the Forest City's as a tool for promoting itself within the region and beyond. This was a common tactic, as baseball was fast becoming America's great secular religion. With the close of the Civil War, the austerity of wartime was supplanted by a return to American optimism. Baseball, the fledgling "national game," became a unifying force, healing regional and denominational divisions while allowing for the construction of a united cultural identity within both communities and the country as a whole. Baseball tournaments pitted top teams from cities across the Midwest in well-attended multi-day festivals; in 1866 Rockford itself hosted a tournament for the "Championship of the Northwest" that drew ten entrants, including teams from Chicago, Detroit, Milwaukee, Dubuque, and Bloomington. Tickets were sold for twenty-five cents. The winning Excelsiors of Chicago received, among other prizes, a regulation-sized baseball of solid 18-carat gold.

It was within this baseball-mad atmosphere that Spalding, in 1865, took it upon himself to challenge the Mercantiles to a game with the Pioneers. At first, the adults refused to even entertain the idea of a match against "the kids." But Spalding, if his memoirs are to be believed, was persistent in his petitioning, and when the game was finally played, it was no contest. With Spalding's pitching confounding the Mercantiles' bats and Ross Barnes, a friend and teammate, slapping hits all about the field, the young Pioneers thrashed their elders 26–2. The result, beyond some bruised egos, was that Spalding and Barnes were immediately drafted onto the Forest City's. At least, this is Spalding's version of events. The truth appears to have been somewhat different. For instance, the Pioneers did not exist in 1865, and there is no record of their having played the Mercantiles the following season. Anyway, it made for a good story, and whatever the circumstances of his rise, he was pitching for the Forest City's in the great baseball tournament of 1866, with Rockford's civic pride on the line. The team was eliminated after two games.

That year marked another notable event for Rockford and its ambitious young pitcher, an event that casts some light on Spalding's rather liberal approach to the idea of truth, at least in the realm of business. On December 4, Phineas T. Barnum, the self-described "Prince of Humbugs," arrived in town to deliver a lecture that had been selling out concert halls across the United States and Europe for several years. Barnum's subject was "The Art of Money-Getting," a task at which he was, indisputably, expert. (Losing money was also a skill he had refined.) Like Spalding, Barnum is best remembered for a business that still bears his name: the traveling circus he dubbed the "Greatest Show on Earth." But the circus was only one of Barnum's many ventures and, hyperbole aside, one of his most reputable. He had in fact made his name producing a series of sensational hoaxes that were exhibited around the country and at his American Museum in downtown New York City. Among his more memorable fabrications were Joice Heth, a former slave woman reputed to be the 161-year-old nurse of George Washington; the Feejee Mermaid, a half monkey, half fish "freak of nature" that was in actuality two carcasses artfully sewn together; and "What Is It," a black dwarf named William Henry Johnson who was advertised as the "missing link."

Contemporary audiences could not get enough of Barnum's extravaganzas, however absurd they may have appeared. When it came to playing the two sides of the American character off against each other—its native skepticism on the one hand, its can-do optimism on the other—Barnum was a maestro. If there was a hoax in the offing, people wanted to see it for themselves, and they'd pay for the privilege. As the historian Neil Harris noted in his biography of Barnum, "Amusement and deceit could coexist; people would come to see something they suspected might be an exaggeration or even a masquerade. Any publicity was better than none at all."

Spalding, by then something of a minor Rockford celebrity, would likely have attended Barnum's lecture—how could Harriet have allowed him to miss it? What he would have heard was Barnum's ten-point plan for achieving and maintaining wealth, a prescription that merged commonsense principle and moralistic cant, all delivered with a showman's flourish:

1: Select the kind of business that suits your natural inclination and temperament; 2: Let your pledged word be sacred; 3: Whatever you do, do with all your might; 4: Use no description of intoxicating drinks; 5: Let hope predominate, but do not be too visionary; 6: Do not scatter your powers; 7: Engage proper employees; 8: Advertise your business; 9: Avoid extravagance and always live considerably within your income; 10: Do not depend on others.

In case Spalding missed the performance, he had more than ample opportunity to review these "golden rules" in Barnum's wildly popular autobiography, *The Life of P. T. Barnum, Written by Himself*, first published in 1855 and periodically updated by the author. The formula presented therein has served countless corporate motivators, self-help gurus, and late-night advertorialists ever since.

Given Barnum's openly dubious business practices and checkered financial history, his admonitions might best have been received with not grains of salt, but mounds of it. Who, of all people, was P. T. Barnum, the man behind the Feejee Mermaid, to lecture on the sacral inviolability of the "pledged word"? Contemporary audiences, however, were generally willing to give him the benefit of their doubt; fame and success conferred authority on Barnum, and his droll treatment of his own antics had absolved him of what otherwise might have been considered foul play. Moreover, in the intellectual universe of nineteenth-century America, a time when robber barons such as Andrew Carnegie, John D. Rockefeller, and Cornelius Vanderbilt commanded the nation's economic imagination, moral and commercial motives seemed inextricably intertwined. "Money getters are the benefactors of our race," Barnum told his audience. "To them, in a great measure, we are indebted for our institutions of learning and of art, our academies, colleges, and churches."

Absent his own father, Spalding was naturally drawn to figures of male authority, and would be throughout his life. Indeed, Spalding would follow Barnum's plan for the accumulation of wealth with almost eerie precision. As a career he chose baseball, a profession that suited his temperament and for which he was supremely qualified, but that was then considered inappropriate for a boy from a family of good standing. (Much of his career would be devoted to changing the negative public opinion of ballplayers.) He was meticulous, if not always forthright, in his business affairs. He was bold, but never foolish. He did not drink to excess, and forbade those who worked for him from doing so (members of his White Stockings were trailed by Pinkerton detectives to ensure their compliance with his temperance policy). His employees were expected to be men of upstanding character. He advertised relentlessly. He was not publicly extravagant. He knew how to delegate, but when matters were pressing, there was no question as to just exactly who was in command.

The tour itself served as both an illustration and product of the ideas Spalding had absorbed from Barnum. He made no secret of the fact that the spread of baseball would mean the expansion of his own baseball empire. Australia, with a rapidly growing population and a vigorous athletic culture much like that of the United States, beckoned as a market for Spalding's nascent sporting-goods business. And he knew that news of the trip would keep his team in the pages of American newspapers on a daily basis through baseball's long winter off-season—a publicity windfall. The

players he would bring with him would not just be athletes, but ambassadors for their game, their country, and Spalding himself. "I intend that
the two ball clubs shall be comprised of men who are not only skillful
professionally, but who are gentlemen in deportment," he had told the
reporters who gathered in his office. "In exploiting the national game in
another country as contemplated, it is desirable to make as good an impression as possible."

The lives of Spalding and Barnum would exhibit a host of odd simi-
larities—both, for instance, built fanciful Orientalist houses and lost political campaigns—but what the two shared, beyond their obvious
intelligence and ambition, was a personal charisma that allowed each
man to assume command and then maintain it. In describing the power
of Barnum's magnetism, Harris wrote, "He was a representative American not simply because of his enterprise and energy, but because of a
special outlook on reality, a peculiar and masterly way of manipulating
other people and somehow making them feel grateful for being the subjects of his manipulation." He might just as well have been describing
Albert Spalding.

It was in the summer after Barnum's 1866 visit to Rockford that Spalding
made his stirring debut on the national stage. That July, a powerful club
team from Washington, D.C., the Nationals, embarked on a cross-country
tour with the express purpose of vanquishing the teams of the "Wild and
Wooly West," which at the time meant any place on the far side of
Philadelphia. Though baseball, with its wide-open playing fields and
leisurely rhythms, is today considered a pastoral game of the American
heartland, it was in fact molded into the modern sport we know in the
cities of the East Coast, and in particular New York. The teams of the
West were considered upstarts, and the trip was undertaken with something of a sectionalist rivalry. Henry Chadwick, the journalist known as
the "father of baseball" (among his many accomplishments was the development of the box score, that charted reduction of a ball game that
has been a standard presence on American sports pages for more than a
century), traveled along with the team, explicitly to report on its progress

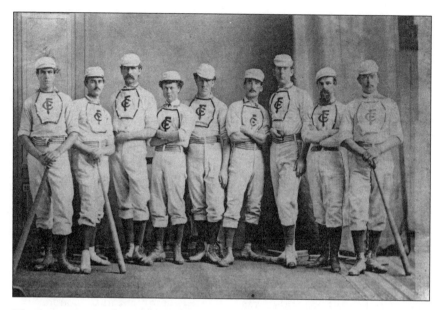

The Forest City's of Rockford, Illinois, in 1869. Spalding is third from the right, a ball in hand.

mowing down opponents. Which is exactly what happened. The Nationals, powered by the hitting of shortstop and team captain George Wright, were indeed a juggernaut, crushing their every foe. Against Cincinnati they won by a score of 53–10. In Indianapolis it was 106–21 (Wright had six home runs). Baseball scores at the time were generally higher than they are today, the result of the ban on overhand pitching, but these were astonishing numbers even by those standards. When the Nationals finally reached Chicago they were undefeated and apparently invincible. There, they were to meet the vaunted Chicago Excelsiors, then considered the top team in the Midwest. But before facing that club they were scheduled for a warm-up match against the Forest City's of Rockford. Albert Spalding, all of seventeen, would pitch.

The game was held at Chicago's Dexter Park on a rainy afternoon. A large crowd had come out for the contest, expecting to see the great Nationals obliterate yet another rival. Even the typically brazen Spalding was anxious. He would later write that as he took the field he had a lump in his throat and could feel the heavy beats of his heart deep in his chest.

Ross Barnes, his old friend, sauntered over from shortstop and advised him to "keep cool," but Barnes's quivering voice betrayed fear. "Every player on the Rockford nine had an idea that their kid pitcher would surely become rattled and go to pieces," Spalding recalled. Things got off to a rocky start in the first inning, when Spalding allowed three runs. Rockford kept close with two of their own, however, and the lead see-sawed over the next several frames, with Spalding keeping the mighty National attack under relative control. Going into the seventh Rockford had a surprising six-run lead, and it looked as though David just might have the measure of Goliath. Then, as George Wright stepped to the plate, he was pulled aside by the Nationals' club president, Frank Jones. Now it was his voice that betrayed fear. Jones ordered Wright to use a lighter bat, and told him, loudly, that "to lose this game would be to make our whole trip a failure." According to Spalding, the entire Rockford team heard him, and it was the decisive moment in the game. "For the first time we began to realize that victory was not only possible, but probable, and the playing of our whole team from that time forward was brilliant." In the end they won 29–23, a victory so unlikely that the *Chicago Tribune* suggested the Nationals had thrown the game. (Jones and A. P. Gorman, another club director—and a future U.S. Senator who would sit on the dais at the Delmonico's world tour banquet—visited the paper's offices and forced them to retract the charge.) The next day, the Nationals took out their frustrations on the Excelsiors, 49–4. But the damage to the notion of eastern superiority had already been done, and Chadwick was there to witness it. What was bad for eastern baseball was good for the game as a whole. "That excursion did wonders in extending the popularity of base ball," Chadwick wrote, claiming, too, that it was "the most enjoyable trip I ever took." Overnight, Albert Spalding was a household name, and "Western" baseball was legitimized.

Spalding's performance against the Nationals precipitated another jump, this time from the Forest City's to the Excelsiors, who knew a good thing when they saw one. At the conclusion of the summer, Spalding bade his mother farewell, and departed Rockford for Chicago, where he had been promised, in lieu of pay, a forty-dollar-a-week sinecure clerking at a wholesale grocery. The going rate for this work was five dollars per week.

Baseball was still considered, at least nominally, an amateur sport. The club game operated under the auspices of the National Association of Amateur Base Ball Players (NAABBP), an organization founded in 1858 at the instigation of the gentlemen members of New York's Knickerbocker Base Ball Club. That group consisted of professional men of accomplishment and standing, what the baseball historian Harold Seymour has described as a "social club with a distinctly exclusive flavor." The Knickerbockers, in their charter of 1845, had codified an innovative set of rules for the game on the field—three strikes and you're out, three outs to an inning, bases set on a diamond, balls hit outside the baselines called foul. In addition to actual game regulations, the Knickerbocker charter also included a series of provisions designed to ensure the club's high social status and enforce proper behavior. Potential new members were subject to blackballing. Article V cautioned that members assembled for "field exercise" caught using "profane or improper" language would be fined six and a quarter cents for each offense. Arguing with an umpire cost twice that much, and complaining to the team captain was a fifty-cent penalty.

The aristocratic mores of the Knickerbockers were carried over to the NAABBP, which by definition forbade professionalism. But by the late 1860s, this prohibition was, in Spalding's own words, a "dead letter." The Knickerbockers may have been satisfied with what their charter called "the attainment of healthful recreation," but many clubs had something a bit more ambitious in mind: They wanted to win. Pride was at stake, and there was a profit to be made. Club baseball had been co-opted by a rapidly growing American middle class that had little use for the Knickerbockers' social pretensions and now had both disposable income and free time to spend on the pastime they considered their own.

Spalding's clerking "job," then, was the Excelsiors' way of skirting the National Association's bylaws. It was also a lesson in how easily rules could be flouted, a circumstance at which Spalding professed no small degree of indignation. "I was not able to understand how it could be right to pay an actor, or a singer, or an instrumentalist for entertaining the public, but wrong to pay a ball player for doing exactly the same thing in his way," he would later write. Spalding did not have to live the lie for long. After only one game as an Excelsior, the grocer who had been supporting him with such a generous salary declared bankruptcy—so much for overpaying clerks—and Spalding's tenure with the club was over. He spent the balance of the winter selling insurance for an uncle (policies on which said relative would later default), and then returned to Rockford, where the Forest City's welcomed him with open arms—and jobs at the Charter Oak Life Insurance Company and the *Rockford Register*, a paper owned by the club's president, Hiram Waldo. Over the next two years, Spalding starred for the club, leading it to a 45–13 record.

———

Spalding was not alone in his dissatisfaction with the blatant hypocrisy of imposed amateurism. In 1869, local boosters in Cincinnati gave Harry Wright, a former Knickerbocker whose father had been a professional cricketer back in England, the funds to build the first openly professional baseball team, the Red Stockings. With a budget of roughly $10,000 for salaries and Wright's younger brother, George, imported from Washington to star at short, the Red Stockings became a national sensation. Women came out to see the men in their risqué uniforms—Wright had them specially designed with knicker-style knee-length pants that revealed a sexy stretch of calf beneath the team's eponymous red stockings. But the real attraction was the team's play. The Red Stockings went undefeated for the 1869 season, including a string of victories against the elite teams of the East. In Washington, they were warmly received by President Ulysses S. Grant, well known as a baseball fan.

Like all good things, the Red Stockings' streak—having reached twenty-four games into the 1870 season, and eighty-one games in all—came to a close, the end arriving with an eleven-inning loss to the homestanding Atlantics of Brooklyn on June 14, 1870. With that defeat, the team's success was transformed, as if by some strange black magic, into acrimony. With their dazzling run over, attendance—and revenues—dropped. Losing exacerbated Wright's problems controlling the team, in particular his star pitcher, Asa Brainard, a notorious hypochondriac with a taste for the nightlife. Soon enough, the team's backers decided they were no longer willing to support their professional squad.

In response Harry Wright picked up his team—name and all—and took it to Boston, where a newly formed club had already declared its intention of running a fully professional team for the coming season. But before coming east, Wright headed in the opposite direction on a recruiting trip. His mission: to sign a young pitcher who could replace the troublesome Brainard. There was no question whom he had in mind: Earlier that year Albert Spalding had led the Forest City's to a 12–5 victory over Wright's vaunted Red Stockings.

Wright offered Spalding a one-year contract at $2,500 ($500 to be advanced upon signature), a deal that would make him the highest-paid player on what would ostensibly be the best team in the country. Later, Spalding claimed (in *America's National Game*) not to have immediately accepted the offer. Wright, he said, was still planning to retain the Boston club's nominally amateur status; it was only at Spalding's own insistence that Wright abandoned this idea. "I was inclined to be obstinate in my views on the matter," he wrote. "The assumption of non-professionalism would not deceive anybody. Why engage in duplicity?"

The duplicity, in fact, was Spalding's. Despite his sterling résumé, he had an unflattering habit of adjusting the historical record to inflate his own accomplishments—often at the expense of a mentor. Wright, who had already pioneered professionalism, clearly arrived at Spalding's door with the intention of bringing openly paid play to Boston, and in any case the young pitcher was hardly in a position to dictate terms. The reality was that professionalism was an unstoppable force. A sizable contingent of NAABBP clubs were clamoring for it, and on a cold night in March 1871, ten team representatives met in a New York hotel and agreed to form a new organization, the National Association of Professional Base Ball Players (NAPBBP). For the first time there would be an organized pennant race, with the ten teams playing each other a minimum of five times per season.

With Spalding's pitching supported by the hitting and defense of George Wright and Ross Barnes—he was also picked off the Forest City's roster—the Red Stockings dominated this new National Association, taking its championship four years running, from 1872 to 1875. Under Wright's tutelage, Spalding perfected his techniques as a pitcher—Wright

The champion Boston Red Stockings of 1874. Spalding, again holding a ball, stands in the back with world tourist George Wright on the ground at his feet.

undoubtedly taught Spalding his famous "dewdrop" curveball, which be-fuddled batters with its sharp curve—making him the dominant force in the game. In his five years with the Red Stockings, Spalding won an as-tonishing 157 games. In his last year he put up what may be, at least sta-tistically, the greatest single pitching season in history: fifty-five wins against just five losses, with an earned run average of 1.52.◆

Fans today often lament the supremacy of large-market teams like the Yankees and Red Sox. It is an old refrain. Well over a century ago, in the 1870s, there was a Boston team so successful that its exploits were seen not only as monotonous but as detrimental to the game itself. That Spalding-led Boston team was in fact so dominant that no other team could credibly compete, and attendance throughout the newly profes-

◆ Earned run average (ERA) represents the average number of runs a pitcher allows over nine innings. Any number under 3.00 is exceptional.

sional National Association fell. Even the Bostonians had trouble turning a profit. Some clubs folded, others moved, and nearly all skipped out on scheduled games (travel being a great expense), leaving fans—soon to be called "cranks"—with little continuity from season to season.

These ills were symptomatic of broader problems within the sport. With no central authority, the National Association was unable to stop players from jumping contracts and moving from team to team, a practice known as "revolving." Ambitious club owners could freely raid opposing squads for players, at once driving up salaries while decimating their rivals. (This is how a team from landlocked Pittsburgh, one of baseball's oldest franchises, would eventually become the Pirates.) Gambling was an equally pernicious problem; the practice of throwing ball games—"hippodroming," in the parlance of the day—was rampant among players, as was drinking, or "lushing." Alcohol was indeed so pervasive that, according to Spalding, "scenes of drunkenness and riot" were everyday occurrences both in the stands and on the field. "Time," he pronounced, "was ripe for change."

Spalding brought that change on a grand scale, and he did so via a bit of subterfuge that would make him a pariah in Boston for years to come. In the midst of the 1875 season Spalding had secretly contacted the president of the Chicago White Stockings, William Hulbert, with the suggestion that he jump his contract and leave Boston at the end of the year. So prompted, Hulbert immediately left for Boston to seal the deal with the game's top pitcher, and while he was there Hulbert signed three other players that Spalding had recruited to join him in his desertion. When word leaked out, the Boston papers were incensed—this was treason!—but Spalding showed little remorse. And he wasn't done with his plundering, either. To anchor the Chicago infield, he helped Hulbert abscond with the first baseman of the Philadelphia Athletics, a rising star named Adrian Anson.

Hulbert, an aggressive Chicago coal merchant, immediately became Spalding's mentor. "I would rather be a lamp-post in Chicago than a millionaire in another city," was a typical Hulbert refrain—it was just this kind of civic bluster, and not the local weather, that was the true source of Chicago's "Windy City" handle. "You've no business playing in

Boston," Hulbert told Spalding as they were consummating their scheme. "You're a Western boy, and you belong right here." Spalding agreed, but he was no rube when it came to negotiating his fee: a two-thousand-dollar annual salary and a quarter of the club's profits. On top of this, a secret contractual rider provided him with another 30 percent of the club's profits—an astonishing early example of revenue sharing. The contract also made him the team manager, and in that capacity gave him broad oversight powers on matters ranging from personnel to game strategy.

Hulbert, perhaps, was willing to cede so much to the capable and ambitious young pitcher because he had bigger things in mind. The National Association, as it stood, was a malfunctioning entity on the verge of irrelevance. There was no reason, however, that it could not be replaced with a more successful organization. America's increasingly urban and middle-class society needed some form of mass entertainment, and an ever-improving rail network provided the groundwork for a baseball league with teams dispersed in large cities across the country. Hulbert envisioned not a loose association but a new league, a National League, with a strong central authority that would keep both players and owners in line. Teams would be forced to play out their schedules; ticket prices would be fixed at fifty cents, high enough to keep out the riffraff; contracts would be strictly enforced; players caught gambling or drinking would be subject to league-wide banishment; teams would be granted exclusive rights to their territories.

With Spalding in tow as his lieutenant, Hulbert cagily approached the three most competitive big-city teams of the West—St. Louis, Louisville, and Cincinnati—and with that consortium on board moved on to the eastern powers of New York, Boston, Philadelphia, and Hartford. And so the National League, baseball's "senior circuit," came into being. Typically, Spalding exaggerated his role in the league's formation, claiming in 1895 that the whole idea had been his own. Later he would suggest it came to Hulbert in a eureka flash when he, Spalding, expressed concern that he might be banished from the National Association for jumping his Boston contract. In truth, Hulbert had the idea well before he recruited Spalding, as evidenced by a story Hulbert planted in the

Chicago Tribune in 1875 that essentially outlined his scheme. In retrospect, there is a desperate poignance to Spalding's fact twisting. Hulbert, much as Harry Wright before him, had become a surrogate father figure to Spalding. Without any special legacy from his own father, it is hardly surprising that Spalding might arrogate credit for their contributions to the sport, augmenting his already considerable achievement so that it might eclipse theirs.

———

Beyond the favorable terms of his arrangement with Hulbert, Spalding had other motivations for returning to Chicago in 1876. If professional baseball was then something of a shaky business, it was clear that baseball as a sport was on the rise, and that the field was open to an enterprising capitalist who might provide Americans with the bats and balls and other equipment necessary to play the game. Albert Spalding would be that man.

Spalding had his eye on the sporting-goods business as early as 1869, when he pasted into one of his scrapbooks (he would keep these throughout his life) a newspaper clipping about Harry and George Wright's intentions to launch a store selling baseball equipment in New York City. In Philadelphia, A. J. Reach, a star with the local Athletics team, had also used his name to open a sporting-goods business. Chicago beckoned as the ideal place for Spalding to launch his empire. There, he would be a hometown hero in a booming city at the nexus of America's transportation network. And so with eight hundred dollars borrowed from his mother, Harriet, and with his brother, James Walter, as junior partner, A. G. Spalding & Bro. was born.

Spalding cleverly parlayed his relationship with Hulbert into a series of wildly favorable endorsement contracts that made his company all but synonymous with the National League. The Spalding company, for instance, produced the official league baseball, a privilege his firm was granted in exchange for the absurdly low fee of one dollar and the provision of a gross of baseballs for each team. Spalding published not only the league's official yearbook but also an annual of his own, *Spalding's Official Baseball Guide*, which despite his claims to the contrary was in no way "official." It did, however, provide generous advertising space for Spalding products.

The guile and aggression Spalding used to build his company into an empire placed him in the company of such Gilded Age industrial barons as Philip Armour, Marshall Field, George Pullman, and Gustavus Swift—Chicago men about whom he read virtually every day in the press. And once more he would receive a boost from family; in 1879, his sister, Mary, married William Thayer Brown, a Rockford banker whose wealth allowed for the purchase of a factory complex. So armed with a sizable market share, production facilities, name recognition, and ample capital, Spalding set out to consolidate his power. In a series of unpublicized agreements, Spalding purchased controlling interests in his greatest rivals—the Reach Company, Wright & Ditson, Peck & Snyder—allowing them to operate under their own names while letting him all but monopolize the sporting-goods market. To this day, no other athlete has so successfully managed to transform athletic prowess and personal celebrity into such corporate dominance.

Spalding's focus on his own business, combined with the trials of running the White Stockings, had a predictably corrosive impact on his play. Successfully juggling so many varied responsibilities, even for a man of Spalding's energy, was an impossibility. His job as team manager encompassed not only on-field maneuvers but also oversight of much of the club's front-office operation, from personnel decisions to travel arrangements, promotions, and scheduling. Spalding would have only one good year of play for the White Stockings: In 1876, he put up a 47–12 record with an ERA of just 1.75 en route to the league title. That would be his last great season. In 1877, Spalding switched positions, moving from pitcher to first base, where he hit a paltry .256—well below his career average. Spalding had complained of injuries, and perhaps could anticipate a gradual decline in his abilities, but what prompted the move, more than anything, was the growth of his sporting-goods firm. "No ballplayer, in my recollection, ever made a success of any other business while he was building up his artistry on the diamond," he would later write. By 1878, at the age of twenty-seven, Spalding knew his time on the field was over.

His leadership from the executive suite, however, made the White Stockings baseball's signature franchise. From the moment he arrived in Chicago, it was understood that he was Hulbert's heir-apparent; when the old man died in 1882, Spalding bought out his stock and formally took over as club president. The next year, he built the team a gleaming new home, Lakefront Park, a steel-framed showpiece with flag-topped pergolas, a bandstand, and eighteen private boxes. A telephone from Spalding's own suite gave the owner direct access to the clubhouse. Two years later, he constructed an even more elaborate stadium, West Side Park, at the corner of Congress and Loomis streets. Here, private boxes were decorated with cast-iron filigree, and a two-story red-brick building contained a ticket office and clubhouse for the players. His own box was equipped with a large Chinese gong so that he might make his displeasure known should his troops fail to properly execute on the lush green diamond below.

On the field, he gave Adrian Anson, his combative team captain, all the tools necessary to create, after his own Boston Red Stockings, professional baseball's second great dynasty. At a time when defense was valued as much as offense, Chicago's famed "Stone Wall" infield, anchored by Anson at first base, was the league's best. So effective were the White Stockings in preventing runs that shut-out teams were said to be "Chicagoed." Looking at the equipment of the day, it's not hard to see why fielding was so highly regarded: Gloves were simple fingerless affairs with padded palms—similar to what bicyclists use now—and a far cry from the familiar webbed mitts that became popular (thanks in no small measure to the Spalding Company) in the 1890s. Error tallies were kept in box scores next to each player's hits and runs.

Spalding, whose sporting-goods business was driven by his own name, was well aware of the rewards and limits of star power. In Adrian Anson he had one of the game's most prized draws. Anson was widely considered his era's greatest hitter. For twenty consecutive seasons, beginning in 1871, Anson's average topped .300. A physically imposing presence, Anson was tall and broad, with frigid blue eyes, close-cropped blond hair, and a prickly brush mustache that seemed to be shaped by the sharp words that so often issued from the mouth beneath it. As a manager, he was a clever and innovative tactician; if he did not invent the hit-and-run play, a cornerstone of modern offensive strategy, he was certainly one of its most prominent early advocates;♦ he regularly used the intentional walk; and, perhaps most critically, he was a pioneer of the spring training season. That he routinely fined players for miscues both on and off the field, however, did little to endear him to his charges. His foul temper was legendary, and he unleashed it, as he grew older, with ever-increasing frequency and at the slightest provocation. Fans came out not just to see him play, but to hear him "kick" at those who upset his fragile composure. "That ain't no shadow, that's an argument," a Chicago player once quipped. "Everywhere Cap goes, the argument goes." Perhaps his insistence on toughness was a reflection of his own harsh experience with the world beyond the ballpark. Like Harriet Spalding, Anson had known great personal tragedy: His three sons had all died within a few days of birth.

———⟶●⟵———

Anson was not Spalding's greatest star. That distinction belonged to the team's catcher, Mike "King" Kelly, a larger-than-life figure whose exploits on the field were rivaled only by his excesses off it. The King's trademark was recklessly spirited—and often spirit-fueled—abandon. Kelly led the league twice in hitting and four times in runs scored. His taste for the high life—clothes, horses, ladies, liquor—was legendary. If these indulgences were occasionally reflected in his performance, the public was willing to forgive him, for the King, despite his moniker, was a man of the people, a dashing and generous character who plainly admitted to his appetites without ever curbing them. Asked whether he would occasionally take a drink during a game, Kelly once quipped, "It depends on how long the game is." Confronted by Spalding with a report that

---

♦ The hit-and-run play calls for runners on base to begin moving forward with the pitch of the ball, and for the batter to swing and put that ball into play. The intention is to force defensive players out of position and allow baserunners a better opportunity to advance.

charged him with drinking "lemonade" in Chicago's notorious Levee district at 3 A.M., the King told the owner flat out it was straight whiskey. "I never drank a lemonade at that hour in my life," he said. Even Spalding seemed to have a genuine affection for him, though he would eventually deal him away for a cash sum so large it left Kelly with a new nickname: the "Ten Thousand Dollar Beauty." It was a wise move; dissipation would take its toll on the King. A popular tune penned in 1889, "Slide Kelly Slide," parodied his once-great talent on the bases. He died broke and broken in 1894.

Before that time, however, Anson, the King, and their Chicago mates would make a historic run, winning five National League titles between 1880 and 1886. This string of successes established Spalding's White Stockings as baseball's premier franchise and, coupled with the continued growth of his sporting-goods business, set Spalding's bold mind toward greater things. Baseball had conquered America, and Spalding had conquered baseball. It was time to expand the stage.

———— ·><·· ————

Though there is no record of precisely when the idea for an international tour began percolating in Spalding's imagination, his own statements indicate it came just as the White Stockings had reached the apogee of their success. When De Witt Ray asked, at that first, carefully orchestrated, press conference, "How long have you been considering this Australian enterprise?" Spalding's quick reply was "For two years." He would later elaborate, claiming he had sent off a series of letters to Australia at that time inquiring as to the potential success of a tour, and that he had also consulted with the champion Canadian sculler Ned Hanlan, who had performed there himself. If we take Spalding at his word, always a somewhat dubious proposition, that meant he began thinking about the trip sometime in 1886, the year Chicago won its last pennant under his reign.

But the seed was likely planted many years earlier. In fact, Spalding had led an international tour of baseball players all the way back in 1874. That trip was the brainchild of Harry Wright, then Spalding's manager on the Boston Red Stockings. An English immigrant, Wright had a long-standing desire to personally introduce his adopted game to his native land. Spalding, not surprisingly, would later take credit for the idea: "It occurred to me that since Base Ball had caught on so greatly in popular favor at home," he wrote in his quasi-autobiography, "a couple of teams could be taken over to introduce the American game to European soil." Although this was not exactly true, Spalding was entrusted with the organization of the tour, no small beer considering that for all his bluster he was still just a twenty-four-year-old ballplayer from a small Midwestern town. Wright had faith in him, however, and in March sent him off as an advance man with letters of introduction to the aristocrats in charge of England's most venerable cricket clubs. "It goes without saying that I had not been hobnobbing with 'dooks' on this side of the Atlantic," Spalding later wrote.

The plan Spalding carried with him was for a series of exhibition baseball matches to be played between the Red Stockings, defending National Association champions, and the runner-up Philadelphia Athletics. But with the brash and inexperienced Spalding doing the negotiating, things did not go exactly according to script; in order to secure support for the proposed baseball games, Spalding foolishly agreed to have the Americans play their English hosts in cricket—a serious tactical error that opened the Americans up to the possibility of considerable embarrassment. When Wright found out about this, he was none too pleased, but the terms had been set. Spalding, for his part, would never forget this rare blunder, and, years later, would try to redress it.

Fortunately, the Americans acquitted themselves fairly well at the English national game. Spalding was particularly adept. Following a match against the famed Marylebone Cricket Club, the *Illustrated Sporting and Dramatic News* reported that "if Mr. Spalding would deign to put a polish on his style, and study the art of defence as well as that of hitting he might well take rank with our foremost English professionals."

Whether or not one viewed the trip in toto as a success was largely a matter of perspective. The reception of the American athletes in the British press was generally positive, if somewhat condescending. "The Americans have a national game and can play it well," wrote the *London Standard*. If nothing else, the reviews embodied Britain's mixed feelings about its erstwhile colony. "The Americans are as a nation so busy, so bent on getting on, that the greatest merit a game can possess in their eyes is that it can be played in three hours. But with us a game that lasts all day, or even two days, is on that account all the more popular," wrote one London paper. The Americans could be condescending in their own right. Anson, who made the trip as the right-fielder for the Athletics, noted the "deep rooted prejudice of the English people against anything that savored of newness or Americanism" and claimed that the game hadn't caught on with Britons "for the reason perhaps that it possesses too many elements of dash and danger and requires too much of an effort to play it."

If anything, the harshest reviews came in the American sporting press, which reported of washed-out games, small crowds, and shoddy play. "It is made very apparent that our baseball representatives have not thus far shown any such skill in their contests as we are accustomed to see here," wrote the *New York Clipper*. When rain dashed attendance for a contest at Liverpool, the paper remarked that "any place that won't turn out more than two hundred persons to see a first-class baseball match ought to be expunged from our maps." The Liverpudlians who did show up, however, seemed to enjoy what they saw. "It is undoubtedly a splendid means for exercising the limbs and muscles, and sharpening the perception and judgment of those who make it a pastime," wrote the *Liverpool Post*. "It may possibly attain some considerable popularity before our American friends return to their native country." The reception was even more enthusiastic in Ireland, ancestral homeland to several of the self-described Yankee "argonauts." The Irish press fawned over these prodigal sons returned home, fortune having smiled upon them. "They are, without a single exception, a fine set of young stalwart fellows, and in excellent form for any manly contest," wrote the *Dublin Mail*.

However one interpreted the aesthetics of the trip's athletics, there could be no debate about its financial results. The trip lost money, and lots of it. Players had their salaries reduced (they had been warned of this possibility before departure), and overall losses were a reported $3,000. Three exhibitions Spalding had hoped to produce in Paris never materialized. (He had traveled there on his scouting trip, and had even managed a demonstration of the national sport with a group of American expatriates

in the Luxembourg Gardens.) And so for all of its success, the trip left
its organizers with something of a sour aftertaste. It is not hard, then,
to imagine a more mature Spalding, now the game's greatest impresario, looking back on that first trip and wishing he could do it all over
again, but this time in a fashion that would expunge any hint of failure
and accrue not only to the benefit of his beloved pastime, but also to his
pocketbook.

"I see great things in baseball. It's our game—the American game. It will
take our people out-of-doors, fill them with oxygen, give them a larger
physical stoicism. Tend to relieve us from being a nervous, dyspeptic set.
Repair these losses, and be a blessing to us." Walt Whitman wrote those
words in 1846, when the modern game was still just an infant. In 1888,
when Spalding announced his world tour, baseball and America had
grown up, and if the two had not quite reached their full maturity, both
were ready to go out and confront the world on their own terms. It was
only fitting that they would make this journey together, and that Albert
Spalding would be the chaperone.

There could have been no better representative for the country and its
pastime than the Chicago magnate. Handsome, athletic, intelligent,
charismatic, self-made, and audacious, he was the very paradigm of
American masculine virtue. The country was on the make, plunging
ahead toward a mechanized modernity that would make it the envy of
the world. Peering out from his office window, Spalding could look out
on a city that, too, seemed to embody America's surging power. Giant
towers, the first true "skyscrapers," grew from its streets in a raucous
battle for aerial supremacy. Washington may have been the nation's capital, and New York its greatest metropolis, but Chicago was "America's
City," a raw and surging wonder of industrial energy. In just five years, all
the world would flock to its shores for the spectacular Columbian Exposition. But for now, Spalding would bring a bit of Chicago's pluck and
dynamism to the rest of the world.

Yes, that telegram Spalding received from Sydney told him just what
he had wanted—and expected—to hear. And so he had a broad and con-

fident smile on his face as he stepped from the four-story Spalding Building on Madison Street and walked off toward the Illinois Central Station, where for a dime a suburban train would take him eight miles south to his wife, Josie, and his twelve-year-old son, Keith. The future was indeed all promise for the Spaldings; nothing made that fact more plain than their home, a picturesque manse constructed in 1884 at 4926 Woodlawn Avenue, in the city's most prestigious new neighborhood, a place that was itself a symbol of Chicago's raging potential: Kenwood.

Spalding's poster advertising the tour featured baseball cards of the players who—he hoped—would make the trip.

CHAPTER 2

THE CHICAGO FAKE?

HAVING ANNOUNCED HIS TOUR, SPALDING WAS LEFT WITH THE considerable challenge of making it happen on the grand scale he had promised that first day in his Madison Street office. This in turn left him with a pair of conflicting motivations, the first being his ever-present urge to exaggerate any potential success, and the second a more realistic imperative to manage expectations. As anyone who knew him could have expected, he would try to do both.

Spalding's take on the financial prospects of the proposed trip seemed to depend, more than anything, on the exigencies of the moment. On the day he made the plan known he was, predictably, full of confidence. "I prefer to assume the entire [financial] responsibility," he told the reporters gathered in his office; he even claimed to have rejected the proposal of "two businessmen of Sydney [who] wanted to share with me or guarantee expenses and divide profits."

Spalding's enthusiasm rubbed off on his team captain, Adrian Anson, who probably should have known better, having experienced firsthand the financial disappointment of the 1874 tour. "The prospects, both from a sight-seeing and a money-making perspective, seemed to be most alluring," he wrote in his 1911 autobiography, *A Ball Player's Career.* Anson was so optimistic that he not only agreed to lead Spalding's White Stockings on the Australia trip, but lobbied for and gained the

ADRIAN C. ANSON.
ALLEN & GINTER'S
RICHMOND. Cigarettes. VIRGINIA.

Adrian Anson, the combative captain of Spalding's Chicago White Stockings and anchor of its great Stone Wall infield. His prickly moustache betrayed a prickly temperament.

right to invest his own capital in the enterprise, a decision he would come to very much regret.

What made the tour's money-making prospects seem so alluring was, of course, Spalding's relentless boosting. To hear him tell it, the tour would be a certain windfall—yet another dramatic triumph to add to his already sterling résumé. Naturally, Anson wanted in. The relationship between Spalding and Anson, one that would last for some three decades before ending in acrimony, was always colored by a deeply repressed but quite real undercurrent of envy on Anson's part. Though Spalding was barely two years his senior, and Anson undoubtedly considered himself the greater athlete, there was no question as to just who had been more successful in business, who was more respected in the game, and who, in the end, was boss. For Anson, a man with such an outsized sense of self, living in another's shadow—and for so many years—could not have been easy, no matter how wide a berth and how much authority Spalding may have granted him. The simple truth was that however brilliant Anson was on the diamond, he could not compete in the halls of business, and his attempts to match Spalding's off-field achievements inevitably failed. (His catalogue of losing ventures included bowling alleys, ice rinks, a to-boggan run, and a ginger beer company.) Adding to Anson's frustration was the unpleasant fact that his wounds were self-inflicted, for the Chicago captain boasted the worst possible combination of traits for a would-be capitalist: horrible instincts bolstered by a massive ego. Spalding shrewdly took full advantage of Anson's ambitions and insecurities. The $3,750 stake in the trip he allowed Anson (the total initial capital outlay was $12,000) effectively positioned the captain as a solid company man, giving him the trappings of authority without any real power. Spalding retained controlling interest in the venture, a fact that would come back to haunt Anson, whose investment would conveniently offset expenses that Spalding, when he was being honest, acknowledged there was little chance of recouping.

In a moment of candor, Spalding spelled out this very truth to Harry Palmer, a writer who served as Spalding's de facto mouthpiece and would make the trip as one of three syndicated columnists. "In my judgement, such a trip would prove a losing venture to any man who undertook the journey with any expectation of making money out of the gate receipts of his games," Spalding told him. "In undertaking such a trip I do so more for the purpose of extending my sporting goods business to that quarter of the globe and creating a market for goods there, rather than with any idea of realizing any profit from the work of the teams I take with me."

Spalding was so skilled in the art of persuasion that he also managed to convince his own advance man, Leigh Lynch, to invest in the trip. Indeed, it may well have been Lynch's enthusiasm that assured Anson as to the safety of his investment, for Lynch—the man who booked the trip's exhibition games and set up its travel arrangements—surely had a good idea of the risks involved in the undertaking as a money-making scheme.

Lynch was the perfect emissary for Spalding, and not just for his willingness to put his own money into the venture. A giant of a man physically, and with a personality as broad as his belly, Lynch was the longtime manager of New York's popular Union Square Theater and the husband of Anna Berger, an established concert musician on the cornet. But he was undoubtedly best known as the agent of Lillie Langtry, the British beauty and former consort of the Prince of Wales who had refashioned herself as an actress. Under Lynch's direction, she had become one of America's biggest box-office attractions. What made Lynch particularly attractive to Spalding was that he had toured Australia as a theatrical agent; his nephew, Will Lynch, was still there and could also do advance work on the tour's behalf. To cap it off, Leigh Lynch was a baseball fan. (His son, Leigh Jr., would even have a brief career with the New York Giants.) Spalding paid Lynch a salary of three hundred dollars a month for his services organizing the tour. Apparently, Lynch thought he could double his money by putting that fee back into the trip.

Convincing the public of the financial benefits of the tour was only a small part of Spalding's challenge. For most fans, profitability was of little relevance. Their primary concern was that the teams being sent across the ocean adequately represent the nation with first-class talent. And there Spalding was finding his case a bit tougher to sell.

Despite Spalding's predilection to think of his White Stockings as the dominant power of the National League, the truth was that they were on the decline. Their last championship had come in 1886, not so long ago, but following that victory Spalding had taken it upon himself to break up the team, an action he justified with the rather dubious claim that "patrons, while appreciating good players, do tire of seeing the same faces year after year." The truth was that he could make a sizable profit by selling off the rights to his top player: the great King Kelly, whose behavior he had long considered "demoralizing to discipline." The deal Spalding arranged with Boston for Kelly netted Spalding ten thousand dollars in cash. Kelly's salary was bumped up from three to five thousand dollars as an inducement for him to go along with the agreement, which he was thus happy to do. Saving himself another large salary, Spalding also released the standout center-fielder George "Piano Legs" Gore, who like Kelly was known as high-liver.

The Kelly sale prompted a considerable outcry. Chicago fans, despite Spalding's assurances that the team's play would not be compromised, were not happy to see a local hero depart, especially with nothing in return except a fat check for the already well-heeled team owner. The transaction, moreover, seemed to observers of the time a microcosm of a broader American social problem: the exploitation of labor by large business interests. Nowhere was this imbalance of power felt more acutely than in Chicago, whose immigrant neighborhoods were hotbeds for worker organization and agitation politics. Recent events had cast the King's sale in an especially provocative light. In May of 1886, in the notorious and polarizing Haymarket Affair, seven Chicago police officers and at least as many civilians were killed when police broke up an anarchist rally. (That rally had been called to protest an earlier killing by Chicago police of demonstrators calling for an eight-hour workday.) Maintaining a safe political distance from the radical left would prove a constant challenge for baseball's labor advocates, but the Kelly deal, even if it worked to Kelly's financial advantage, seemed to galvanize public sentiment for some kind of reform. The ill treatment of players by imperious league owners had already prompted, in 1885, the foundation of a fledgling union, the Brotherhood of American Base Ball Players. And just a few months after the Kelly deal was completed, John Ward, star shortstop of the New York Giants and Brotherhood president, penned a provocative article for the August 1887 issue of *Lippincott's Magazine* entitled, "Is the Base-Ball Player a Chattel?"

Spalding, who had absorbed Barnum's lesson that all publicity is good publicity, was only too happy to exploit the Kelly controversy for his own ends, and had no problem playing the role of villain to King Kelly's popular hero in the local press. "It was understood between us that he was at liberty to play the 'poor base-ball slave' act to the limit." Spalding later recalled. "He did his part with such splendid effect that I soon had the whole press of Chicago applying to me names that, to say the least, were far from complimentary. I had learned to know the value of good newspaper advertising, and it came good and plenty as long as Kelly remained to weep and wail over his sad fate in being sold away from the city he loved so well."

When the uproar abated, Spalding's White Stockings were left without two of their most productive performers, Kelly and Gore, and they wound up in third place for the season, six and a half games behind pennant-winning Detroit. Spalding, however, had not quite learned his lesson. Following the 1887 campaign he once again sold off a top player, this time pitcher John Clarkson, who had accounted for a league-leading thirty-eight wins and 237 strikeouts. Clarkson was a notorious grouch and it has been suggested that a feud with the slugging shortstop Ned Williamson may have prompted his departure. But Spalding and Anson generally were able to keep players in line—if not by carrot then by stick—regardless of their personal issues. They were also shrewd judges of talent, and should have realized that finding effective replacements for their team's top batsman and top hurler in consecutive years would be difficult at best. Looking back in *America's National Game*, Spalding would admit that when it came to selling off players, he "overdid the matter a trifle."

Buoyed by the Stone Wall infield, the White Stockings of 1888 were still a good team, perhaps even a very good team. That said, they were hardly the juggernaut Spalding had advertised. Spalding, however, seemed immune to the idea that his team might finish anywhere but in first place, and that this might have an adverse effect on his planned trip. "I have not thought of it," he told the *Sporting Life* on August 22. "We are *bound* to take the championship. Nothing can stop us." But this was absurd talk; at the time they were already eight games behind the league-leading New York Giants.

Worse still, the team appeared to be sleep-walking through the season. "In the name of decency, for the sake of old Chicago, and the good of base ball, isn't there some means of waking the boys up?" asked Harry Palmer, the most sympathetic of reporters, in his *Sporting Life* column. Things were going so badly at the plate for second baseman Fred "Dandelion" Pfeffer that he gave up smoking. When his batting didn't improve,

Spalding's second-place Chicago ball club of 1888. Team captain Adrian Anson stands in the back row, directly behind helmeted "mascot" Clarence Duval. Fred Pfeffer is on Anson's left. In the front row, from the far left, are DeWolf Hopper, James Ryan, Digby Bell, and Ned Williamson.

his mother advised him to retake the habit, and he began smoking four cigars before each game.

Not only was the team foundering on the field, but the players, for all Spalding's talk of gentlemanly comportment, were engaging in the same sordid behavior that had, a few years earlier, led private detectives hired by Spalding to compile an inch-thick dossier cataloguing their debauchery. Now, on September 21, less than a month before the trip's scheduled departure on October 20, three Chicago players—catcher Tom Daly and outfielders James Ryan and Marty Sullivan—were arrested for "flirting" with one Mrs. Seth Blood, proprietor of a house situated just beyond the outfield wall of West Side Park. Apparently the boys were in the habit of waving handkerchiefs at Mrs. Blood and her pretty friends, a fact that caught the attention of spectators at the ballpark and also a rather talkative Pinkerton detective named Kelly, who happened to be one of Seth Blood's neighbors. When Blood heard tell of Kelly's comments regarding his wife's respectability, he threatened to "thump" the detective, and soon enough everyone was in custody. "I know the lady, but I know nothing wrong about her. As far as I know her house is very respectable," Ryan told Police Justice Woodman, who took him at his word. Blood was fined one·dollar and the case was dismissed.

———◆———

More problematic than incidents of bad behavior was Spalding's apparent difficulty in recruiting players to make the journey. "The securing of teams for this voyage in the interests of [the] Base Ball missionary effort was not easy," he would recall. "To openly ask for volunteers was out of the question, because it would be certain to result in a deluge of applications from undesirable players in the fraternity. To choose the best equipped to play the game meant the asking of many who could not go." His solution was to extend invitations to a select group of ballplayers whom he considered to be, at least theoretically, not only top-flight athletes but "men of clean habits and attractive personality, men who would reflect credit upon the country and the game." The terms Spalding offered these prospective tourists were by his standards generous: a fifty-dollar weekly salary on top of an all-expenses-paid, first-class trip across the country and then to Australia (including stops at Hawaii and New Zealand along the way). With costs anticipated at more than nine hundred dollars per man, Spalding essentially considered the trip a paid vacation that gave each player the ancillary bonus of being celebrated, both at home and abroad, as a globetrotting American hero.

Unfortunately, many of Spalding's invitees were not inclined to share this view of things. Chicago's backup catcher, the grizzled veteran Frank "Silver" Flint, made no secret of his disdain. "No Australia trip for me," he told the *Sporting Times*. "I don't care who goes, but you can rest assured that 'Silver' doesn't. America is good enough for me, and don't you forget it." Flint's rejection was of little consequence, as Spalding had managed to convince the rest of his White Stockings to make the trip.

An early baseball card of Mike "King" Kelly, the most flamboyant of nineteenth-century players, and one of the greatest. When he gave up alcohol during the 1888 season, the story made national headlines. He fell off the wagon within weeks.

(Fred Pfeffer, however, had to be given the concession to sell scorecards before and during games as an incentive.) Reserve pitcher John Tener agreed to come along both as a player and tour treasurer (he later became governor of Pennsylvania).

Putting together the All-America squad, however, proved significantly more difficult. As of September 19, Spalding had still not secured a full roster for the picked team, and O. P. Caylor, one of the nation's leading baseball journalists, felt compelled to comment on the matter in *Sporting Life*: "Much to my surprise, I find that there is a disposition on the part of ball players to shirk that Australian trip. They seem to have an idea that Spalding, besides paying the tremendous expenses incident to the trip, should throw upon them a munificent salary. Why, a ballplayer should be glad to make that trip without a cent of compensation. It will be five months out of his life that he will always look upon with pleasure. A visit to Australia with no responsibilities or expenses is something very few men are favored with. My advice would be to all ballplayers who are wanted on that trip and can get away is to go. I believe the ocean voyage will do them good."

No player caused Spalding more consternation than Mike "King" Kelly, the famed Ten Thousand Dollar Beauty himself. Never one to let his own posturing get in the way of his business interests, Spalding set aside his avowed intention to take along only "men of clean habits" in favor of a bankable star—Kelly. Indeed, in the years since his departure from Chicago, Kelly's off-field antics had only intensified. After a particularly wild bender just four months before the trip's departure, the King had announced to the *Sporting News* that he was "giving up drink," a revelation that garnered a front-page headline. But he wasn't on the wagon for long. On August 3, Boston Manager John Morrill fined him for lushing, and Kelly walked off the team.

Notwithstanding these foibles, Spalding signed Kelly to serve as the All-America catcher, with an "iron-clad" contract for a reported one hundred dollars—twice what he had offered other players to make the trip. The truth was that Spalding had always liked Kelly, and no doubt saw something of himself in his erstwhile star. Both men were fatherless (Kelly was an orphan), both craved attention, and both had a penchant for twisting the rules of whatever game they might be playing to suit their favor. (Kelly was notorious for tricks on the diamond, like skipping bases when an umpire's gaze was distracted.) If life had dealt each man an early blow, both had struck back against fate with talent and guile and an outsized personality. Spalding, perhaps owing to Harriet's strong maternal hand, had managed to direct his energies toward constructive ends. Kelly's behavior was more often self-destructively hedonistic.

Whatever their relationship, Spalding's desire to contract his irresolute protégé inevitably devolved into a protracted will-he-or-won't-he-go saga that played itself out in the press on a near-daily basis—added attention that may well have pleased the magnate. Just a week before the trip's departure, the question remained wide open, nevermind the contract. "No one in Chicago has any idea how it will terminate," wrote the *New York*

Clipper. "Spalding expresses a confidence that Kelly will come up smiling at the eleventh hour. Mike's old friends here do not take that view of the situation."

Three days later, on October 16, the matter was still unresolved. The *Chicago Tribune* reported that "all reports to the contrary" Kelly would make the trip, and that Spalding had received a cable assuring him of the fact. But it was the King's friends who were correct. As the *Clipper* wrote, "It so happens that Mike is most prolific of expedients to escape from a disagreeable situation." His latest excuse was a real corker: He claimed to be quitting baseball altogether in favor of the hotel business. With a partner, Kelly planned on opening The Two Kells, a rooming house and saloon at Thirty-first Street and Sixth Avenue in New York. "I shall be very sorry if Mr. Spalding holds me to the contract," he told the *Sporting Life.*

Spalding, no longer amused, responded in sarcastic fashion in the *Clipper.* "Yes, and I am [also] told that Kelly says he can't go to Australia because his wife is sick. Tomorrow he will probably have some other excuse—probably be summoned to Ireland to receive a fortune which has been conveniently left him." He closed with a none-too-veiled threat: "I know Mike through and through. I submit that I ought not be trifled with—I don't think Mike will be so shortsighted as to break the contract."

But Kelly did break the contract, and he was not the only player to do so. On October 19, Spalding received a telegram from "Silent" Mike Tiernan of the New York Giants, a rising star whom Spalding had signed on as the All-America's right-fielder. The missive was short and to the point: "Am sorry, but it is impossible for me to go, as I am unwell." The excuse might have carried some weight had Tiernan not played in a game earlier in the day, appearing the picture of health. Walter Spalding, representing his brother, publicly offered to have Tiernan examined by doctors in New York, Chicago, and San Francisco with the promise of an unconditional release if any of the physicians found him too infirm for the journey. Tiernan declined.

The withdrawals of Kelly and Tiernan were particularly embarrassing for Spalding, as he had already included their likenesses in a large, full-color poster he had commissioned to advertise the tour. Printed by the Orcutt Lithographic Company of Chicago, it featured the baseball cards of the players Spalding had signed up for the trip superimposed over a panoramic view of a game in progress at Chicago's West Side Park. (The poster was in fact modeled on one made for baseball cards produced by the tobacco company Allen & Ginter.) Along the top, banner type reading "Spalding's Australian Base Ball Tour" sat adjacent to the Australian seal of arms. Below was an image of the S.S. *Alameda*, which would carry the teams across the Pacific. The poster was to be distributed along the route of the tour in advance of its arrival to help drum up attendance. Engravings and line drawings of the players were also provided to local newspapers. This publicity onslaught was successful: as the tour made its way west from Chicago, audiences came out expecting to see King Kelly and Silent Mike in action. Their absence was not well received.

———

While the press was in general willing to tolerate Spalding's embellishments—they made for great copy, after all, and in any case a bit of hyperbole seemed to be the order of the day—there was at least one paper eager to expose any hint of fabrication in his claims: the *Sporting News*. Founded in St. Louis in 1886 by an aggressive sports editor named Al Spink, the *News* rapidly developed a national reputation as the self-professed "bible of baseball." Spink was never a Spalding fan, a fact derived in no small measure from his connection to the American Association, a down-market rival to the National League.

Known to its detractors as the "beer and whiskey league," the association had been founded in 1882 by a consortium led by four midwestern brewers who, quite understandably, had little interest in upholding the National League's ban on alcohol. With a twenty-five-cent admission (as opposed to the National's fifty-cent ticket) and a commitment to Sunday ballgames, the American Association aimed squarely at the blue-collar audience neglected by a National League that had been bent on "respectability" from its inception. Before starting the *Sporting News*, Spink had helped form the association's most successful franchise, the St.

Louis Browns, and remained a confidant of team owner Chris Von der Ahe, a portly German immigrant whose heavy accent and apparent bungling made him an easy target in the press. "Nutting is too goot for my poys," was a favorite refrain of "Der Boss President." It was only natural that he became something of a comic foil to the more patrician Spalding, who treated him with thinly disguised disdain.

A low-grade hostility characterized the relationship between the two leagues, though they came to an uneasy peace in 1883. One of the fruits of that conciliation was the inauguration of the World Series. In 1885 and 1886, St. Louis and Chicago, winners of their respective leagues, faced off in the championship, and in both cases Von der Ahe's Browns won. Spalding was hardly magnanimous in defeat, dismissing the event as an afterthought incomparable to the National League crown. Behind closed doors, however, he sought to co-opt the new league and its teams, a practice of monopolistic consolidation he was also pursuing in the building of his sporting-goods empire. It was in this spirit that Spalding approached three of the American Association's premier players—St. Louis's captain, Charlie Comiskey; Brooklyn's ace pitcher, Bob Caruthers; and Bid McPhee, a standout Cincinnati second baseman—in the hopes that they might join his trip. But he had gravely miscalculated.

In its September 22 edition, the *Sporting News* gleefully reported on Spalding's recruiting troubles. After claiming that the entire trip was merely a front for the sporting-goods magnate to "find a new market in which to dispose of his ancient and decrepit wares," it wrote that "the Chicago fakir has agents scouring the country in search of players to make the Australian trip." McPhee, already tired from the season, had turned Spalding down. "Seven months of ball playing is work enough for any man of ordinary strength and intelligence," he told the *Sporting News*. "Any player having the interest of his club at heart cannot afford to make these long winter trips."

There was also the money issue. Baseball salaries, though generous compared to what the average worker might bring home in a year, were not the kind of astronomical sums that would set a man up for life, and so for many a ballplayer, the off-season was a time to supplement their income or perhaps establish themselves in business. It was for this reason that Comiskey, too, flatly rejected Spalding's offer. "I might have gone had Spalding offered anything like a fair inducement," he told the paper, adding that the proposed fifty-dollar salary "would not have been cigar money."

Spink's initial attacks in the *Sporting News* were followed up, a week later, by a far more damaging broadside. "The Chicago Fake" was the headline of a story that pulled no punches: "The best friends of Spalding now admit that the Australian trip is to be a gigantic fake. All along Spalding has claimed that he would have two nines to make the trip among whom would be found all the leading professionals in the country." This, the newspaper proclaimed—in bold capital type, no less—was "A FRAUD ON ITS FACE! Not one half of the men mentioned in the All-American team will make the trip." In addition to Comiskey, Caruthers, and McPhee, it noted that Kelly and Tiernan were planning to opt out, and suggested as well—correctly—that Pete Conway, the star Detroit pitcher, would not go. In their stead, the paper claimed, "Spalding is signing a lot of fourth rate men who will make the trip to keep themselves from starving through the winter." Adding insult to injury, or perhaps injury to insult, Spink had the temerity to send personalized copies of the article to all of the would-be tour participants on both the Chicago and All-America clubs.

Spalding's response to the attack and its attendant act of sabotage was swift and harsh. "The blackmailing character of the paper is so well known that I need say nothing of that," he told Harry Palmer, his mouthpiece at the *Sporting Life*. "Some months ago I withdrew my business advertisement from its pages, and this, I think, is the secret of the paper's attack. Had I sent them a contract of $4 or $5 per week—it would not have taken more than that—the sheet would have extended to me its heartiest co-operation and assistance. This would not have materially helped my enterprise, however, for the sheet is a 'fake'—a scissors and paste pot concern out and out, as anyone can see by a glance at its pages."

Spalding left the real dirty work of smearing Spink and the *Sporting News* to Palmer, who would be traveling with the tour. Through Palmer, Spalding intimated that one of the disinclined association players was an

inveterate gambler who welched on his personal debts, that another un-
named deserter (presumably Kelly) had an addiction to whiskey, and a
third (Comiskey) was a "coyote" and "no good as a manager." But the
greatest scorn was reserved for Von der Ahe, who was perceived as the
dark force behind the attack. "Were the man possessed of a single grain
of consideration, generosity, or square dealing proclivities there might be
room for wonder that he should exhibit the contemptible, narrow-
minded characteristics that have shown themselves more prominently
than ever during the past two years," Palmer wrote. "His pig-headedness
has made a fool of him in the Association, and his invariably grasping
narrow-gauged policy upon every matter connected with the game is
rapidly winning him the disgust of the public." He went on to attribute
Von der Ahe's animus to a fear that the tour might somehow hurt the
gate at the World Series, which the Browns were set to play against the
New York Giants just as the trip got under way.

For all of Spalding's genuine troubles, Spink and Von der Ahe probably
oversold their case, and the enmity they engendered in the process only
played to the Chicago magnate's favor. In truth, Spalding had convinced
several high-profile players to join the tour. If none of them came from
the American Association, which he happily dismissed as an inferior circuit, that was hardly a critical setback.

Spalding could also point to a major recruiting success, for he had
managed to land the one player he wanted to captain that All-America
team: John Montgomery Ward, charismatic shortstop of the New York
Giants and leader of the fledgling players union. Ward was the ideal
public face for the tour, a dynamic presence on the field and a handsome
and intelligent figure off of it. While playing for the Giants he had
worked his way to a law degree from Columbia University. In 1880, as a
right-handed pitcher for the Providence Grays, he threw major league
baseball's second perfect game. The previous season he had put up
forty-six wins while leading Providence, then managed by George
Wright, to the National League pennant. When arm troubles ended his
career as a pitcher, he taught himself to throw from the left side, and he

JOHN M. WARD.
ALLEN & GINTER'S
™ Cigarettes
RICHMOND,   VIRGINIA.

All-America captain John Ward earned a law degree from Columbia University while starring as shortstop for the New York Giants.

became one of the league's most productive offensive players, a whiz on defense, and a team captain. Like Anson, he was a gifted strategic thinker: The primer he published at the opening of the 1888 season, *Base-Ball: How to Become a Player,* was a popular and nimble introduction to the game, with lively sections on technique and strategy, and an obsessively researched overview of the game's origins. One of his recommendations concerning proper training habits surely impressed Spalding: *"Keep away from saloons."* The italics are Ward's.

Ward preached temperance, but his own behavior was hardly above reproach in other areas of personal comportment. A notorious Lothario, his reputation as a man about town made him a popular figure in New York City. In 1887 he had married an independently wealthy actress, Helen

Helen Dauvray's ambitions for stage glory did not please her husband, John Ward. This studio portrait, a gift to journalist Henry Chadwick, was inscribed "Avec les amitiés de Helen Ward." She was not French.

Dauvray, a minor light of the New York stage who had an interest in fashion and a taste for ballplayers. Dauvray was a small woman, with the broad figure fashionable at the time. Men found her round face, which was open and slightly puggish, somehow appealing. When Ward and Dauvray met, she was already a divorcée with a well-developed sense of drama—

and not just on the stage. Together, they made for a combustible pair, their marital doings often appearing in headlines, and not always the good kind. More than anything, Ward wanted his wife to give up the stage, to become a more traditional spouse. Toward this goal, he convinced her to join him on the trip, and also persuaded Spalding to allow her to design the All-America's uniforms. For these, she settled on cream-white flannels with blue trim, letters blocked in blue, and a silk American flag that ran around the waist and was cinched at the left hip. "It is an exceedingly pretty design," Harry Palmer wrote in the *Sporting Life*—a phrase that, while perhaps true, also seems somewhat short of endorsement.

Dauvray was not the only woman in Ward's life. As the tour departed, he was in the midst of a heated affair with another beauty, a twenty-year-old named Jessie McDermott, who remained in New York. (She would eventually reinvent herself as the great stage actress Maxine Elliott—an intimate, in her later years, of Noel Coward, Douglas Fairbanks, and Johnny Weismuller.) Dauvray was almost certainly aware of the romance, and since her own sister, Clara, was then seeing and would soon marry Tim Keefe, a pitcher for the Giants, it's hard to imagine that the affair wasn't an open secret throughout the gossipy and close-knit world of the National League.

Ward's position as president of the Brotherhood of Professional Base Ball Players undoubtedly augmented Spalding's interest in bringing Ward—philanderer or not—along on the trip. Having the union chief under his captive gaze over the course of the winter would prove, at the very least, highly informative. Ward, for his part, seemed uncharacteristically oblivious to the fact that Spalding might have ulterior motives for bringing him on the trip. Indeed, he may well have seen the tour as a prolonged opportunity to plead the players' case with the league's most influential owner. Besides, Ward had other reasons for accepting Spalding's invitation: he planned to use the trip as leverage in his own contract negotiations with the New York Giants. As the 1888 season came to a close, speculation was rife that he might be sold away from that team, a prospect he did not find appealing. In response, he threatened to take Spalding's trip and then extend it for himself, completing a journey around the world instead of coming home directly from Australia with the other tourists. The message was clear: if Ward was not satisfied with his contract for 1889, he would not play at all.

The All-America squad included several other players of note, among them Ward's fire-balling New York teammate Ed "Cannonball" Crane. No one threw any harder than the big right-hander out of Boston, though his head was all too often clouded by alcohol. To play rightfield for the All-Americas, Spalding brought in Ned Hanlon, captain of the National League's Detroit franchise and Ward's chief deputy in the Brotherhood of American Base Ball Players. (Chicago's Fred Pfeffer was also a union director). Hanlon was a fine player, and would go on to become one of the most influential managers in baseball history. Playing center was lighting-quick James Fogarty of Philadelphia, a defensive specialist who would prove to be the tour's irrepressible practical jokester. Boston's Tom Brown, another speedster, was to play left. At first base was Fred Carroll, a Californian largely forgotten by history, but in his day a feared hitter.

The All-Americas may not have been stocked head-to-toe with stars, but as a team they were formidable—and fast. Ridiculously fast, and at a time when base-running was a far more crucial part of the game than it is now. In the 1889 season, Ward, Fogarty, Brown, and Hanlon alone would account for a stunning total of 277 stolen bases.♦ George Howe, president of the American Association's Cleveland Blues, who would see the All-America team play at an exhibition on its swing through England, declared it the "strongest base running and batting team he ever saw," and suggested he'd gladly spend $30,000 for its roster. Taken in combination with Spalding's White Stockings, who rebounded to a second place finish in the National League, the All-America squad represented an impressive aggregation of star power, baseball intelligence, and

---

♦ With deep fences and a comparatively dead baseball that was played all game long, home runs were harder to come by in that era; the single-season record, owned by Chicago's Ned Williamson, was just twenty-seven, and even that was an aberration, the product of a one-year quirk that allowed hits that would normally have been scored as ground-rule doubles to be counted as homers in Chicago's Lake Front Park. (The previous record was just fourteen.)

ability—certainly a group distinguished enough to impress a foreign audience unfamiliar with the game's intricacies.

Never one to leave anything to chance, however, Spalding acquired the services of a sideshow attraction to boost attendance. Before each game, a one-eyed "aerialist," the self-styled "Professor" C. Bartholomew, would ascend to an impressive height while suspended beneath a small hot-air balloon. After a series of acrobatic gyrations, he would then jump clear of his rigging and parachute back to earth, all the while performing a series of trapeze stunts beneath his chute. The Professor's missing eye might have been an indication that things did not always go according to plan, an eventuality that would come to pass with rather disturbing, though thankfully not fatal, consequences during the tour.

Spalding also knew he could count on baseball's most distinguished journalist for support. Henry Chadwick, the "Father of Baseball," was an enthusiastic advocate of the trip, and spoke with enough authority to quash Spinks's attacks in the *Sporting News*. "Unquestionably the base ball event of 1888 will be Spalding's grand tour of Australia, not only on account of the widespread interest it will create in both hemispheres, but also for the beneficial effect it will have on the future of our National game," Chadwick wrote in his *Sporting Life* column. His greatest praise, however, was reserved for the trip's architect: "It has to be said here that Albert G. Spalding is the only base ball magnate of the country who has had the pluck and spirit of enterprise in him to undertake the task of extending the popularity of base ball outside of the American continent. No one but him would have run the financial risk that he has done in this spirited venture of his. . . . The more I write of this Australian trip the more anxious I am to go." Unmentioned was the fact that Chadwick was on the Spalding payroll; since 1881 he had been editor of *Spalding's Official Baseball Guide*.

Spalding had an even more dramatic endorsement in mind. For years, he had been the tireless leader of an informal campaign to establish and promote baseball as the definitive national pastime, an enterprise he deemed essential to the game's long- term success. The game's origins, however, were obscure, and the subject of two competing evolutionary theories.

The first, promoted by the ever-authoritative Chadwick, posited that the game was a direct descendent of a British children's game, rounders, then understood to be a cousin to cricket. The alternate school of thought, of which John Ward was a leading advocate, argued that the game was in fact a native product, one that had naturally evolved through a series of progressively more complex bat-and-ball games, all home-grown. "The assertion that base-ball is descended from rounders is a pure assumption, unsupported even by proof that the latter game antedates the former and unjustified by any line of reasoning based on the likeness of the games," Ward wrote in his book, *Base-Ball: How to Be a Player.*

At the time of the tour, these arguments had reached an esoteric stalemate among cognoscenti, with a certain chauvinistic disposition in favor of Ward's position offset by a reverent faith in Chadwick. For most fans, who by default assumed baseball was an American game, the whole argument was of marginal consequence. "Only a minority know anything about it, and the vast majority care less," wrote the journalist W. I. Harris in 1889. In fact, both theories were wrong, though both were more plausible than the tale Spalding would promote at the beginning of the twentieth century—namely, that the sport was invented by Abner Doubleday on a dusty street in Cooperstown, New York, in 1839.

For the moment, however, Spalding diplomatically supported Chadwick, but couched his endorsement in a veil of nationalist pablum. Whatever its ancient genetic origin, it seemed incontrovertible to him that baseball was, as he would later write, the "American game *par excellence,*" the very embodiment, in his alliterative catalogue, of "American Courage, Confidence, Combativeness; American Dash, Discipline, Determination; American Energy, Eagerness, Enthusiasm; American Pluck, Persistency, Performance; American Spirit, Sagacity, Success; American Vim, Vigor, and Virility." This was the patriotic spirit in which Spalding had envisioned the tour. Barnstorming through the American heartland and then halfway around the world would effectively demonstrate—both at home and abroad—that baseball was, without question, *the* American game.

For the purposes of wrapping the game in the flag, only one man's endorsement would do. And so it was that Spalding's Chicago White

Stockings found themselves, at two o'clock on Monday, October 8, standing in the East Room of the White House and waiting patiently for the arrival of President Grover Cleveland, who was at present busy installing his new chief justice, Melvin W. Fuller. The players had spent much of their afternoon preparing for the reception. Third baseman Tom Burns had waxed his red handlebar mustache into a tight curl. Fred Pfeffer had a watch-chain elegantly passed through the buttonhole of a new suit. The group, as a whole, looked "as prim as a squad of theological students."

The meeting with the president had been arranged through the good offices of Congressman Frank Lawler of Chicago, who earlier in the afternoon had paraded with the White Stockings from their downtown hotel on Vermont Avenue, the Arlington, to the executive mansion. The team had arrived in the capital over the weekend for their final series of the season against the Nationals. Spalding, however, had not made the trip, the consequence of this circumstance being that Anson was left to handle ceremonial duties with the president. That was a mistake.

When Lawler called the White Stockings' captain forward to introduce him to Cleveland, a red-faced and paralyzed Anson simply stood there stammering. Anson, the National League's most intimidating personality, its most notorious kicker, became tongue-tied in the presence of the nation's chief executive. The awkward moment was only broken when Fred Pfeffer and Ned Williamson nudged Anson forward.

Clutching Cleveland's hand, Anson finally managed to get a few words out before losing his train of thought. "Mr. President, on behalf of the Chicagos, the famous . . ." Silence.

"Exponents," Williamson said helpfully.

". . . the famous exponents of the national game, I have come to ask you a little favor." At this, the smile disappeared from Cleveland's face, and the president's eyes rolled toward the ceiling. Anson, however, was only beginning to embarrass himself.

"We sail from Chicago the twentieth of October," he blurted.

"From *where*?"

"Mr. President," he began again, now entirely flustered. "We intend to sail from Chicago, that is we will. . . we are anticipating, as it were, anticipating. . . ahem. . . anticipating sailing from Chicago. . . . That is, we are going to Australia. And we would like a letter of endorsement saying we are what we represent."

Cleveland, ever the politician, agreed to consider the request. With that, Anson managed to chirp out, "We are all Democrats, and will vote for you in November!" This no doubt pleased Cleveland, who at the time was desperate for votes wherever he could find them. The rotund president had barely squeaked past his Republican opponent, James G. Blaine, in the vicious 1884 general election. (Allegations of a bastard child led to the derisive slogan, "Ma, ma, where's my pa? Gone to the White House, ha, ha, ha"). Four years later, Cleveland was facing a more daunting challenger: Benjamin Harrison, a Civil War veteran and the grandson of William Henry Harrison, the ninth president. This race, too, would take a turn for the nasty. For the moment, however, Cleveland was happy to shake hands with the players and wave them a hearty goodbye. A few days later, his letter certifying Anson and his men to be exponents of the great national game of baseball arrived at Spalding's Madison Street office.

CHAPTER 3

GOING WEST

WHEN THE DAY OF DEPARTURE, OCTOBER 20, FINALLY arrived, a chill wind was blowing through Chicago's West Side Park, and Albert Spalding, standing in the center of the diamond, could well have been forgiven for asking just what he had gotten himself into, at least on this one frigid day. A few hours earlier the members of his White Stockings and All-America teams had met at the ballpark and set out on a brief send-off tour through the streets of the city before returning for the first game of the tour. Donned in their respective uniforms—Spalding had brand-new ones made for every player—they had boarded a series of horse-drawn carriages draped in black broadcloth banners that read "Spalding's Australian Base Ball Tour." A full military band led the parade, and soon found itself separated from the rest of the party as the carriages were engulfed by admiring crowds.

When the convoy finally made it back to the park, the grandstand had filled with dignitaries and die-hards who had braved the elements so they might witness the opening game of Spalding's historic trip. The most prominent among the assembled, Spalding's friends from the Chicago Board of Trade, had even managed to convince the magnate to come out of retirement and pitch the first few innings for his beloved White Stockings, which explains the predicament Spalding found himself in as umpire Dave Sullivan called the All-America's first batter to the plate. Sure,

Spalding was still fit for a man of thirty-eight, but it had been a decade since he had last pitched in the big leagues, and here he was facing an all-star team that he had selected himself. Normally, at game time, he was happily ensconced in his private box, ready to bang on his gong if proceedings were not running in Chicago's favor. Today, that gong might just toll for him. Indeed, the line among the cranks in the bleachers was that Spalding and his old-time delivery would be walloped all over the park. They should have known better. Underestimating Albert Spalding had always proved a foolish enterprise.

Whether Spalding threw a ball or strike with his first straight-armed pitch to pesky Ned Hanlon, who led off for the All-Americas, is a fact lost to history. But it can be said that the first inning did not go particularly well for the magnate, though it was no fault of his own. Chicago's great Stone Wall infield became porous in the frigid conditions, allowing four runs to score, all of them unearned. Fortunately, the All-America fielders didn't seem to be any more immune to the weather than their opposition. As Harry Palmer reported in *Sporting Life*, what developed was "a good natured, happy-go-lucky kind of game"—a nice way of saying the run of play was exceedingly poor. Together, the teams combined for a whopping nineteen errors, a large total even by the elevated standards of the day. Three of those miscues were Anson's.

When Spalding's turn at bat came in the first, he was greeted by a rousing ovation from the crowd, and in response promptly lashed what should have been a two-out double into the outfield. He was no longer the limber base-runner of his youth, however, and pulled up at first. With a difficult journey ahead, this was no time to risk injury. In the next frame, he walked and scored, and the Chicagos came back to tie the game at four. But it was his pitching that most impressed. After the shaky first inning he had settled down, puzzling the All-America hitters with his trusty off-speed pitches and darting curveballs. He struck out three and allowed just two singles before he was relieved in the fifth. By that time, the Chicagos had built a lead they would never relinquish; when the game was finally in the books, they had an 11–6 victory capped by a Marty Sullivan home run that had sailed clear over the outfield wall and onto Congress Street.

Spectators may also have been surprised by the man they saw scampering around behind the plate for the All-Americas: Mike "King" Kelly. The King stole two bases in the losing effort and was at his very best throughout—"full of ginger," according to the *Sporting Life*. His appearance had come following an hour-long meeting held in Spalding's private office the night before. When the two men emerged, a dour Spalding made a statement to the press: Kelly would play in the tour's inaugural game the next day. Following this, he would immediately return to New York to attend to his hotel business, and then join back up with the tour in Denver. (Ward and Cannonball Crane, who were currently playing for the Giants in the World Series, were also scheduled to meet the tour in Colorado.) The true result of that closed-door meeting, however, was quite different, a fact betrayed by the distinctly unhappy look on Spalding's face. In all likelihood, Kelly simply agreed to play in that first game and then keep quiet about his plans to abandon the trip. It would, Spalding knew, take some time before news that he was not actually playing caught up with the teams as they barnstormed their way west across the country. This much is certain: Kelly never showed up to meet the tourists in Denver, nor anywhere else.

After exchanging farewells with the crowd, which had streamed onto the field from the grandstand and bleachers, the players made their way to the clubhouse, changed into their traveling gear, and headed back out to the horse-drawn carriages that would take them to the Union Depot, a hulking red-brick pile just a short drive across town on the corner of Canal and Adams streets. When they arrived, the station was already packed with hundreds of well-wishers there to see them off: tearful mothers and wives and girlfriends, relatives, acquaintances, business associates, and, of course, fans. Dodging the crowds and their own steamer trunks, the men forced their way toward the gleaming two-car train that the Burlington Route Rail Road had outfitted especially for them. Yet another "Spalding's Australian Base Ball Tour" banner, this one with black type on white linen, was slung from its customized dining car, named the

The Burlington Route Rail Road published a handsome program to promote the tour's swing west—and its new "Cosmopolitan" dining cars.

"Cosmopolitan." Behind it stood a first-class Pullman sleeper, the "Galesburg," polished and gleaming in the electric light.

Spalding was naturally at the center of the commotion, soaking up and feeding off the attention. On his arm was his proud mother, Harriet, now white-haired but still erect in posture and as dignified as ever. Trailing behind was his personal secretary, Harry Simpson. Adrian Anson also had family along with him: His wife, Virginia, was accompanying him on the tour, and now she was busy calming their crying daughters, Grace and Adele. They would be staying home with a nurse. Ned Williamson, too, was taking his wife, Nellie. The couple seemed especially excited to be making such a momentous trip together; in nine blissful years of marriage they had rarely been separated.

Bachelors Jimmy Ryan and Fred Pfeffer, each surrounded by a cluster of admiring young ladies, stood on the platform waiting for the final boarding call. A few yards away the All-Americas George Wood and John Fogarty, both from Philadelphia, chatted amicably beneath a light standard. Chicago pitcher Mark Baldwin talked to his parents, nervous at the prospect of their son's departure. On the periphery, taking it all in, was Harry Palmer, notebook in hand, already composing his first story for the newspapers that would run his syndicated coverage of the tour: the *Chicago Tribune*, the *New York Herald*, the *Boston Herald*, and *Sporting Life*. Those who had watches synchronized them with the time shown on Union Depot's grand clock. By 5:55 P.M., having said their last good-byes, everyone was on board. Then, right on schedule, a whistle blew and at six o'clock the great iron locomotive slowly chugged its way out of the station. Spalding's historic expedition was finally on its way.

Speaking at Chicago's 1893 World's Columbian Exposition, the historian Frederick Jackson Turner famously declared that the American frontier was closed. Sport, both professional and recreational, would provide a physical outlet for the restless pioneer energy that had gone into conquering the frontier. But as Spalding and his men began their trip across the country's wide-open prairie, they found themselves confronted with a place that was, although no longer wild, not quite domesticated, either. "No American can form any adequate idea of the grandeur and extent of his own country until he has made this journey," Palmer later wrote of the trip. "The days of the bison, the Indian scout, and the red raiders of the immigrant settlement are over, it is true, yet on every hand one sees evidence of life so crude, when compared with the methods and surroundings of an existence in the large cities of the East, that the people, their striking characteristics, their broad Western accent, their evident thrift and enterprise, and the apparent, though as yet imperfectly developed, resources of the country, are as interesting a study as any to be met with in a journey around the globe."

That journey was made possible by one of America's most impressive achievements: its railroad system, already the most extensive in the world. As Spalding and his men embarked on their trip across country, they were riding on a network of roughly 160,000 miles of track, nearly half of it laid during the 1880s. Progressive improvements in technology increased the capacity and speed of the trains that rode those rails, and the establishment of time zones in 1883 allowed for the synchronization of schedules across the transcontinental system. Modernization did not come without cost, however. Construction and operation of the network, built with private funds on land granted by the government, was often wildly abusive and corrupt. The Crédit Mobilier scandal of the early 1870s had revealed that men at the highest levels of government and finance were guilty of exploiting the railroad boom for personal gain. Just a year before the tour departed, in 1887, President Cleveland signed into law the Interstate Commerce Act, which finally gave the federal government authority to regulate the unwieldy rail system.

Spalding and his men hardly had such issues on their minds that first night of their adventure. Their mood, like that of the country, was buoyant. The economy was sound, and the future bright. Shortly after departing Chicago, the group gathered in the Cosmopolitan for a formal dinner that left everyone in festive spirits. These feelings only grew as the train of fun-loving ballplayers was cheered by large crowds at whistle-stops along the route. But as evening passed into night and the crowds began to dwindle, boredom set in and the players found themselves naturally turning to what Anson called "the solace of the traveler"—cards. The women were packed off to bed, and so many cigars were lit that a thick blue veil of smoke hung throughout the train. Poker was the game of choice, and a specialty of the White Stockings, who were notorious around the league for their gambling ways. "The Chicago players are probably the most nervy gang of bettors in the country," the *Sporting News* observed, noting their willingness to seek out any venue where they might try their luck. "It little matters whether it is a horse race, a dog fight, or poker, so long as it is within a day's journey of where they happen to be." By the time the last hand was folded, the players' precisely calibrated watch hands had all moved well past midnight.

The following morning they found themselves in St. Paul, their train surrounded by fans anxious to greet them. After a quick breakfast, Spalding set up in the Cosmopolitan and, like a king at court, began to receive a continuous stream of supplicants. At eleven, these guests were ushered out and the players put on their uniforms. Spalding, a driving force in the National League's ban on Sabbath games, had organized a pair of Sunday exhibitions for his traveling ballplayers. Principle, it seemed, had given way to profit, a fact that was not lost on the *Sporting Life*, which noted the "radical departure from long-established rule" by one of "the greatest sticklers for strict observance of the prohibition of such desecrating games." The first of these desecrations was a contest between the Chicagos and the All-Americas. In the second half of the double-bill, the Chicagos would face the top team from St. Paul, the Saints. It was this second game that was to be the big draw. Spalding had wisely anticipated that large numbers would come out to see their local heroes attempt to make good against the vaunted pros from back east.

When the Spalding party arrived at Athletic Park, the crowd was already waiting in the cold for the first game to begin. Sadly, the performance to which they were treated was no more impressive than the teams' effort the previous day in Chicago. Again, frigid conditions made fielding a problem, but on this day there would be no hometown pass, and, to make matters worse, there was no King Kelly to liven the mood. Behind the plate for the All-Americas was the curmudgeonly Frank "Silver" Flint, who had agreed to travel with the tour as far as San Francisco. Kelly's name, however, remained on the program, and no announcement was made about the substitution. The ruse just might have worked—this was, after all, a time before uniforms carried names and numbers—had Flint not struck out five times, calling attention to himself with each feeble swing. The White Stockings, meanwhile, scored three runs in the first inning, and muddled their way to a thoroughly unimpressive 9–2 victory.

Having expended their energy in the cold on the front end of the doubleheader, the Chicagos were, understandably, less than thrilled to play a second game, in particular against a team with something to prove. The Saints, for their part, "played ball for all they were worth," and the locals cheered them on with gusto—this, after all, was what they had been waiting for. The Saints did not disappoint. Behind the pitching of "Cyclone" Jim Duryea, who struck out ten Chicago men in just seven innings, the Saints rolled to an 8–4 win. "Anson Annihilated" read the next morning's headline. Humbled, the Chicago captain agreed to a rematch the following afternoon in Minneapolis, again to be the second half of a twin-bill with Chicago playing the All-Americas on the undercard.

Despite the disappointing result, at least for the tourists, the trip to the ballpark the following afternoon was altogether more celebratory than it had been the previous day in St. Paul. A drum major with a scarlet coat twirled a large silver baton and a twenty-one-piece band led the players, riding in a dozen landaus drawn by horses in golden plumes and blankets, into the park. It was traditional for visiting teams, even in major league cities, to parade to local ball fields from their hotels—both to help promote the games and because clubhouse facilities were generally limited or nonexistent—but this procession was unusual in its scope and grandeur. Unfortunately, another cold-weather day restrained the festivities considerably. On the field, play was uninspired, "a disappointment to all," according to Newton "Mac" MacMillan, who traveled with the tour as a correspondent for the Chicago *Inter Ocean* and the *New York Sun*. Only four innings were played (the All-Americas won the shortened game 6–3) and "no one asked for or wanted any more."

It was the rematch between the Chicagos and the Saints that the fans, about one thousand in number, had come out to see. The hometown heroes put on quite a show, playing with "vim and snap," but a controversial play left them on the losing end of a hotly contested game. With one out in the fifth, Chicago's Fred Pfeffer attempted to steal second base, and was apparently caught dead in his tracks. The umpire, however, ruled him safe, and after a passed ball and a sacrifice fly, Pfeffer gave Chicago the only run it needed, as pitcher Mark Baldwin shut down the St. Paul offense.

If the loss didn't sit well with the Saints and their fans, they had good reason to be upset: The umpire in question was Herman Long, who was filling in as shortstop for the All-Americas until John Ward joined up with the tour in Denver.

After five games in three rather frigid days, the players and their entourage were happy to have a relatively quick dinner in the Cosmopolitan, smoke a few cigars, and then retire to their bunks early. Those hoping for a restful sleep, however, would be sorely disappointed, for Chicago catcher Tom Daly had a few surprises in store for his companions.

His first victim was Tom Brown, the All-America's right-fielder. Brown was sleeping peacefully when a dampness at the foot of his bed brought him to consciousness. He awoke to find a large chunk of ice fished from the Galesburg's water-cooler melting uncomfortably at his feet. Next in line was Long, who had suffered the taunts of the Minneapolis cranks earlier in the afternoon. Now, as he faded into a sleep that would put the day's events behind him, Daly pulled the drapes shut on his berth and filled the compartment with smoke from a cheap West Virginia cigar. Moments later Long tore out from behind the curtains screaming vengeance, but he was coughing too hard for Daly to take the threat seriously. Anyway, Daly had protection—an audience of ballplayers who had fallen in behind him eager to take part in the "raid." All-America pitcher John Healy was unfortunately not a member of that group. Punishment for his sound slumber was a face artistically painted with lampblack.

Daly's pièce de resistance came at the expense of Silver Flint, who had taken a few nips at the bottle before hitting the sack and so remained unconscious through the excitement—indeed, he was snoring away at considerable volume. Daly, meanwhile, had retrieved one of the red warning lanterns from the rear platform of the Galesburg. With the rest of the party now in tow, he approached Flint's berth. Pulling back the curtain, he held the red light before Silver's eyes, bent down to his ear, and let out a scream for all he was worth. Palmer described what followed:

> The lurid glare of the red light blinded the old player and scattered his terrified thoughts beyond all hope of re-collection. Slowly he raised himself into a sitting posture, never once taking his wide open eyes off the horrible thing before him, and then as the climax of his fear was reached, gave a gasping, terrified howl and plunged through the curtains into the aisle, striking his head with a resounding thump against the top of his bunk as he went.

With that, Flint fell to the ground, unharmed but disoriented, only to recover as peals of laughter burst forth throughout the car. By the time Silver got to his feet, Daly had disappeared, wisely. No one saw him again until breakfast.

That meal took place with the Cosmopolitan parked on a track at Union Depot in Cedar Rapids, Iowa, as fans filed past, hoping for a peek at the dining ballplayers. In his tour diary, Chicago's Jimmy Ryan reported that the tourists "excited as much curiosity as Barnum's circus." With "big league" ball still confined to the territory east of the Mississippi, the arrival of Spalding's all-star aggregation was in fact a major event not just for the city, but for all of eastern Iowa. Six special trains had been run through the region to bring in fans, including one from Marshalltown that carried a large contingent of Anson supporters anxious to see their town's most famous son in action. This delegation was led by Anson's own father, Henry, a former semi-pro player himself who joined the tour and traveled with it as far as San Francisco.

For its efforts, Cedar Rapids was rewarded with a beautiful day and a first-class contest. Spalding called balls and strikes. Anson, to the delight of the crowd, had a hit. Bill Hutchinson, a Cedar Rapids native whom Spalding had signed for the coming season, pitched effectively as a substitute for the All-Americas. (Chicago won, however, 6–5.) Back on the Cosmopolitan, the tourists celebrated the successful event with local dignitaries and a case of Mumm's champagne before resuming their journey west. The next day, in Des Moines, the two clubs put on another exhibition, this time won by the picked stars, 3–2. All-America won again in Omaha, 12–2, thereby taking a one game edge in the series. But the tour's stop in that city was notable not so much for the performance of the teams on the field, as for the acquisition of a new member for the traveling party: a diminutive African-American minstrel named Clarence Duval. Members of the White Stockings knew him well; earlier in the year he had served an ill-fated term as the team's mascot.

This, in and of itself, was not unusual. Team mascots were a commonplace of the era, though they were most often children, freaks, or entertainers, and not the oversized, fur-suited characters we're familiar with today. Their function, however, has evolved little over time: Then as now, the mascot's duty was to energize crowds during rallies and between innings, harass opponents, and divert attention after miscues. In an especially superstitious age, they were also thought to be good-luck charms. The New York Giants, for instance, had spent much of the 1888 season with Broadway star DeWolf Hopper filling the role of luck-bringer, but when his presence coincided with a series of home losses, he was replaced with a fourteen-year-old street urchin, Fred Boldt, who had been on hand for a pair of wins against Spalding's White Stockings. During their champion run in the mid-1880s, the Chicagos had had their own boy mascot, Willie Hahn, but by 1888 he had grown out of the job. It was then, on a road trip through Philadelphia, that Anson came across Duval, who seemed to fill nearly every requirement of the mascot bill: Being less than five feet tall he was no larger than a child (he was reputedly fifteen years old), his blackness made him something "other," and he was a gifted entertainer—"a singer and dancer of no mean ability," according to Anson, whose "skill in handling the baton would have put to the blush many a bandmaster of national reputation." Anson outfitted him in a blue suit with brass buttons, and Chicago had a mascot.

That is, until the team arrived in New York for a series against the Giants. There, Duval abruptly quit Anson's White Stockings to rejoin a traveling theatrical company led by one Vernona Jarbeau, a second-string diva of the comic-opera stage and the headliner of *Starlight*, a musical farce in which Duval had appeared earlier in the year. Like Anson, Jarbeau was a force to be reckoned with; a woman of considerable means with a taste for extremely large diamonds—most notably a sixteen carat stone she wore on a silver bracelet. Despite her ample girth, Jarbeau attracted no shortage of admirers, including the anonymous but acrostically gifted poet who composed this ode:

> *Juno, herself, might envy thee,*
> *Art's devotees before thee fall*
> *Responding to thy siren call.*
> *Bright bird! whose notes possess a charm*
> *Earth's doleful visions to disarm,*
> *Accept this tribute fairly paid*
> *Unto thy genius, lovely maid.*

Anson was outraged at Duval's "desertion." In lieu of an explanation, Anson groused that life on the stage held more attraction "than a life on the diamond" for the "little rascal." The real cause of Duval's departure was more likely mercenary, and perhaps driven by Anson's virulent bigotry. Even in his autobiography, which he might well have sanitized, Anson refers to Duval as, by turns, "a no account nigger," "a little darkey," and "a little coon."

Anson's racism was by no means limited to Duval. In the early 1880s there was as yet no entrenched color line in baseball, but Anson's actions against the small number of black players who had managed to break into professional ball by that time would help set the game on a terrible course it would follow for more than half a century. In 1884, Anson's traveling White Stockings were scheduled to play an exhibition match against the American Association's Toledo franchise, which then had on its roster the African American brothers Moses and Weldy Walker. Anson refused to field the Chicago team until the duo was benched. Three years later, Anson again refused to field the White Stockings against a team on which Moses Walker played, this time the Newark franchise of the International Association. The next day, that league's directors voted to ban all future contracts to black players, thereby placing the first formal block in the barrier that would effectively keep blacks from the majors until Jackie Robinson's 1947 debut with the Brooklyn Dodgers.

Though Anson was the most visible proponent of the movement to keep blacks out of organized baseball, he was hardly alone in his desire to do so. The working-class urban population from which so many players were drawn had been historically antagonistic to African Americans—New York's draft riots of 1863, in which largely Irish mobs sought out and attacked blacks, brought that animosity to violent form. Fear of competition for the limited pool of baseball jobs compounded the prejudice of many white players. There were some, however, with slightly more progressive attitudes on the subject, among them John Ward, who was rumored to have unsuccessfully campaigned to have Walker and his teammate George Stovey added to the Giants' roster in 1887. Five years later, in 1892, Ward participated in a rowdy game between two all-black teams outside Jacksonville, Florida. In a dispatch to the *Sporting Life* after the event, he suggested, perhaps with tongue in cheek, "If you hear of any clubs in quest of talent refer them to the colored population of Florida."

Spalding remained disappointingly quiescent on the issue. From the outset of his career he had considered the maintenance of a "respectable" middle-class audience a necessity for the survival of baseball in general and his National League in particular (hence its ban on gambling, drinking, and Sunday games). If that meant segregation on the ball field, it was apparently a compromise he was willing to make. In any case, he rarely traveled with the club, and its day-to-day management—including the scheduling of exhibitions—was a job he had happily delegated to Anson. Certainly, he was smart enough to avoid any publicity on such a controversial matter, a strategy that has effectively left his name untarnished through time while Anson, once considered the game's greatest player, has become, perhaps to an unfair degree, a pariah of history.

———

This, then, was the state of affairs when Chicago third-baseman Tom Brown spotted Duval while the tourists were being paraded through the streets of Omaha, the obligatory military band once again out in front. (No parade was complete without one.) Duval was dusty and tattered and only too happy to see the White Stockings' familiar faces; earlier that day he had been fired by the imperious Jarbeau, and was now desperate for work. Reunited with the Chicagos, he immediately took up his old responsibilities, leading the team onto the diamond while performing a series of feats with a cane he substituted for his absent baton. The crowd loved the act, though the band's actual drum major, having been relieved of his duties, was less than pleased.

Anson wasn't any happier himself. "Where'd you come from, boy?" he asked.

"Miss Jarbeau done gimme my release this mornin'," said Duval.

"Well, you're blacklisted from this party, d'ye understand? We got no use for deserters."

"I reckon you're right, cap'n. But I've had a mighty hard time of it since I left you all."

"I don't doubt it. You look as though you had, and you deserve it. But we've done with you."

So ended the exchange. The players, however, convinced Anson to relent, and put together a fund to pay Duval's way to San Francisco.

Spalding was not on hand for any of this. At Cedar Rapids, he had taken a brief leave from the tour to travel to Kansas City, where he recruited Jim Manning, captain of the Western Association's Blues, to round out the All-America roster. When he reconnected with the party at Hastings, a railway junction town on the Oregon Trail in south-central Nebraska, he immediately signed up Duval for the remainder of the trip. A group of players took Duval on a shopping expedition, outfitting him with a checked suit and matching Panama hat, patent leather shoes, and a new cane. Anson was still unimpressed. "This reminds me of the new suit I gave you in Philadelphia, last spring," he told Duval. "It should not surprise me a bit if you should desert us at San Francisco."

Spalding's tourists may have considered themselves exponents of America's myriad virtues, and in many ways they were. But so too did they represent the vices of the Jim Crow era, and Clarence Duval would not be the only victim of their prejudice.

Hastings played host to the sixth game between the Chicagos and All-Americas—but not before a small disaster struck, one that could easily have cast a pall over the entire tour. As in Cedar Rapids, the traveling tourists had drawn fans from across much of the surrounding area. (Hastings itself was just a small prairie town, incorporated in 1874.) Indeed, the tour was so successful in attracting spectators anxious to see the pros in action that the local ballpark, which was not constructed with such audiences in mind, was practically overrun. Just as the players were taking the field, a section of the grandstand collapsed, dropping several spectators some twenty feet to the ground. Miraculously, there were few serious injuries and no fatalities. After order was restored, the two teams played their game, which Chicago won, 8–4, behind the pitching of Mark Baldwin. When the tourists rolled out of Nebraska, the series between the teams was tied at three games apiece.

The players awoke early the next morning to find their train chugging across the prairie toward Denver. Overnight they had climbed into the mile-high Colorado air, and now, in the distance, they could spot the snow-capped Rockies spiking majestically into a crystalline blue sky. As the train closed the distance, the purple mountains seemed to grow so near that the tourists could practically reach out and touch them. A kindly conductor informed a table of breakfasting ballplayers that this was but a happy illusion: "They deceive nearly every one who looks at them for the first time and is unaccustomed to estimating distances upon the prairies in high altitudes," he said. "It is no trick in this country to see from forty to fifty miles, and at some seasons of the year even further than that."

When the tourists finally arrived in Denver they found a city that, thanks to the staggering mineral wealth of the American West, was rapidly transforming into a great metropolis. Downtown, an industrial district had sprung to vigorous life on the broad streets laid out in front of Union Depot. Uptown, the brand new State Capitol, with its gigantic golden dome and hyper-baroque architecture, symbolized the go-go spirit of the city. But for all its energy, Denver still relished its identity as a frontier town. The lead story of the *Rocky Mountain News* on the day the tour reached the city was "The End of a Bad Man: A Cowboy Murderer Hanged at Rawlins." The front page of the previous day's *Post* warned of "Crows on the Warpath" in Dakota territory.

The arrival of Spalding and his men had been widely anticipated. Local papers tracked the tour as it made its way toward the city, reporting on the scores of the games and providing colorful background on the players and their journey. The *Rocky Mountain News* ran a feature, "Base Ball in Australia," slugged with the headline "Dangers of Flirting in the Bush." The story proceeded to outline the perils that would confront the players in the Australian outback: "Travelers who have traversed the island continent say that one of the brite [*sic*] ways of expressing love practiced by the dark-skinned but intensely affectionate maidens of the bush is to offer her lover as a toothsome tid-bit to her cannibalistic chieftain father. What a fricassee Jimmy Ryan would make! How the tears would well up into the eyes of the dusky beauty as she sharpened her teeth on his femur." An illustration accompanying the article suggested just what such a scene might look like. When the tourists finally did arrive, they were met at the station by dignitaries and enthusiastic fans and were then escorted in a procession to the Windsor Hotel, the city's great luxury hotel.

By all accounts the tour's first game in Denver, held the afternoon of its arrival, was a disaster. Though attendance was high—the *Rocky Mountain News* put it at roughly five thousand—the venue, River Front Park, was a sloppy mess. Denver's "rarefied atmosphere" didn't help matters either. The players spent so much time wheezing that the next morning the *Denver Republican* ran a sarcastic cartoon that pictured Anson pumping a barrel of Chicago air into his players' lungs. More galling to the locals, however, was the apparent lack of effort on the part of the visiting stars—and this after spectators had put up the stiff fifty-cent National League ticket price for the privilege of attending the game. Only Anson, who tripled twice, and Ryan, who homered, "played ball as though they meant it." After nine shoddy innings, Chicago walked off with a 16–12 victory. There were twelve errors, including three by the Chicago shortstop, Ned Williamson. "A chump exhibition," was the assessment in the *Rocky Mountain News*. Indeed, the only thing that seemed to keep the fans happy was the fancy riding of Myrtle Peek, an equestrienne hired to perform tricks on horseback between innings.

Having failed to deliver much entertainment for the citizens of Denver in the afternoon, the tourists spent their first evening on the town searching for a little amusement themselves—a practice that would characterize their behavior for the rest of the tour. Certainly, the Mile High city offered plenty of options. For the swells on the trip, there was the Tabor Grand Opera House, supposedly America's finest, built at a cost of eight hundred thousand dollars in 1881 by Horace Tabor, the notorious "Silver King," who was the state's most illustrious citizen. There were also opportunities for those with something less posh in mind. At the Collander Billiard Hall, Anson handily dispatched the local pool champion, using the personal cues he carried with him in a baize case—Anson never traveled without them.

The next day the players returned to River Front Park with redemption on their minds, and this time they brought reinforcements: Ward and Cannonball Crane had arrived on an overnight train, fresh from the Giants' World Series victory over Von der Ahe's St. Louis Browns. This second game, unlike the previous day's affair, was well played from the outset. Ward made his presence felt with three hits. Anson again tripled twice. The lead seesawed back and forth through the game, and the score was tied at eight in the bottom of the eighth when Ryan went back on a deep fly ball and "gathered it in," as the *Rocky Mountain News* would have it, "as gracefully as a maiden would pluck from their virgin stem a cluster of lilies of the valley." An even more spectacular play was in store. In the top of the ninth, Chicago's Marty Sullivan stepped to the plate with the game still on the line. Again, the *Rocky Mountain News* did it justice with purple prose:

[Sullivan] got the ball just where he wanted it, and the way he lit into it was simply appalling. It took off into the azure, coursing toward far center, that was truly enchanting. During the silence that followed it grew beautifully less in size, as did Hanlon in his mad race into the far center field. It was a race in mid-air and on terra-firma that was supremely exciting. On and on sped the winged sphere over the kid's grandstand, and on went Hanlon, his legs oscillating with the rapidity of a jig saw until the ball lowered almost to earth, when the fleet-footed flyer fairly flew up into the air, gathered in the battered bun and fell in a heap upon the ground, not without holding the ball, however. The excitement knew no bounds. Yells, cheers, huzzahs and vehement exclamations of exultant joy knew no end. The vast audience were on their feet in a deafening pandemonium. Such a scene was never before witnessed in Denver, and doubtful if anywhere else.

In the tenth, Anson instructed Chicago Pitcher Mark Baldwin to intentionally walk Tom Brown, who had homered earlier in the game—an unconventional strategic move Anson had helped pioneer. Finally, in the eleventh, Ward singled home the winning run for the All-Americas, leaving the crowd fully satisfied. The next day, the generally reserved *Republican* described it as "one of the finest games of ball ever seen in the city." The hometown *Denver Times* simply called it "the best game ever played in Denver."

⸺⸱⸺

Having redeemed themselves, the players made their way back to Union Depot, where—with their time aboard the plush Burlington Route Rail at an end—they transferred their luggage to the narrow-gauge Denver & Rio Grande Line for the overnight trip to Colorado Springs. There they were to play a single exhibition game before continuing on by rail through the Marshall Pass and into the Utah Territory.♦

When the sun began to rise over Colorado Springs the next morning, the tourists had already arrived at the station, where a handful of horses and carriages waited for them. As a treat for the party, Spalding had arranged for a little side-trip before the day's ballgame. The plan was to depart at seven—the men on horseback and the ladies in the carriages—for the spa town of Manitou, about ten miles away, where they would breakfast. From there, they would tour through the Garden of the Gods, a formation of dramatically upturned sandstone rocks, and then move on for a panoramic view of Pike's Peak. For some reason it didn't occur to anyone that this was far too ambitious an itinerary, given that their procession to the ballpark from the depot was scheduled to begin at 9 A.M.

The result, when the players realized just how late they were running, was a mad dash back to Colorado Springs. In the rush, Ward, who wasn't much of a horseman, wound up flying head-first over his mount after crashing the poor animal into a post. (Neither man nor beast was seriously injured.) Making matters worse, when the party did make it back to the depot, Spalding was informed that the tour's train would be leaving in one hour and could under no circumstances be delayed.

♦ Utah did not achieve statehood until 1896, the chief impediment being the practice of polygamy.

The teams finally arrived at the Colorado College ballpark at half past ten, and the crowd had already become restless. What they saw hardly made them feel better. "It was positively the worst game of ball ever seen on the grounds," wrote the *Colorado Springs Gazette*, a "scramble to see which side could get out the fastest." The crowd jeered the players as they raced off the field at the end of the "game." Following closely behind them with two large sacks of silver coins—the tour's profits for the day—was John Hart, the man who had been engaged to serve as tour general manager as far as San Francisco. The train was already moving when he got to the station and jumped on board.

"Roasted," screamed the *Gazette*'s banner front-page headline the next morning, "A Colorado Springs Audience Badly Sold." The official scorer didn't even have time to compute the final figures. (Palmer recorded it as a 13–9, six-inning victory for Chicago.) "There was talk of arresting Spalding for obtaining money under false pretenses, but it amounted to nothing," noted the *Gazette*. The citizens of Colorado Springs did exact some revenge, however. "Telegrams have been sent on ahead warning people further west to protect themselves and it is hoped they will be forced to play better ball or walk home."

What Spalding and his party gave up in luxury with their switch to the Denver & Rio Grande they more than made up for in dramatic vistas; the route they traveled, promoted by the railroad as the "Scenic Line of the World," was unrivaled in its dramatic beauty. An observation car was added to the rear of the train shortly after its departure from Colorado Springs, and soon after that the tourists found themselves winding their way through the Grand Canyon of the Arkansas River. At Royal Gorge a frothing torrent of white water raged almost 900 feet below as they passed over the highest suspension bridge in the world. The train pressed on, clinging to tracks nestled between towering rock formations and plunging escarpments. The view inevitably set the tourists to reflection. "How fearful must have been the convulsions, and how terrible the throes through which 'Mother Earth' passed ere these imposing masses were piled in such wild confusion," Palmer wrote. A year later, Rudyard

Kipling, traveling the same route, echoed Palmer's sentiments: "There was a glory and a wonder and a mystery about the mad ride, which I felt keenly," he wrote. "I had to offer prayers for the safety of the train." The path, which had opened in 1882, was one of the great feats of nineteenth-century engineering, blasted out of some of the most demanding terrain in the West using a new and highly volatile explosive: nitroglycerine.

The train halted at Salida, a small mountain stopover, and the group ate a brief dinner. From there, they continued on their tortuous way, soon arriving at the snowy apex of the Marshall Pass, some 10,845 feet above sea level. Once again the players debarked from the train, this time into deep white powder. "Imagine it," wrote Palmer, "six hours before we had been playing ball under a hot sun at Colorado Springs, and now we were indulging in a game of snowball on the top of the Rocky Mountains." Back on board, Hanlon, Manning, and Palmer gathered on the observation car's rear platform where they gazed out in the moonlight as the train passed by the skyscraping granite Curecanti Needle and along the rugged cliffs of the Black Canyon of the Gunnison. No one got much sleep that night, but there was plenty of time for rest the next day as they traversed the Utah Territory toward Salt Lake City. They didn't arrive until evening.

When they did, Spalding checked them into the Walker House, a four-story brick structure on Main Street in the heart of the city. The next morning, an intrepid group that included Daly, Brown, Fogarty, Palmer, and Ryan rose early for a horseback tour of the chief sites of interest in and around the "Mormon stronghold." The first stop was Fort Douglas, a red sandstone encampment named for Senator Stephen Douglas of Illinois, Lincoln's renowned debate adversary. "We arrived there in time to see the soldiers drawn up in line on the parade ground and saw the daily routine of a private's life upon the frontier," Ryan wrote in his tour diary.

The group returned to the city center and Temple Square, site of the Mormon Temple, Tabernacle, and Assembly Hall. After passing through a gate in the fifteen-foot-high adobe walls that surround the square, they came to the Tabernacle, an eight-thousand-seat auditorium with an egg-shaped dome, unobstructed sightlines, and acoustics so sensitive that a whispered utterance at its pulpit could be heard throughout. Adjacent to the Tabernacle was the Temple itself, a towering neo-Gothic pile still under construction after years of work and costs totaling more than three million dollars. Least impressive of the trio of buildings was the Assembly Hall, though Ryan did note the beauty of its "very fine pipe organ."

The afternoon meant a return to the field and yet another in the teams' string of less-than-exhilarating performances. Warnings from Colorado Springs and signs of malevolent weather—as play began a storm was already gathering force over the nearby Wasatch Mountains—did little to dissuade the fans of Salt Lake City from venturing out to the ballpark. By the fourth inning, a driving rain had turned the field to mud. "The water did not come down in drops, but by the bucketful," said Anson. Play was finally suspended in the top of the fifth with the All-Americas claiming a slippery 9–3 victory.

When the teams met on the same field the following afternoon, the situation was even more dire; overnight the puddled diamond had been covered over by frost and snow. A layer of sawdust was thrown down on the infield to add traction, but to little effect. The outfield might just as well have been a lake. "Conditions could not have been more antagonistic to good ball playing," wrote Palmer. "The black mud on the runways gradually worked itself up through the sawdust, and soon our boys looked like a lot of street laborers in rainy weather." The players persevered, however, and their gutsy showing endeared them to the crowd. Later that evening, more than two hundred of those cranks showed up at the Walker to bid Spalding and his men a fond farewell.

The tourists did not get far before they were forced to change trains. Only thirty-seven miles from Salt Lake City was Ogden, end of the line for the Denver & Rio Grande. It was here, on May 10, 1869, that the final golden spike had been driven in the transcontinental railroad, connecting America's East and West coasts by rail for the first time. Now, Spalding and his men transferred to the Union Pacific Railroad, which would carry them across the bleak Nevada desert to the promised land of California.

After their exhilarating trip through the Rockies, this portion of their journey was inevitably something of a letdown. "A long dusty ride it is,"

Ryan wrote in his diary. "There is nothing to amuse the passengers save a few forlorn looking Indians, who are always found around the railway stations, clothed in a red blanket and trying to look as majestic as the Bartholdi statue." If the empathetic spirit embodied by New York's Lady Liberty seemed to elude the group, at least they were beginning to understand the magnetic power of the American landscape. "Until one has traveled it," Palmer wrote, one can "form no conception of how broad and rich and unequaled by those of any other [country] in the world are the great pasture-lands of the United States."

When the pasture-lands became tiresome, there was always the opportunity for high jinks. A pack of snarling wolves spotted in the afternoon inspired the All-America's James Fogarty to form the "Order of the Howling Wolves," a group of pranksters committed to the annoyance of their fellow passengers. Ward, in a communiqué to the Chicago *Tribune*, for whom he had agreed to file the occasional dispatch, complained about the group's constant yowling, which might be triggered at the "slightest provocation" and in character resembled "as nearly as possible the wailing of a moonstruck dog." If Ward thought their behavior was irritatingly juvenile, the Howling Wolves didn't seem to care. Despite all threats of "vengeance," they continued to howl away with their favorite song:

> "We are the Howling Wolves,
> And this is our night to howl,
> And we howl thus: Wooo!"

CHAPTER 4

A LAND OF MILK AND HONEY

W HEN THE TOURISTS AWOKE THE NEXT MORNING THEY
FOUND themselves in a landscape so radically different from
the desert wastes of Nevada that it seemed almost the product of fantasy. Wheat fields, vineyards, and orchards of incomparable
lushness stretched out before them to either side of the Union Pacific
tracks. Wild geese circled overhead. At Sacramento, where they stopped
for breakfast, the tables spilled over with nature's bounty: apples, pears,
peaches, and grapes in great bunches. California, wrote Harry Palmer,
presented itself as "a veritable Garden of Eden."

The state, with its endless riches, had been a dreamland for years—
from a time long before there were motion pictures, let alone a film industry. Statehood had come in 1850 for California, only two years after it
had been ceded to the United States following the Mexican War, and just
one year after the great rush that brought so many "forty-niners" west in
search of an elusive fortune in gold. What California did not have was
major league baseball—the Giants and Dodgers would not arrive until
1958—and for that reason the coming of the Spalding tourists had generated considerable excitement. Spalding's Chicago and All-America teams
would face off against each other for this audience, but also take the field
against the top teams of the California League, allowing fans from the
Golden State to see just how they measured up against the great powers
of the East.

At Suisun, some fifty miles from San Francisco, the tourists were joined by an advance team of local baseball officials and sportswriters who had come out to share in the glory of their arrival. The Howling Wolves gave them a hearty welcome bark, frightening several bystanders on the platform. Further down the line, at Port Costa, a conductor handed Spalding a telegram: "We welcome you to our city and to the Baldwin Hotel. You will find carriages waiting at the foot of Market Street." It was signed by none other than E. J. "Lucky" Baldwin, proprietor of the hotel that proclaimed itself the "finest west of New York." Baldwin's Hotel was a resplendent six-story masterwork of Empire style that also housed the Baldwin Theater, and when the tourists arrived at its doors on the wedge-shaped corner of Market and Powell Streets the owner was there to greet them in person. The tour must have appealed to the hotelier's personal sense of adventure; Baldwin had acquired his nickname in the course of a journey across the Pacific twenty years earlier. In 1867 he departed San Francisco for the Orient having left directions that his considerable fortune in mining stocks be sold off at the first sign of a market tumble. That crash came, but Baldwin's stock certificates were locked in a safe and no one could find the key. He was busted. But by the time he returned the market had rebounded, and Baldwin found himself ahead of the game. With his profits Baldwin built the grand hotel that Spalding and his men would call home for the next two weeks. (Baldwin's luck didn't hold, however; the hotel burned in 1898, and it was not insured.)

However much they may have wanted to, Spalding and Baldwin had little time to engage in private conversation that first afternoon. After a quick change into evening wear, Spalding joined Anson and Ward for an early dinner with the sporting press at Marchand's, one of San Francisco's finest tables. For two hours, the magnate entertained the party with stories of his past life on the diamond, embroidering the details here and there as was his custom. Several bottles of California wine, one imagines, did little to restrain his imagination. After dinner, he led the group back to the Baldwin Theater, where they and the rest of the traveling party sat in boxes decked out in their honor for a command performance of *The Corsair*.

The evening did not end when the curtain fell—it would continue for some time, for the American presidential election was only three days off, and the Grand Old Party had sponsored a suitably grand late-night parade to promote its candidate, Benjamin Harrison. (In its early days, California was staunchly Republican territory.) The pageantry and fireworks would run deep into the night. Though the majority of Spalding's tourists no doubt counted themselves as Democrats—and the White Stockings had personally promised their votes to President Cleveland just a few weeks back—the men were more than happy to join in the revelry. What's more, many of them, in particular those of Irish descent (Jimmy Ryan, John Tener, Tom Daly, and James Manning) might well have been turned against the incumbent by a recent scandal. In late October, Lord Lionel Sackville-West, the British minister to the United States, had suggested, rather obliquely, that Cleveland's re-election might foster a "spirit of conciliation" between Britain and the United States. At the time, relations between the two nations, though cordial, were strained by a dispute over the Canadian-American border. More crucially, the traditionally Democratic Irish-American voters who made up much of Cleveland's base were vehemently anti-British. Sackville-West's supposed endorsement had come in a reply letter to a private citizen, a "Mr. Murchison," who had solicited his opinion on the matter. When that letter was leaked to the press, the Republican machine seized on it, and Cleveland was saddled with a political mess. Though he responded with a stern denunciation and a demand that Britain recall West, considerable damage had been done to his campaign.

At eleven-thirty the next morning, in the wake of the Republican festivities, Spalding and his players gathered in the Baldwin lobby, ready to begin their own parade out to San Francisco's municipal ballpark, the Haight Street Grounds. A military band led the way, and behind it followed a convoy of six carriages carrying the White Stockings, the All-Americas, and a host of dignitaries, sportswriters, and hangers-on. The procession wound its way through the San Francisco streets until the players finally made it to the field, whereupon they were given a raucous ovation by a record crowd of 18,463—by far the largest they would play for on their journey. If those fans had any idea of what they were about to witness, they would surely have stayed home and saved their fifty cents.

Things began inauspiciously for Chicago when shortstop Ned Williamson muffed Ned Hanlon's easy grounder to lead off the game. Two wild pitches from the White Stockings' Mark Baldwin moved Hanlon to third, and a triple by All-America second baseman George Van Haltren brought him to the plate. The All-Americas scored twice more in that first inning to take a 3–0 lead. The game proceeded from there in slipshod fashion, with the players alternately striking out (fifteen times, but not on account of stellar pitching) and then flubbing the balls put in play (there were sixteen errors, including seven by the supposedly impenetrable Stone Wall infield). When it was over, the score was 14–4 for the All-Americas, but nobody was pleased with the result.

"I never saw men work harder or try more determinedly to play good ball; but it was no use," wrote Palmer. That was a generous appraisal. A more accurate assessment was that the previous night's indulgences had left the great exponents of America's national sport exhausted and hungover; Cannonball Crane was in such bad shape that he was scratched from the lineup. According to the teetotaling Anson, the whole group was "in no condition to do ourselves justice." They paid the price in the next morning's papers. "Disgusted Thousands: A Poor and Unsatisfactory Game," read a typical headline. Most upset were the large number of women who had come out to see the game. They had been promised free admission as part of a "Ladies' Day" promotion, but the deal was somehow amended on the morning of the game so that women did not get in free but were charged twenty-five cents, half the regular fifty-cent admission. The *Sporting News* happily described the switch as one of the "dirty and contemptible tricks of Spalding and his crew."

The man responsible for the change was probably James Hart, whom Spalding had brought on to manage the westward swing of the tour and then, after its departure from San Francisco Bay, handle the White Stockings' daily business back in Chicago while Spalding himself was touring the globe. Hart had caught Spalding's attention back in March, when, as manager of the Western Association's Milwaukee franchise, he told a local newspaper that Spalding's planned trip was "merely an advertising dodge to keep Spalding's name before the public." What's more, it seemed that Hart was planning his own trip across the Pacific. "I may take a team out to the Antipodes myself," he told the paper. "I inquired particularly of several gentleman from Australia regarding sports there and have it all figured out." Spalding, following one of his practiced business strategies, simply co-opted the competition—much to the chagrin of Anson, who quite rightly saw Hart as a threat to his own authority.

Anson responded with a demonstration of utter political ineptitude. In appreciation for Hart's work in getting the tour to San Francisco, the players of both teams decided to present him with a diamond stickpin. Anson flatly refused to chip in, and let his displeasure with the gift be known. That little bit of ingratitude would come back to haunt him. But for the moment Anson and the women of San Francisco got a bit of inadvertent revenge. When the tourists' boat finally took off across the Pacific, Hart's luggage was mistakenly stowed somewhere in its bowels. Unfortunately, Hart was heading back to Chicago.

San Francisco, a small Mexican outpost named Yerba Buena as recently as the 1840s, had exploded into a genuine metropolis in the decades following the 1848 discovery of gold at nearby Sutter's Mill. By 1888 it was the first city of California (though not its capital). On their third day in this booming town, with no game scheduled, Spalding and his tourists were free to explore San Francisco's many sites of interest. Jimmy Ryan scaled Telegraph Hill, which afforded broad views across the city and the Golden Gate. (Alcatraz Island, sitting out in the bay, then housed a military prison and naval station.) From there, he traveled by cable-car up to the wildly exuberant mansions of Nob Hill. Built for the captains of California industry, these palaces of ostentatious Victorian ornament, with their riot of towers and spires and cupolas, made Spalding's genteel Kenwood manor seem practically impoverished by comparison.

The evening was given over to less salubrious activities, beginning with a night-time excursion into San Francisco's fabled Chinatown, already a de rigueur stop on the tourist trail—"No one should leave the city with-out visiting it," advised Karl Baedeker's 1893 guide to the United States. The time to go was after dark, and then in the company of a licensed guide—generally an off-duty police detective—who for five dollars would lead a tour of the area's most sordid opium dens, joss houses (temples), brothels, and betting parlors, the trip culminating with a late-night plate of chop suey on Dumont Street.

The press of this industrialized tourism inevitably led to the staging of the illicit activities the tours were meant to showcase. Spalding was al-most certainly a victim of such a ruse. Walking down one of the district's seamier alleys, his guide, Sergeant Burdsoll of the San Francisco Police, pointed out a sleepy-looking tough ostensibly guarding a back-room casino. "That fellow looks half asleep, doesn't he," Burdsoll prodded.

"Yes," said Spalding. "He certainly doesn't look as though he is stand-ing to his post."

"Well now, you just watch him," replied Burdsoll, who charged toward the doorway. On cue, the tough blocked the officer and let out a warning cry that brought the steel doors behind him slamming shut. Burdsoll walked back to the party, pleased with his demonstration.

"Can you not batter down doors and make prisoners of them?" asked Palmer, who was in Spalding's party.

"My dear sir," Burdsoll replied, "it would take three hours to enter these places, and when we got in not a Chinaman would be inside. What would be the use of it anyway? No power on earth can check the crime and vice that exist in these quarters to-day."

If nothing else, Chinatown had a dramatic impact on the tourists; An-son went back several times. "The memories of these after-dark trips still linger with me even now, like the shadow of some dark dream," he wrote in his autobiography. Palmer didn't share Anson's romantic view; he was simply appalled: "No religion is known in Chinatown; virtue is unknown there. The people have brought the heathenish customs and horrible practices of their barbarous country to San Francisco, and cling to them with a tenacity that shows the hopelessness of converting them to our views of life and religion and of their ever becoming desirable citizens." This opinion was reflected in U.S. government policy. Just a few days before the tourists arrived in California, Congress had passed legislation re-inforcing the 1882 Chinese Exclusion Act, which had placed a ten-year ban on Chinese immigration. Perceived as interlopers on American soil, the Chinese of San Francisco were subject to more calumny and vituper-ation from the tourists—many of whom were immigrants or second-generation Americans themselves—than any other ethnic group they would encounter on their trip.

Meanwhile, the night of revelry was not yet over, at least for some mem-bers of the tour. While Spalding and Anson, those champions of sobriety, returned to their rooms at the Baldwin, several of their charges sought out the libidinous pleasures of the Barbary Coast, the notorious San Francisco tenderloin that Herbert Asbury, the great chronicler of Amer-ica's underworld, claimed to be more glamorous "than any other area of vice and iniquity on the American continent." The center of this zone of corruption and depravity, "Devil's Acre," was found just a short walk from their hotel, on the triangular block bounded by Broadway, Kearney, and Montgomery streets.

Perhaps the All-Americas were still reeling from the previous night's adventures when they arrived at the ballpark for their next game, an ex-hibition match against the Oakland team of the California League. An-son umpired and Cannonball Crane pitched for the All-Americas, who were beaten handily, 12–2. The only event of note came in the fourth in-ning, with All-America already down five runs and the bases loaded. John Ward stepped to the plate, and as he set himself in the batter's box he let Anson know just what he thought about the job Anson had been doing calling the game. It was not an endorsement. Anson suggested a wager on the outcome of Ward's at bat, and Ward agreed, guaranteeing a base hit. But like everything else on this afternoon, things didn't go Ward's way. After a tapper back to the pitcher, he owed the Chicago cap-tain five bucks.

For Anson, a man who could hold a grudge, the wager must have rep-resented a bit of sweet retribution. In the October issue of *Cosmopoli-tan*, then a general interest magazine, Ward had published an article on the state of the national game in which he explicitly attacked Anson and his credibility, writing: "He will go to the outside limit of the rule every time, and, while his claims may be legitimate so far as the rule is concerned, they are not always in accord with a sense of fair play." Ward then complained that Anson would "occasionally stoop to certain questionable tricks upon the field." In other words, not the ideal umpire. The cranks of San Francisco, however, were hardly interested in the intramural squabbling of Spalding's tourists. They had once again shelled out good money for a bad game. "Players cannot train on late hours and alcohol and win," scolded the *Daily Examiner*.

While the All-Americas were struggling against the Oaklands, their Chicago mates had another day free to explore the riches of San Francisco. Ryan toured Golden Gate Park, Cliff House, and the Seal Rocks—still favored sites on any San Francisco visitor's itinerary. The next day everyone was free, and a large contingent headed out to the Presidio to hear the military band that played there in the afternoons. Anson, Daly, and Palmer took a ride by horseback through the city's suburban residential districts. In his autobiography, Anson offered this description of the local flora: "Roses in California greet you at every turn, not the hothouse roses of the East, that are devoid of all perfume, but roses that are rich with fragrance and that grow in great clusters, clambering about the doorways of the rich and poor alike, drooping over the gateways and making bright the hedges." If it seems impossible that such florid prose could have been the work of the famously coarse-mouthed captain, it is for good reason. Anson, in addition to some of his other less-than-endearing qualities, was a wanton plagiarist. Wide swaths of *A Ball-Player's Career* were drawn verbatim from other books, in particular the account of his riding mate, Harry Palmer.

No one enjoyed the amazing fecundity of the California landscape more than Ward, who spent the following afternoon on a quail-shooting expedition despite the fact that his All-Americas were playing an exhibition against the San Francisco Pioneers, also of the California League. The All-Americas struggled without him, and his absence was most assuredly not appreciated by the crowd, his teammates, or Albert Spalding. As it was, the All-Americas faced Joe "Peachblow" Purcell, whose sweeping curveball proved an impossible target for the visitors' bats; without Ward, they managed only six hits and struck out eight times in an ugly 9–4 loss.

After so many poor performances, the press that had been so welcoming upon the tour's arrival was beginning to turn on Spalding's party. "Can the tourists play ball?" begged one story. "That is the question that is agitating the minds of the San Francisco public at present." Another was less generous: "Perhaps they may be able to play ball, but no one, not even their most intimate friends, will accuse them of having attempted to do so since their advent in this city." Worse still, it cautioned that before Spalding "attempt[s] to introduce base ball in a foreign land with the All-Americas [he] should introduce the game to them first."

No publication reported on the travails of "the Chicago fakirs" with more undisguised glee than the *Sporting News*. Back in St. Louis, word of the tour's failings were received as validations of the paper's early attacks. "I can not tell you with what disgust the people of San Francisco look upon the recent exhibitions given here by the Chicago and All-America teams," its California correspondent reported. "I can not dignify the affairs by calling them base ball games. I can honestly say that the *Sporting News* has made thousands of friends on the coast by showing up these alleged ball teams before they came among us."

While Ward was out hunting and the All-Americas were flailing against the Pioneers, Spalding and the White Stockings had already started down the road to redemption in Stockton, home of the state insane asylum and of the California League's champion baseball club. There, some twenty-five hundred fans were treated to a well-played contest, the first by the tourists in the Golden State. It was a pitcher's duel on a warm, crystalline afternoon. In the first inning, Marty Sullivan homered to put the visiting Chicagos into the lead, and they carried a 2–1 advantage into the bottom of the ninth. But with two outs in the inning an error by Anson allowed Stockton's third baseman to reach first, and when Williamson threw away a grounder on the next play, the Stocktons tied the game—or so they thought. The umpire saw things differently; he called the runner out, ending the game. The crowd would not stand for the loss, however, and a heated discussion began behind the plate. After ten minutes, the various parties decided discretion was the better part of valor, and the game was called a draw on account of darkness.

The tourists would have their revenge. The next day, Friday, the Stocktons met the other half of the Spalding contingent back in San Francisco, but this time there would be no darkness to save them. Crane pitched for the All-Americas, striking out twelve while making "monkeys of the Stocktons" at the plate. On the attack, his teammates ran unhindered on the base paths. Seventeen bases were stolen by the All-Americas, seven alone by James Fogarty. The final score of the wild game was 16–1. "The All-Americas showed yesterday that they know something about the great American game of base-ball," read one lengthy San Francisco headline. Indeed, the tourists now seemed to be on a roll. On Saturday, the Chicagos beat another California League team, the Haverlys, 6–1, behind the solid pitching of Mark Baldwin. "Anson Made Happy" crowed the *San Francisco Chronicle*. "'Cap' and His Fellow-Travelers Play a Good Game of Ball."

Building on that success, on Sunday, November 11, the White Stockings and the All-Americas met for what would be their final confrontation in San Francisco. More than seven thousand spectators, an impressive number, came out to the Haight Street ballpark for the two o'clock game. Unfortunately, not all of Spalding's players were present when play was scheduled to commence: Ward and Hanlon were missing. Spalding was livid. After twenty minutes, he instructed Healy and Crane, pitchers who had been given the day off, to rush down to the clubhouse and suit up. The audience, bored in the cold, sat on its hands and watched as the two teams stalled, trying to leaven the situation with impromptu demonstrations of juggling and pepper.♦ Then, just as their replacements were making their way onto the field, Ward and Hanlon arrived, now forty-five minutes late and sheepishly begging forgiveness. Somehow, they claimed, they had confused the starting time of the game. (This, at least for Ward, was nothing new; during the regular season he

---

♦ Pepper: a drill in which a ball is slap-hit among a small circle of players.

was so often late that his New York teammates took to calling anyone who failed to show up on time a "Johnny Ward.")

On this day, all transgressions were excused, as the teams put on another fine showing; after so much floundering, they had finally found their rhythm. Anson was the offensive star of the game, with three hits, two of them doubles. The fielding, Palmer wrote, was of a character "I have never seen surpassed for brilliancy. . . . The enthusiasm of the crowd knew no bounds." When the final out was made, the scoreboard read 9–6 for the All-Americas. They had won the last four matchups between the teams, and now led the informal series eight games to six.

Having thus rescued their reputations, the full Spalding contingent departed San Francisco for a two-day jaunt south to Los Angeles, then the capital of California's fruit-growing industry. The trip, by Southern Pacific Rail, was a twenty-two hour ride across a varied terrain that eventually gave way to the arid plain surrounding Los Angeles. According to its boosters, a mild and healthful climate made this city the most attractive in the country. Of these men, none was more prominent than Harrison Gray Otis, publisher of the *Los Angeles Times*, who was no doubt still basking in the warm glow of a political coup when Spalding and company rolled into town. Just a week earlier, Benjamin Harrison, his favored candidate, had defeated Grover Cleveland in the presidential election, this despite widespread allegations of voter fraud and Cleveland's winning the popular vote. Otis could take some personal satisfaction in the victory. His paper had been the first to print Lord Sackville-West's notorious letter. The man to whom it was addressed, "Mr. Murchison," was in actuality George Osgoodby, a Republican operative from Pomona and a friend of Otis's. Sackville-West—and Cleveland—had been suckered.

When Spalding and his fellow tourists arrived in Otis's city they were taken immediately by coach to the first-class Hotel Nadeau, on the corner of Spring and First (now site of the *Los Angeles Times* headquarters). That afternoon, the teams played their first game in Los Angeles, at Prospect Park, "the finest base ball grounds in California," according to the *Sporting News*. Chicago won in a 5–0 shutout before some seventeen hundred fans. The next day, the All-Americas got their revenge, a 7–4 victory, this time with an attendance of just eight hundred. With that, the two teams promptly left for the station and their train back to San Francisco. If the tourists' stay in Los Angeles had been a successful one, at least artistically, it was no more memorable than the play they witnessed on their one night out on the town: the long forgotten *Natural Gas*. In that pre-cinematic era, the city had but two serious theaters; its glory as both a baseball and entertainment capital lay in the future.

The Southern Pacific returned the party to San Francisco just in time for what would be one of the signature events of the tour: a grand banquet, paid for by Spalding, at the Baldwin Hotel to celebrate the trip's departure for Australia the next day. Actually, they arrived a bit late for the dinner. Although the guests were invited for ten-thirty, the group did not make it back to the Baldwin until eleven o'clock, and by the time the festivities got under way it was practically midnight. This time, however, no one seemed to mind their tardiness. Spalding had spared no expense on the event, and there was free-flowing champagne—Perrier Jouet—and a twenty-piece orchestra to keep the seventy-five waiting dignitaries happy.

The guests found the Baldwin's banquet hall aglow beneath a row of crystal chandeliers. The centerpiece of the room, displayed on a flower-strewn table, was an elaborate assemblage of bats, balls, masks, mitts, and other paraphernalia of the game, all carefully constructed out of nougat. The hand-stitched menu—or "scorecard"—was in the shape of a baseball. Beneath an injunction to "Play Ball" was a staggering inventory of dishes, each made to correspond with the adventure:

MENU, BALDWIN HOTEL

"Play Ball"

Eastern Oysters, on the "Home Run"
Green Turtle à la Kangaroo
Queen Olives, Radishes, Celery
Petit pâté à la Spalding
Pommes Parisiennes à la Palmer
Fillet of Beef, larded à la Antipodes
Asperges à la "Willow"
Sweet Breads, sauté, à la Anson
Petit Pois Français à la "Over the Fence"
Stewed Terrapin à la Ward, Short Stop
Fresno Turkey à la "Foul"
Mashed Potatoes à la "Soft Ball"
Baked Sweet Potatoes à la "Hot Grounder"
String Beans à la McMillan [sic]
Sorbet au Kirsch à la Frank Lincoln
Shrimp Salad à la Colorado Springs
Roast Mountain Quail, garni de cresson à la "Fly Catch"
Dressed Lettuce à la "Full Tog"
Gallantine de Dinde, sur socle à la Burlington Route
Pâté de Gibier
Saumon au Beurre à la S.F. Press Club
Jambon, garni, à la Jim Hart
English Plum Pudding, à la "Hard Hit," Brandy sauce à la "Hot Ball"
Meringue Pyramid à la "Chicagos"
Macaroon Pyramid à la "All-Americas"
Champagne Jelly à la Captain Morse
Tutti Frutti Ice Cream à la "Cold Day"
Desert à la "Gazzam!" Café Noir à la "Mascot"
Fruit, "Allah Be Praised!"

Falstaff himself would have been impressed with the repast. The Baldwin's tireless wait staff filled and refilled champagne flutes and ferried dishes to the tables deep into the night. Among the revelers, conversation turned back and forth from baseball to recent political events. After the final course was cleared, cigars were passed about, and speeches made. Ward, Anson, and Spalding all gave thanks to the San Franciscans for the warm reception and (mostly) forgiving coverage they had received during their stay. By the time the titanic repast was complete and the men pulled themselves from their seats, it was nearly 5 A.M. No one seemed to mind. As Ryan wrote in his diary, "It was a jolly good time."

The trip's departure, originally scheduled for the following afternoon, was delayed one day to wait for a mail shipment from the East Coast, which allowed the players a welcome bit of time to recover from their feast and to spend a last few hours on native soil. The holdup would come to pose "a serious complication," as Spalding put it, but for the moment it was a blessing. Most everybody slept in. A few walked down to the pier to inspect the S.S. *Alameda*, the liner that would carry them across the sea. Trunks were given a final inspection. Leigh Lynch, Spalding's advance man, had wired from Australia with packing recommendations for the players: a light spring overcoat, a few flannel suits and shirts, two pairs of pajamas, and formal wear for ceremonial events. It was taken for granted that they would all bring their revolvers, still considered standard equipment for a long journey. (Although by the late 1880s Baedeker guides considered arms "unnecessary" for travel within the United States, elsewhere they remained obligatory. The list of recommended items in John Murray's popular 1891 handbook for travelers to Egypt included, "guns, magnesium wire and a lamp—for properly seeing in tombs.")

The traveling group now also included several new faces, the most prominent among them being George Wright, Spalding's old teammate on the Red Stockings and co-owner of the sporting-goods concern Wright & Ditson, and Irving Snyder, one half of the Peck & Snyder sporting-goods company. Wright was brought along as an umpire and cricket coach; Snyder claimed to be on a mission to unload thirty thousand pairs of roller-skates rusting away in a warehouse. Their appearance suggests that, although formal arrangements would not be announced for several years, Spalding had already begun the work of assembling their respective companies under the umbrella of his own. Professor Bartholomew, the one-eyed aerialist, also joined the party in San Francisco, as did Frank Lincoln, a popular entertainer who it was hoped would lighten the mood on the long journey. Finally there was Leslie Robison, a retired president of the Peoria Electric Light Company and a lifelong fan of the game who thought nothing could be more appealing than a trip across the ocean with America's greatest "baseballists." There was only one conspicuous absence: Helen Dauvray. "Urgent business" had called John Ward's actress wife back to New York. That business would eventually demand Ward's presence as well, though for the moment he was probably happy to see her go.

In the evening, this motley group came together for one last meal before their expedition began in earnest. This time it was a relaxed affair in the Baldwin dining room, without pomp or pageantry or fancy menus—though there was plenty to drink. And on this night it was not Spalding or Anson or Ward who would make the final toast. That was left to Ned Williamson, the much-respected White Stockings shortstop: "To-morrow we bid a fond adieu to the shores of our native land. Never did a ship bear more precious freight. Treading the planks of the noble vessel, with only the sheering keel beneath us, will be the men who are the pride and boast of every true American. Who could replace us should the envious sea, lashed by some unknown fury, gather us to its never-ending embrace? Think, if you are sober enough, of the glory that has been ours." Glory had been theirs, if not always, at least intermittently. Whether they would continue to find it overseas—well, that remained to be seen.

CHAPTER 5

AT PLAY WITH THE KING OF
THE CANNIBAL ISLANDS

THE VESSEL THAT WOULD BEAR SPALDING'S "PRECIOUS FREIGHT" to Australia was the iron-hulled *Alameda*, pride of the Oceanic Steamship Company. Built in 1883, it boasted two large funnels amidships and, spaced evenly over its decks, three masts rigged for sail. "Neat and trim looking," was Palmer's assessment of the 3,000-ton ship when he came upon it for the first time. Further exploration, on the morning of departure, revealed it to be "a world in itself." As big as it may have appeared, it was actually no match for the giant liners that made the Atlantic run; the thiry-four person Spalding party comprised nearly a third of its passengers. The staterooms they occupied were cramped and poorly ventilated, and had the unfortunate tendency to grow intensely hot in the equatorial sun. If escape was to be found, it was under the broad awnings that shaded the ship's decks. Time could also be whiled away in a grand dining room, a saloon, a card room, and a library. Commanding it all was a figure whose imposing presence inspired confidence in even the most anxious traveler: Captain Henry G. Morse, a self-described "sea dog" who had spent more than twenty years plying the waters of the Pacific.

It was shortly after two o'clock when Morse gave the signal to raise the *Alameda*'s gangplank and unleash the ship from its moorings. Back

on the pier, several hundred well-wishers waved hats, handkerchiefs, um-
brellas, and called out their final farewells to the tourists. Moments later,
the liner's throbbing engines began to churn water, and the ship pulled
out into foggy San Francisco harbor.

There was something irresistibly romantic about this sendoff—the
pageantry, the anticipation of adventure, the sadness of leaving home, the
fear of the unknown with all of its attendant risks—that left even these
hard baseball men soft with emotion and perhaps a bit apprehensive. For
those of humble, working-class background international travel was indeed a novelty, and certainly an occasion for celebration. In the past, the
touring classes had been comprised almost exclusively of the extremely
well off. Only those with considerable resources of time and money could
afford the luxury of a transoceanic voyage. But the industrial revolution
was changing that. Modern technologies dramatically reduced the costs
of movement and allowed for the development of a broad middle-class
with expendable income and the means to take time away from work. The
result was a gradual democratization of travel. "God's earth, with all its
fullness and beauty, is for the people; and railways and steamboats are the
results of the common light of science, and are for the people also," wrote
Thomas Cook, the British entrepreneur who created the package tour in
the early 1840s. His services were wildly popular, both in Europe and with
Americans. Mark Twain vouched for Cook, and President Grant was a
client. The world, which had once seemed impossibly large, was beginning to shrink; if its farther shores remained out of reach for most Americans, they were, for the first time, not beyond some kind of reasonable
aspiration. Spalding and his itinerant, blue-collar ballplayers would serve
as an avant-garde for those Americans, venturing forth to return with colorful stories of strange peoples and places and things. Meanwhile, in the
lands they would visit, Spalding and his men would be nothing so much
as harbingers of a not-too-distant future when American tourists would
roam freely across the globe.

The pervasive air of sentimentality that engulfed the *Alameda* as it
pulled out of dock was soon broken by Anson, who had begun taking

bets and laying odds before the ship even passed through the Golden
Gate. Who would be first to lose it over the rail from sea-sickness? What
kind of soup would be served at lunch? How far would the ship travel in
the next day? There was no subject on which he would not make book,
and no man he would not challenge to a wager. When Captain Morse
mentioned at dinner that clear weather was forecast for the night, Anson
bet him five dollars it would rain before morning. (It did.) By day three of
the voyage, Anson's gambling had become a running joke, and over
breakfast James Fogarty decided to have a little fun at his expense.
"Twenty-five to one that the ship does not go down before we reach Honolulu," he called out. "I will take you!" Anson replied. The room burst
out in laughter.

On the second day out of San Francisco, gale-force winds drove waves
over the *Alameda*'s decks, and the ship pitched violently in the rough waters. Sea-sickness plagued nearly all of the tourists. Sullivan was the first
to feel the nasty effects of the roiling ocean, and soon Burns, Fogarty,
and Wright were similarly ill. (Members of the White Stockings took to
calling out "New York" while tossing over the side in a mordant salute to
Ward's National League champion Giants.) Anson, after his book-
making the previous afternoon, had left himself with few allies on this
front. "Every one seemed to want to see Anson right sick," Ward wrote
in a dispatch back to the *Chicago Tribune*. Only Anson's stubborn pride
kept his fellow passengers from getting much satisfaction. In his own
correspondence he admitted to being in "vile condition" and as "pale as
a cleanly brushed home plate." In any case, he was in no worse shape
than Chicago's Jimmy Ryan. "Oh! If I could but get off and walk," he
scribbled in his diary. A day later, feeling slightly better but no less embit-
tered, he wrote of his plan to "get on shore and stay there and then find
the author of *A Life on the Ocean Wave* and punch his head."◆

By day three the storms had passed and the men had begun to acquire
their sea legs. The balance of the trip to Hawaii would be smooth sailing,
the days languorous and uneventful in the tropical heat. In the evenings,

---

◆ *A Life on the Ocean Wave:* An autobiographical account of British sea captain
George Bayly's adventures traveling to Australia.

to keep cool, they abandoned their poorly ventilated staterooms for the *Alameda*'s breeze-swept decks, where they slept, pajama-clad, in cane-seated steamer chairs. In the mornings, at around five, the crew came out to spray those decks clean with saltwater, chasing the men back to their cabins. The players would return shortly thereafter, now only with towels, to be hosed down themselves, and for a quick cup of coffee and a biscuit before dressing for the day. Palmer would always remember this portion of the trip with fondness. "The sun shone down upon us from a cloudless sky. The salt air was pure and healthful," he wrote. "Looking back over our journey around the globe, I can recall no part of it that was pleasanter than those days upon the Pacific."

It was, indeed, an indolent time, and with the players made complaisant by the heat and the natural boredom of the journey, Spalding calculated the moment was right to reveal, ever so carefully, a secret he had been guarding for some time: The grand adventure on which he and his men were presently engaged was about to be extended into something more ambitious than anyone had previously imagined. Spalding's Australian Base-Ball Tour was about to become Spalding's Around-the-World Base-Ball Tour.

For just how long this change had been set in Spalding's mind is something of a mystery. John Ward had raised the possibility of extending the trip into an around-the-world tour, at least for himself, several months earlier. Before that, in the winter of 1887, the adventurer Thomas Stevens had completed a three-year circumnavigation of the globe on a Columbia "High-Wheel" bicycle, and his account of that journey had been serialized in the popular magazine *Outing*, which Spalding read.

If these men provided inspiration, the enthusiastic crowds that greeted the tour as it barnstormed across America assured Spalding that the country would be eager for news of the players wherever they traveled. The prospect of redressing one of his few professional failures—that ill-conceived 1874 tour of England with the National Association's Boston and Philadelphia clubs—must have been appealing. But more than anything, it must have been the very idea of a world tour—its boldness, its extravagance, its romanticism—that appealed to Spalding's sense of scale and audacity. If he could not compete with the timetable set by

Jules Verne in his 1872 classic, *Around the World in Eighty Days*, he knew that he could present Americans with something that was, in many ways, altogether more powerful. In place of Phileas Fogg, Verne's punctilious British protagonist, Spalding would be leading a charismatic gang of working-class heroes on a mission to spread the gospel of baseball, that most beloved and potent symbol of the American way. And his madcap group, just as had Fogg, would be racing against the clock: Spalding and his men would have to be back by April 24th—opening day of the 1889 season.

It was with this spirit of possibility that Spalding had called the London agent of the Burlington Route Rail Road into his suite at San Francisco's Baldwin Hotel, informed him of his new plan, and sent him off to make preparations for the party to travel on from Australia to India, Egypt, Palestine, Italy, Germany, France, England, Ireland, and then back across the Atlantic to America. In the meantime, Jim Hart, his new lieutenant, was ordered back to Chicago, where he would launch a campaign to promote the tour in the American press.

These steps were undertaken in at least provisional secrecy. Anson, a "partner" in the venture, was informed, as were Ward and the three syndicated correspondents traveling with the group—Harry Palmer, who was supplying four papers with his reports, Newton MacMillan of the *Chicago Inter Ocean*, and Simon Goodfriend of the *New York Sun*—but they were instructed to keep the new plan to themselves. Lining up the players for the Australian journey had proved a major headache for Spalding; he was not about to risk any more last-minute defections before the ship cast off from its pier. Keeping word of the new itinerary from the men until they were already floating across the Pacific would neatly forestall that possibility. As it was, the contracts they had signed made no mention of the route by which they would return to the United States; on that front, he had them, as the *Sporting News* would soon report "dead to rights."

With his audience captive aboard the *Alameda*, all that was left was for Spalding to inform the players of the new route without inciting a mutiny. He dismissed the idea of assembling the group for a bold change-of-mission statement as potentially inflammatory. Instead, he shrewdly calculated that the best way to win the players' favor would be simply to allow the news to leak. Palmer, Spalding's usual mouthpiece, and Ward, the leader of the players' union, were presumably the sources of a rumor that Spalding was "considering" the possibility of an extension of the tour into a complete circumnavigation of the globe—a genuine baseball odyssey.

As the enticing news became public, Spalding equivocated, letting the players, increasingly excited about the possible extension of the tour, twist in the ocean wind. "I want to state emphatically at the outset that nothing definite in regard to a trip around the world has yet been decided upon," Spalding told Goodfriend. "Personally, I should like to make such a voyage as I shall probably never again have such an opportunity of carrying out one of the strongest desires and ambitions of my life. But the tour I contemplate is one of such great magnitude, involving such an enormous amount of labor and expense, that I hesitate to approach the scheme until the matter has definitely been decided upon." Hesitation, however, did not keep him from boasting of stops in India, Egypt, Constantinople, and virtually every European capital, including ten days in Paris—all, of course, merely being "an outline of a trip that has not yet been decided upon."

The ploy worked to perfection. Lured in by his come-on, the players spent the remainder of their time on the *Alameda* raiding the ship's library for works on the countries they hoped to visit, speculating on possible routes, and otherwise fantasizing about their would-be adventure. Fortunately, the ship was well-stocked with guidebooks, one of the great fruits of the new tourist industry, from which they could feed their imaginations. By 1888, there was nary an inlet not described by such publishers as Appleton, Bradshaw, Cook, Harper's, Murray, and of course Baedeker, king of them all, exhaustive and definitive—a virtual university faculty in your pocket.

Spalding, meanwhile, was only too happy to let the men think the trip's extension was their own prerogative. Tener, who shared Spalding's stateroom (the magnate, always prudent with a dollar and insecure since he was sent off to Rockford in his youth, preferred company even in sleep), claimed in a letter home that he was "instrumental" in persuading Spalding to continue on around the world. Little did anyone realize that Spalding had already set in motion a publicity campaign advertising the new route back in the States. When he finally came clean and formally announced the new plan—nearly a month later, in Melbourne—the men burst into applause.

Spalding's little ruse was not the only machination going on behind the players' backs. On November 22, while the *Alameda* was still sailing on the Pacific and was days from Hawaii, the kingpins of the National League gathered at New York's Fifth Avenue Hotel for their annual winter meetings. In their absence—and, more critically, that of John Ward, president of the players' fledgling union—the league's directors came to an agreement on a wholesale revision of its labor policy. The form of this restructuring was the so-called Brush Classification Plan, an accounting system that divided players into five payroll categories, with annual salaries staggered from a maximum of $2,500 for "Class A" players down to $1,500 for those in "Class E." Determination of class would come at the unilateral discretion of league management, and would be based not only on such measurable (though certainly debatable) criteria as performance, but also on a player's personal conduct both on and off the field.

Not surprisingly, the National League players, at least those who remained in the United States, were livid, but with their leadership incommunicado and potentially out of the country for the next four months, they were all but powerless and were forced to begin their off-season contractual negotiations with the new terms in place. "Won't Ward and the others be mad," Tim Keefe, star pitcher of the New York Giants, wryly noted to a *Sporting News* reporter after the announcement of the policy. Spalding's role in the whole matter was certainly a question on many people's minds. Had his Australian tour, now extended around the world, been nothing more than a pretext to remove the owners' chief antagonist from the scene? Or could it be that Spalding, too, was floating west across the Pacific blissfully ignorant of the scheming taking place back home?

The call of "Land ho!" came from the *Alameda* bridge early on the morning of Sunday, November 25, one day after the scheduled arrival date. The rugged slopes of the extinct volcano Diamond Head, rising above the verdant Hawaiian shoreline, had been spotted through the predawn haze by the steamer's lookout. Though it was only five-thirty, much of the party was already on deck, having been driven from their close quarters by the oppressive heat. Roused from their loungers, they assembled along the rails at the bow of the ship, anxious for a first glimpse of the land they had already taken to calling the "paradise of the Pacific" and the "Cannibal Islands." Hawaii was then a romantic island fantasy, a spectacularly lush (if mosquito-ridden) independent kingdom still known to much of the world as the Sandwich Islands, the name Captain Cook had given the group upon his arrival there in 1778.

The tourists were not disappointed by the view that gradually revealed itself to them as they stood gazing out along the *Alameda*'s rails. Newton MacMillan was so overcome that he attempted to capture the whole experience in one rambling, Victorian masterpiece of a sentence:

> Our friends at home can perhaps understand how full were the hearts of every man of us when, after ploughing the waves of the great ocean for seven long days, without once seeing or speaking to any living thing beyond our ship's rail, or gazing upon ought else than the seemingly limitless expanse of ocean that rolled about us, we sailed into the beautiful harbor of Honolulu, nestled at the foot of the picturesque Nuuanu Valley, with great verdure covered mountains towering sentinel-like above it, the bright sunlight gilding the rippling waters of the peaceful harbor and outlining the broad porticoed houses, the coconut and banana groves, and the extensive acres of the distant sugar plantations along the shores.

Word that the *Alameda* had been spotted off the Hawaiian coast traveled through the streets of Honolulu with similar excitement. A general holiday had been called the previous day in anticipation of the ship's arrival, and now, some twenty-four hours later than expected, an eager crowd once again began to assemble on the Oceanic pier. Across the harbor, the officers and crew of the U.S.S. *Alert*, on hand to safeguard American interests in the island kingdom, saluted the ballplayers as they steamed past. (Annexation would not come until 1898, and statehood until 1959.) Meanwhile, the tugboat *Eleu*—carrying a small reception committee, a harbor pilot, the port physician, and several native boys with lei-filled baskets—was dispatched to reel in the liner.

By the time the *Alameda*'s gangplank was lowered, the crowd on shore had grown to more than two thousand, and the Royal Hawaiian Band, decked out in crisp white-duck uniforms, had begun to play. Henry Berger, the band's indefatigable master, had long made it a practice to greet incoming ships with a serenade, and now he happily drilled his musicians through a series of tunes chosen especially for the baseball tourists, among them "The Star-Spangled Banner," "Yankee Doodle," "Auld Lang Syne," and "Alohe oe," the last being a tune he had scored himself. The arrival of a steamship at port was always a well-choreographed affair in Hawaii, then still a remote territory unconnected to the wider world by that most modern of conveniences, the telegraph.

This last fact meant that results of the American presidential election had not reached Hawaii in advance of the tourists—the *Alameda* was the first vessel to arrive since the contest—and so as the men stepped onto terra firma they were besieged with questions from the local American contingent as to its outcome. But there was another question on the minds of the many baseball cranks who had come out to greet the tourists: Would they play? A doubleheader had been promised and for a week the local papers had hyped the event with illustrated feature stories on the players and the trip. (Harry Simpson, Spalding's secretary, had arrived a week in advance to seed the press and make arrangements for the tour's arrival.) But those games were scheduled for Saturday, and that day had passed. Now it was Sunday, the *Alameda* was set to continue on to Australia just after sundown, and strict blue laws imposed by Hawaii's missionary class forebade public entertainments of all kinds on the Sabbath. Would there be a special dispensation for the baseball-playing visitors? Would they simply flout the law? Spalding's position on the matter of Sunday ball had already proved malleable. More crucially, the game's most ardent supporters were in control of Hawaii's political apparatus. These factors alone may have lent encouragement to the fans gathered on the Oceanic pier. But there were larger forces at work. Over the coming hours, Spalding and his men found themselves caught in the uncomfortable center of a triangular showdown between a vociferous band of baseball fans, the purported guardians of Hawaii's moral welfare, and a chastened native king out to assert his own independence. Who knew paradise could be so complicated?

The tourists' first stop was the Royal Hawaiian Hotel, an elegant three-story structure that was to be their base of operations for the day. A sumptuous breakfast spread had been laid out in their honor in the hotel's formal dining room. Tropical fruits spilled from bowls on the finely set tables: bananas, coconuts, guavas, mangos, oranges—all, as Palmer noted, "taken from the parent branch not half an hour before." While the players indulged themselves, Spalding stood in the hotel's reception hall greeting a string of island power brokers who had come to pay their respects. The day's schedule was the primary topic of discussion. An audience with the king had been arranged for the tourists later in the morning, and there would be a luau, a feast, at the residence of the queen in the evening. Whether baseball would be played sometime between these two events remained an open and highly charged question. Throughout the morning Spalding was "buttonholed and pulled off into different corners" by those pitching their various agendas. Members of the formal reception committee, bolstered by local business interests and chaired by William Smith, a distant Spalding cousin, were anxious for the teams to play. Another faction, one that included Hawaii's attorney general, Clarence Ashford, and its finance minister, William Green, was less willing to see any break in precedent on a matter of moral authority.

Nothing had been resolved when the U.S. minister, George W. Merrill, arrived at ten-thirty to escort the group to their meeting with the king, David Kalakaua. Though his Iolani Palace sat in an enclosed ten-acre garden catty-corner from the Royal Hawaiian, it was nonetheless decided that a formal parade through the streets of Honolulu was in order, and a procession was formed in front of the hotel. Clarence Duval, who had been outfitted with a new drum major's uniform in San Francisco consisting of a scarlet jacket, khaki pants, black boots, and a braided cap, was sent out to lead the way. He was followed by Berger and his band (they had come from the docks), the ballplayers in double file, and a carriage for the ladies of the party bringing up the rear. The group made for quite the spectacle as it meandered through town, with Duval tossing his baton high in the air and the band playing the Civil War anthem "Marching Through Georgia." (The song, a celebration of Sherman's victorious sweep, was an interesting choice for men on a jingoistic mission of their own.) Whatever the locals thought of this merry group, what most impressed the tourists was the apparent harmony of Hawaii's diverse population, which Newton MacMillan described with typical sensitivity, writing that "windows and doors in the low-browed houses bulged with dusky humanity. The curb was crowded with barefooted and open-mouthed Kanakas [native Hawaiians], Chinamen, half-castes and whites mingled in picturesque confusion."

The group eventually made its way back to where they had started, finally passing the bellicose bronze statue of King Kamehameha, erected by Kalakau in 1883, and then entering the palace grounds through the ceremonial Kauikeaouli Gate. Its lintel boasted an elaborate coat-of-arms and the motto "*Ua mau ke ea o ka aina i ka pono*" ("The life of the land is perpetuated in righteousness"). The Iolani Palace, which still stands, is a grand, vaguely Italianate affair that had been built by Kalakaua over four years, from 1879 to 1882, at a cost of more than three hundred thousand dollars. From the start, opinion on its merits was divided. "Though rather free from exterior ornamentation," wrote Palmer, it "presents a dignified and imposing presence." Goodfriend, however, thought it a "gaudy and unsubstantial affai—stuccoed without and glaring with white plaster within."

Upon entering the palace, the party was ushered into the Blue Room, a broad chamber hung with formal portraits, where protocol required that they cool their heels. Soon enough a chamberlain notified them that the time was at hand to meet the monarch, and the party once again formed into double file. With that they were led, with Merrill and Spalding at the head of the line, into the Throne Room, a long hall with red velvet carpet and gold-trimmed walls. Kalakaua, dressed in a handsome brown suit cut in the English style, stood waiting for them at the other end of the room, flanked on either side by an attendant in white hat and yellow cape. For Merrill and Kalakaua, it must have been an awkward moment.

Barely a year earlier, the diplomat had walked into the same room to inform the king, in no uncertain terms, that his time running Hawaii had come to an end. His message was simple: The leaders of the white community, backed by their own military force, were rewriting the constitution, and he could either peacefully accept a new position as a figurehead or lose his kingdom altogether. He chose the former. (The United States, at the time, was satisfied with a reciprocity treaty that allowed it exclusive rights over Pearl Harbor, and wanted nothing more than that the little island kingdom remain well behaved—hence the presence of the *Alert*.)

Despite Merrill's intercession, the Hawaiian political climate remained fraught, and now it was a game of baseball, of all things, that was stirring up passions. On this day, however, there would be no ultimatums, and if there was tension between Merrill and Kalakaua it was camouflaged by the formalities and niceties of the royal court. William Smith, sensing the moment for action was at hand, stepped up to introduce his kin: "This is Mr. Spalding and this is his mother." Spalding gave a small bow, took up a position at the monarch's side, and proceeded to present each member of the party. Kalakaua, who spoke English with only a slight accent, made a winning impression on the tourists. "He was courteous yet dignified, held himself erect, and looked every inch a Hawaiian King," wrote Ward. Palmer thought he had "a fine face, with dark, expressive eyes and a kindly expression that grows more interesting as one looks into it." There was no stammering from Anson, who by his own account "seized the imperial flipper and squeezed it with all the ardor of a howling wolf." He was less impressed with the king than his fellow tourists, however. "The monarch of the Sandwich Islands needs exercise," wrote the captain. "His flesh is soft and I don't believe he could do a hundred yards in less than two minutes."

After the introductions, the king mingled with the players and chatted with Spalding. The monarch was a fan of the game, which had been imported to the islands in the early nineteenth century by New England missionaries who had come to Christianize the population. The natives took up the sport, which they called *kinipopo*, and it had grown increasingly popular over the years. Kalakaua claimed to have played the game himself, and his kingdom could boast some baseball royalty of its own: Alexander Cartwright, secretary of the pioneering New York Knickerbockers, had landed in Hawaii as a tourist in 1849 and stayed on permanently.

Small talk aside, there was the question of whether the Chicagos and All-Americas would perform later that afternoon. King Kalakaua was anxious to see a match, if for no other reason than to flout the laws of those who had stripped him of his power. The irony that this would come through the agency of the invaders' own favorite pastime must have made the prospect all the more appealing. In fact, the very same men who had orchestrated his downfall—including Attorney General Ashford—were those who had been instrumental in organizing the reception of the ballplaying tourists in the first place. This left Spalding in an awkward position, to say the least. How do you say no to a king? The obvious answer is that you don't, at least not to his face. Spalding thus assured Kalakaua that, of course, he very much hoped to play. And then he beat a hasty retreat.

While Spalding and his charges were hobnobbing with the king, Hawaii's baseball cranks, fearing the worst, had taken to the streets on a petition drive, and in the span of just a few hours had accumulated more than one thousand signatures in support of play. When Spalding's party returned to the Royal Hawaiian from the palace, a swell of fans was waiting, and the documents were handed over:

> To A. G. Spaulding [sic], Esq.
>
> Sir,
>
> We the undersigned request you to play a game of baseball today and guarantie to defray any expenses of whatever nature.

Below this pledge was a roll of both Anglo and Hawaiian signatures. "I was importuned, almost with tears, to ignore the law," recalled Spalding. As further incentive, the reception committee offered a bonus purse of one thousand dollars.

Confronted with this groundswell of support, Spalding quickly set off with a lawyer to review his options with the city marshal, who informed him that the injunction against play would be enforced. This left Spalding with little room for negotiation: An arrest, though unlikely, would be disastrous—the *Alameda*, which was set to sail that evening, would not wait, and the episode would be a publicity debacle back in the States.

Explaining this to the potentially dangerous crowd that had gathered on the Royal Hawaiian's front lawn, however, would require considerable tact. To make the announcement, Spalding ascended to a veranda that overlooked the garden, and with the petitions clutched aloft in his hand saluted the audience for its support. A certain soothing tone, a calm but authoritative demeanor was required under the circumstances, and by all accounts Spalding hit just the right note. He was obliged to tell them, unfortunately, that the law was beyond his control, and despite his special pleading on their behalf there would be no baseball on this day. When his brief talk was over, the crowd's anger had been deftly converted to disappointment, and sympathy was fully with Spalding and his charges. A rather tame cry of "rats" was the harshest note anyone could muster. Ward, who watched with lawyerly detachment as the scene unfolded, summed up the young magnate's performance with undisguised admiration: "What Al Spalding does not know about diplomacy is of no possible use."

For their part, the tourists were happy to be relieved of the obligation to play ball, and broke off into smaller groups so they might take full advantage of their one day on the island paradise. Wright, Snyder, Palmer, and Daly hired a carriage, and made first for Makiki Field, the local ballpark. An extra grandstand with space for eight hundred spectators had been constructed to accommodate the overflow crowds the players had been expected to draw—the base capacity was roughly one thousand—and Palmer deemed the field itself to be in "splendid condition." From there, the group moved on to the Pali, a mountain precipice with stunning views across the Nuaanu Valley. "No one who saw that glorious picture of nature withdrew his gaze from it without a feeling of regret and felt that his time had been all too small to absorb its beauties." Tom Burns, who had traveled to the same spot, most assuredly felt this way, and decided the best recourse was to abscond with one of those beauties. With the assistance of John Ward, he climbed over an iron rail guarding the 1,100-foot drop and—hanging precariously from a cane—plucked a white flower from the wall of the cliff.

Spalding, meanwhile, spent the day with his mother, first dining at the home of his cousin George Smith, and then setting out on a tour of Waikiki. The principal stop on this expedition was Ainahau, home of the widower Archibald Cleghorn, said to be the most beautiful estate on the island. Here, the Spaldings were introduced to Cleghorn's daughter, the fourteen-year-old Princess Kaiulani. (Cleghorn had been married to Princess Likelike, a cousin of Kalakaua; she died in 1887.) After a pleasant visit, in which the princess impressed all with her intelligence and beauty, the Spalding group moved on to the home of the sugar baron John Cummins before finally returning to the Royal Hawaiian to prepare for the evening's festivities.

<hr>

The culmination of the tourists' short stay in Hawaii was a grand luau thrown in their honor by King Kalakaua. More than one hundred guests were invited to the event, which took place on the estate of Queen Kapiolani, an Eden of coconut, date, banana, and royal palms ringed with torches and set aglow by countless hanging Japanese lanterns. "A perfect fairyland," recalled Harriet Spalding. "Certainly the most novel, if not the most gorgeous event in which we participated during the tour," echoed Palmer.

Gorgeous was just how the hot-blooded American ballplayers found the many young Hawaiian women on hand to garland them with leis. "We were all too much astonished for the moment but to do much else than stare at the dusky beauties as they stood before us," Palmer reported. Their revealing traditional outfits, which left "their shapely arms exposed—and the brown skin of their rounded shoulders only partly concealed," made for quite a contrast to what the men were used to back in Victorian America, where so much as a bare ankle was considered risqué. The elderly Harriet Spalding, as if to accentuate the difference, was on hand in her matronly uniform of neck-to-toe pitch-black silk.

The players had been wondering just what was in store for them at this native feast for most of the afternoon; the transformation of Polynesian dining into a hokey cliché of tiki huts and mai-tais by so many Trader Vics would not come for generations. "All of us knew, or thought we knew, that a luau was a barbaric festival, fraught with that pagan abandon which obtained in the Sandwich Islands before the day when the good missionaries came and converted their Hawaiians from their wickedness and cannibalism," wrote MacMillan. Whatever their expectations, they were savvy enough to pick up on the larger political implications of this feast: the palpable friction between their native host and his supposed vassals. MacMillan noted, "We knew that these same missionaries, or their descendants, had interdicted a Sunday game of ball and we shrewdly suspected that the King, having no sympathy with this inhibition, had hit upon the luau as a partial reparation to his guests and a bit of revenge upon his sabbatarian subjects."

In any case, King Kalakaua liked to entertain; his penchant for lavish party-giving had earned him the sobriquet "the merry monarch." One of his first actions upon assuming the throne in 1874 was to launch a campaign to restore and elevate native culture, a project that did little to endear him to Hawaii's white planter and missionary classes. And so it was that when Spalding and company arrived at the queen's estate, they found the king dressed in a traditional white tunic, seated informally on a stool in front of his "birth tree," a sturdy palm planted some fifty-two years earlier. Rising to greet them, he casually flicked away a cigarette and with a wave of his burly arms welcomed the ballplayers to his wife's home.

Following another brief round of introductions, the party moved to a tent for champagne punch and conversation. The king apparently took a particular shine to Harriet Spalding, and—his wife being ill and not in attendance—had specifically requested that she take the queen's place of honor beside him during dinner. Harriet obliged, but only reluctantly; she had earlier wanted to skip the whole affair, and was only convinced to attend after a bit of prodding by her son back at the hotel. "Mother, you speak as though you were in the habit of being escorted by kings," Albert chided her. As for just what a Polynesian king with a reputation for revelry might have found entrancing in a sixty-two-year-old Midwestern dowager is anyone's guess—in all likelihood, he was simply showing a bit of courtesy to an elder—but at least he could offer her a bit of advice on her travels, for he, too, had circumnavigated the globe; he was the first reigning monarch of any nation to do so. In 1881, Kalakaua had set off on a ten-month journey on which he met the emperor of Japan, the king of Siam, the pope, the queen of England, and the American president, Chester A. Arthur, among other dignitaries. How could she not be impressed?

The feast itself took place in an open wooden *loual*, or pavilion, erected on a platform in the center of the queen's garden. A large, U-shaped table had been set on low boards, and the diners sat, Indian-style, on woven mats placed neatly along its side. At the head was Kalakaua, who shared a specially embroidered silk mat with Harriet. The table itself was a *horror vacuii* of elaborately presented traditional foods and decoration. Each place had a glass for water, a champagne flute, and a bottle of beer. There was roast suckling pig, turkey draped in garlands, whole fish wrapped in leaves, and game of all kinds. The centerpiece was a towering composition of tropical fruits, flowers, and fronds. The general impression, said MacMillan, was a sense of "barbaric plenty. Not a square inch on that huge board was but covered with some dish, pan, platter, tureen, bowl, or other receptacle for food."

Of all the comestibles, what fascinated the Americans most was *poi*, the native Hawaiian porridge of mashed taro, which was ladled into hollowed-out coconut shells and eaten with a dip of the finger. Kalakaua himself opened the festivities with a demonstration of proper poi-eating technique, inserting his right forefinger into a large calabash and removing it with a flourish. "This he deftly inserted into his mouth, swabbed it about for a moment, and then presented a clean finger and a pair of glistening lips to the gaze of his admiring guests," wrote MacMillan. "The

King is always right; the King eats poi with his finger; it is right to eat poi with one's finger." So instructed, the tourists followed suit, though none seemed to enjoy it so much as the monarch. "It doesn't tempt the adventurous finger, nor does the finger, once imbued with the flaccid mess, tempt the palate," was MacMillan's assessment. Ward felt it had both the consistency and flavor of poster paste. Harriet thought it an unpleasant combination of "mashed potato, turnip, and sugar," though when her mat-mate asked if she approved she had the good sense to respond, "Oh yes, I like it very much." Anyway, she enjoyed the fish.

The luau proper concluded with a series of after-dinner speeches, the first being a lampoon of after-dinner speeches by the tour's traveling comic, Frank Lincoln. This he followed with a routine on the "artistic mixing of a soda cocktail." (The details are lost, but by all accounts it was quite a knee-slapper.) After Lincoln came Attorney General Ashford, who, speaking for the king, made a simple toast to the health and good fortune of the players. Spalding responded with a brief toast of his own—Harriet, always the nervous mother, "trembled head to foot" with the practically inconceivable notion that Albert might embarrass himself—this on a day when he'd already proved his mettle in a far more difficult situation. Now, he provided a quick recap of the tour's progress, and thanked the king for his hospitality. When he was heartily applauded, Harriet could finally relax.

With that, the party returned to the garden for a bit of socializing, and, it turned out, dance. Clarence Duval, who had been pressed into duty as a steward during the feast, was pushed into performing one of his "plantation dances" to the hand-clapping accompaniment of Ryan, Burns, Fogarty, and Pfeffer. Kalakaua was so impressed with Duval's "maze of rapidly flying legs and arms" that he rewarded him with a ten-dollar gold coin. In Hawaii, however, there could be only one main dancing attraction: the final activity of the evening was a performance of the hula, a dance considered so pagan and libidinous that it had been banned by the forces of missionary propriety. Kalakaua had revived the custom as part of his broader mission to resuscitate Hawaiian culture, and now was only too happy to put on a demonstration for the tourists, who were equally happy to see it. But before the demonstration could begin, once again the authorities, ostensibly in the person of Ashford, stepped in. A luau on the Sabbath was already a blasphemy; a hula dance would be untenable. And so the king was forced to announce that the spectacle would be reserved for the tourists' next visit.

But that was not the end of the matter. Having come so far, and having already noted the alluring qualities of the local populace, the tourists were not about to be denied. The queen's garden was large, allowing the men to draw off the nubile performers for private performances of the devilish dance. "The lithe forms, graceful movements, and wondrous eyes of the charming Kanaka dancers will haunt the boys for many days to come," Ward informed the *Tribune*'s readers. Anson was no less effusive. "Such supple maidens I never before beheld," he wrote. "The earth upon which they tripped seemed to have an elasticity about it which sent them rollicking off into the air. And such eyes! If my boys had them we would lead the batting for years to come."

When it was finally time to leave, the players collected themselves in a group and offered the traditional baseball salute—three cheers!—to the king, to their Hawaiian friends, and, especially, to the fair maidens of Honolulu. By ten o'clock they were back on the decks of the *Alameda*, still a bit tipsy as they watched the tropical paradise recede into the distance. Standing at the rail, a wistful Harry Palmer hummed a tune he had picked up earlier that day:

> Fair Honolulu, City of the Sea,
> On Oahu's shores, where stately mountains rise,
> To dwell forever there, with thee,
> Would be to live in earthly paradise.

CHAPTER 6

KIWIS AND KANGAROOS

HAVING DEPARTED HAWAII, LIFE ON BOARD THE *Alameda* returned to its lethargic monotone, the players' senses lulled by the heat and the inexorable churn of the ship's engine. There was little for them to do but loaf about in the shade, read, smoke, eat, and then loaf about some more. The women of the tour—Harriet Spalding, Virginia Anson, Nellie Williamson, and Anna Berger, the cornet-playing wife of Leigh Lynch—gossiped among themselves. The most strenuous activity in which the players seemed to engage was the growing of pointed, Van Dyke–style goatees, said to be fashionable in Australia. In the evenings, they drank and traded stories with their fellow passengers. Most curious among this group was a tall, bearded gentleman of late middle age with a steely glare and a bronzed complexion that betrayed many years in the hot sun of the subcontinent.

That man was Major General T. Bland Strange, formerly of the British artillery, who was now returning to England via the Antipodes after a rather eventful final posting in Canada. Strange's forbidding appearance was, at least in this environment, deceptive; the tourists soon found that the general liked nothing better than to sit back with a cigar and a whiskey in the *Alameda*'s saloon, where he might recount the exploits of a life spent advancing the interests of the British Empire. He was already at work on a memoir, *Gunner Jingo's Jubilee*, that when published in 1891 would stand as one of the more preposterous works of military history ever committed to print. (In the book, Strange refers to himself almost exclusively in the third person, and then as "Jingo," a frighteningly militant and insufferably pompous officer with a fondness for classical allusion).

Strange was the scion of a distinguished military family: His grandfather fought at Waterloo and his father, also a soldier, was an intimate of King William IV. Strange himself could boast of a thirty-year military career, one that had taken him to posts on four continents. In contrast to Spalding and his merry band of baseball exponents, with their rather happy-go-lucky mission to bring American culture to the world, Strange had few illusions about his role as an unrepentant enforcer of British power. "If we are to maintain an Empire we must first be strong—by sea and land," he wrote in the conclusion to *Gunner Jingo*. (It is one of the book's few straightforward passages.) Most recently, his overzealous suppression of a rebellion by the Métis, an independent group in Northwestern Canada, had resulted in his temporarily being relieved of both his commission and his pension.

Of all Strange's stories, the one that most captivated the tourists was his firsthand account of the Siege of Lucknow, a key episode in the Indian insurrection then known as the Sepoy Mutiny. Trouble had started in May of 1857, when native soldiers—sepoys—in the service of the British mutinied against their colonial masters in the city of Meerut, in northwest India, setting off a revolt that quickly spread across the north of the country. The roots of the uprising were many, but the violence itself was triggered when Muslim and Hindu soldiers were disciplined for refusing to bite the tips off of rifle cartridges supposedly greased with pig and cow fat. In Lucknow, more than a thousand British soldiers, citizens, and loyalists were trapped in a fortified residential compound. The bloody siege lasted through November, when the residence was finally evacuated by a force in which Strange was then a junior officer. In the aftermath of the Mutiny (in India, it is now known as the First War of Independence), the siege assumed considerable symbolic power as a demonstration of the resilience of the British colonial system, a meaning that was no doubt transferred, at least in the minds of the tourists, to General Strange himself.

Anson, who was predisposed toward such tales of fortitude and discipline, was certainly impressed by the general. Inevitably, he looked with alarm at his own troops, concerned that their days and nights lazing about the decks of the *Alameda* would leave them as "stiff as old women and as fat as aldermen." The ship's menu wasn't helping any on this front; a typical dinner included oysters, steak, lamb chops, veal cutlets, sausages, peas, rice and gravy, boiled and fried potatoes, corn bread, toast, fried bananas, coffee, and chocolates. Clearly, some program of exercise was required to keep the men in shape and their skills sharp. A proper regimen had in fact always been one of Anson's preoccupations; with Spalding, he had been a pioneer of the spring training season. His White Stockings typically opened the year in Hot Springs, Arkansas, where they could "soak out" and play themselves into shape before moving north. Now, trapped aboard the *Alameda*, things were a bit more complicated. Out of sheer boredom, the players had already taken it upon themselves to try tossing a baseball around on deck, but Spalding had put a stop to that after the fifth from their limited supply went "over the fence." The solution came from George Wright, who asked and received permission from Captain Morse to construct a batting cage some forty feet long on the promenade on the port side of the quarterdeck. Here, enclosed by sheets of canvas, the men could play ball, and Wright could drill them in the fundamentals of cricket, which they would be expected to play in Australia in addition to baseball. Despite his age, it was Spalding who was most facile as a bowler—"as energetic as when he used to stand in the pitcher's box," according to Palmer. Anson, who could not tolerate the thought of a public humiliation, put in a good four hours of practice a day with the unfamiliar bat. Overall, the cage had just the effect he desired; when the ship finally reached Australia the players, said Palmer, were "in the pink of condition."

In the meantime, they would be forced to sweat out their days. When the *Alameda* crossed the equator on the eve of Thanksgiving, the mercury on board was pushing ninety degrees. In lieu of roast turkey and cranberry sauce, the group entertained itself with the mock trial of one of their fellow passengers, Sir James Willoughby, a louche British aristocrat on permanent holiday. Willoughby, who was rarely seen without a drink in hand, had for some reason—perhaps it was the drink—agreed to participate in the shenanigans. General Strange served as judge of this kangaroo court, and Ward stood as lawyer for the defense. "Sir Jimmy" was charged with the crimes of traveling under false pretenses (impersonating a peer) and the carrying of a concealed weapon ("an eight-ton gun"). One "witness" identified the accused as a clerk in Macy's ribbon department. It was all Ward could do to have his client throw himself on the mercy of the court, and he won a sentence that pleased all: a round of drinks. James Fogarty, serving as bailiff, was happy to enforce the fine.

The political entanglements of Hawaii were strictly low-grade compared to the situation in Samoa, the *Alameda*'s next port of call. A pair of rival chiefs, Malietoa and Tamasese, were facing off in a civil war on this ostensibly independent island chain. Just offshore, the navies of the United States, Germany, and Great Britain were engaged in their own standoff, jockeying for control of the archipelago and its strategic harbors. Even Kalakaua, having badly misjudged the situation, had tried to insert himself into the mix. In an effort to expand his power base in the Pacific, the Hawaiian king had in 1887 dispatched an envoy to meet with Malietoa, ostensibly to discuss a plan for a confederation of Oceanic states. (On this front, he also suggested the United States cede the Midway Islands, located 1,300 miles northwest of Honolulu, to Hawaii, a request that was, not surprisingly, rejected out of hand.) The larger powers were none too pleased with Kalakaua's interloping, and even less happy when a Hawaiian "warship"—actually, a converted guano hauler—crewed by reform school students and captained by a notorious drunk—joined their navies on the scene in June of 1888. That ship, the *Kaimiloa*, was soon dismissed, and luckily so, for in March of 1889 a hurricane scuttled the three American and three German warships on patrol in the Samoan waters, leaving but one British vessel, the *Calliope*, afloat—and just barely at that.

Matters were still at a stalemate when the *Alameda* pulled in on the night of December 2, 1888. The ship was scheduled to dock for the evening; the next day, while it was taking on coal, the tourists were to put on an exhibition of the American game in the port town of Pago Pago. But here, just as in Hawaii, there would be no game. Spalding and his men never even made it off the boat; the situation on the ground was simply too unstable. Instead, they dropped anchor a few hundred yards offshore and the passengers were left to ogle the mountainous coast by the light of the moon. The only communication with the natives came when a dory pulled up alongside the ship and a broad-chested islander in blue coveralls and a plaid shirt clambered aboard with a mail bag. The purser took the islander's sack and offered him a large glass of gin, which he drank down in one quick gulp before disappearing over the rail. The next morning, before dawn, the *Alameda* lifted anchor and steamed off toward the Antipodes.

Harry Palmer was the first of the tourists to catch sight of the New Zealand coast on the night of December 8. It was yet another stifling evening aboard the *Alameda*, and Palmer had come up on deck for a smoke and a reprieve from the heat when, at 3 A.M., he spotted a revolving lighthouse beacon on the horizon. The *Alameda* would reach Auckland by sunrise, and the time could not pass quickly enough for the eager passengers. It had been two full weeks since their last landfall, in Hawaii, and everyone was anxious to walk on solid ground once again.

Their greeting, the following morning, lacked the pomp and circumstance of the Hawaiian reception; owing to the original delay leaving San Francisco, the *Alameda* once again arrived early on a Sunday morning, a day later than expected. In place of a military band and a cheering crowd, they found only a few reporters and Will Lynch, who had been assigned by his cousin Leigh, then in Sydney, to make preparations for their arrival. But there was some good news: The *Alameda* would be staying overnight for coaling, and they would be able to get in a game the next day.

After a hot fortnight at sea, however, Spalding and his men seemed less concerned with ballplaying than with some relief from the *Alameda*'s gut-busting menu. Of particular interest were the local strawberries, larger and sweeter than their American cousins, which they picked up from vendors along the wharves. For the next twenty-four hours, Jimmy Ryan wrote in his diary, "it was a common sight to see ball players walking down the street, munching berries from a box." When they were done with their first bout of fruit shopping, they boarded a pair of four-horse carriages Lynch had organized to take them on a tour of the city. What they found was a quaint town that had been founded in 1840 as a British colonial settlement. Situated on an isthmus between two fine natural harbors, Waitemata and Manukau, it was the colony's commercial center and largest city. But on a cool Sabbath morning heavy with fog and drizzle, Auckland's streets were practically desolate. And so the undisputed highlight of the morning's perambulations was an audience with a Maori chief, his face "fancifully" tattooed, who greeted the players with a welcoming call of "Boys!" in his native tongue. The visit, which had been organized by members of the local press, also included the viewing of an eighty-foot-long Maori dugout canoe, ornamented fore and aft with carvings made with wood and stone tools.

For lunch, Spalding commandeered the dining hall of the Imperial Hotel, Auckland's finest, for yet another memorable meal. English duck, new potatoes, green peas, cauliflower, and, of course, strawberries were served. "They know how to live in New Zealand, even though they be colonists," Palmer wrote. There was more exploring to be done following the repast, though the drizzle had developed into a steady rain. The featured event on the afternoon's itinerary was a trip to the summit of Mount Eden, an extinct volcano offering panoramic vistas and the terraced ruins of a Maori *pas*, or fortified village, on its slopes. Through the rain drops, they could just make out the *Alameda*, taking on coal in the harbor below.

While the tourists were traipsing about in the rain, Will Lynch was busy upholding his family's well-earned reputation for promotional skill. Already, he had convinced the local papers to greet the arrival of the tour with all the weight and ceremony of a formal state visit. "The treat promised by the battle between the two great teams of players who will visit us on Saturday will be one of no ordinary merit, and will certainly mark an epoch in the annals of Auckland sport," beamed the *Auckland Star* in a preview. The *New Zealand Herald* promised a game by "the two strongest ball combinations that have ever been got together even in that country of 'big things'"—a bit of rhetorical embellishment that would have made even Spalding proud. These planted stories were supplemented by player profiles and features complete with explanatory diagrams that promised to decode the "mysteries of the Yankee national game." And even more exciting than a game of baseball played by its leading practitioners was the promise of an aerial performance by Professor Bartholomew, billed in the *Star* as "one of the most novel and thrilling spectacles ever presented to the public of Auckland."

Who could resist such come-ons? A crowd of more than ten thousand, nearly one fifth of the city's population, was expected at Potter's Paddock, the local rugby ground, where the game was to be held. The better-kept cricket fields were in the Auckland Domain, a public park where Spalding would have been precluded from charging his proposed one-shilling entry fee. Auckland's cricket association postponed all of its Saturday matches so as not to conflict with the exhibition, and the manager of the Auckland Tramway Company agreed to run a special service from Queen Street, the city's main thoroughfare, to accommodate the crowds. Lynch himself supervised the laying of the diamond, and saw to it that the grandstand was enlivened by two long stands of flags—the Stars and Stripes alternating with the Union Jack in each row.

All of this had been set up for Saturday; when the *Alameda* arrived a day late, Lynch found himself scrambling to recover. This dire situation brought him to the office of Alfred Devore, the mayor of Auckland, late on Sunday afternoon. Once again channeling a bit of Spalding's audacity, he requested that Mayor Devore declare Monday a civic holiday so that all the town might have the opportunity to see the Chicagos and the All-Americas play. It is a testament, perhaps, to the zeal with which New Zealanders have always appreciated sport that Lynch was not tossed out on his ear. Though the mayor did not accede to the presumptuous request, his solution was nearly as good. He could not shut down the city entirely, but he would close the municipal offices in time for a two o'clock start. And of course he would be happy to attend the match himself, if only to give it an air of official sanction. What's more, it would be his pleasure to personally escort Spalding and his fellow travelers on a tour of the city's public library and art gallery the next morning.

———

Spalding and his men were not, in fact, the first to introduce baseball to New Zealand. Some four years earlier an attempt had been made to develop a baseball program at the local elementary school. More recently, several games had been played by a black-run vaudeville troupe, the Hicks-Sawyer Colored Minstrels, one of several such companies that took their shows abroad, where they were treated more fairly than by American theater owners. The Hicks-Sawyer company also bucked the conventional trappings of minstrelsy—avoiding in particular the stereotypical "plantation slave" character Clarence Duval so often found himself playing—in favor of a less demeaning portrayal of African American life. To supplement its earnings, the Hicks-Sawyer group played baseball exhibitions, and the week before the arrival of the Spalding contingent they had played in a game organized by Lynch as a part of his promotional campaign. Anson might not have approved if he had known about it, but he was still on the *Alameda*.

When the Spalding contingent did finally take the field, a frigid wind was blowing in from the harbor, making life uncomfortable for the mayor and a fairly impressive crowd of spectators, twenty-five hundred strong, who had come out for the demonstration of America's national game. The fans were not the only victims of Mother Nature's unleashed forces. In the difficult conditions, the All-Americas seemed incapable of making even the most routine plays (third baseman Ned Hanlon had four errors). The one-sided thrashing by the White Stockings began in the first inning with a three-run, inside-the-park home run by Fred Pfeffer. He hit another in the third, sandwiching clouts by the right-fielder, Robert Pettit, and diarist Jimmy Ryan. By the end of the sixth, the score stood at 20–5 in favor of Chicago.

The gusty weather was also wreaking havoc on the main attraction of the day—not a baseball game, but Professor Bartholomew's balloon ascension and subsequent parachute leap back to earth. In addition to those who had assembled to witness the jump at Potter's Paddock, an-

*Professor Bartholomew, in performing attire, before a
poster advertising his balloon ascension and subsequent
"leap from the clouds." The leap he had mastered.
Landing was a problem. Photo from around 1888.*

other large group had gathered at the summit of Mount Eden, hoping
for an elevated perspective of the professor's derring-do. The winds were
too dangerous for him to try his flight, however—a reality that did not sit
well with the aggressive Kiwi crowd. "They seemed disposed to handle
him roughly," wrote Goodfriend. If Bartholomew's academic title and
effeminate costume—a full-body black leotard with frilly white shorts
and matching cuffs and collar—gave anyone the impression that he was
an easy mark, well, they were sadly mistaken. The aerialist was not a

man to be trifled with. He had, after all, lost an eye and broken more bones than he cared to recall over the course of his career. And so when an attempt was made to liberate a swatch of fabric from his balloon, the professor pulled a pistol from his sack and coolly announced that "the man who attempts to cut a piece out of that will have to cut a piece out of me." Anyone who looked into his one remaining eye knew that he meant it.

Thus, it was on something less than a high note that the tourists made their way back to the *Alameda*. But at least they had left an impression, and when all was said and done the New Zealanders seemed happy with the brief visit by the Spalding contingent. Nearly a thousand fans, including the ever-hospitable Mayor Devore, gathered at the docks that evening to wish them a safe voyage. Just a few months earlier New Zealand had sent its own sporting ambassadors on a trip around the world. The New Zealand Native Football Representatives, forerunners of the country's famed All Black national rugby side, would play more than one hundred games in Australia and England before returning home. That team hadn't received anywhere near the fanfare accorded to Spalding and his intrepid baseballists.

Rough seas made the four-day trip due west from Auckland to Sydney one of the more difficult legs of the tour, but the welcome Spalding and his men received as they pulled into Woolloomooloo Bay and the city came into view was grand enough to fully brighten their spirits. All of Sydney, or so it seemed, had been mobilized for their arrival. On South Head, the white stone tower of Macquarie Lighthouse was decked out in red, white, and blue bunting. An entire flotilla had been assembled to accompany the *Alameda* into the harbor: tugs, yachts, steamers, rowboats, dinghies—every craft that would float was sent out to greet the arriving baseball tourists. The reception committee, led by Leigh Lynch, was jammed onto a large harbor boat, the *Admiral*. Even a pack of dolphins, curious about the hubbub, joined the commotion, bobbing along next to the *Alameda*. Onshore, hundred of fans waited in the late-afternoon sun waving flags while brass bands issued forth with American standards. "It was glorious! It was stirring! It was in every way a complete surprise, in that it so far exceeded all that we imagined it might be," Palmer recalled. "The scene was one that brought joy and then tears," echoed Ward. "From that moment Australia became not a foreign land, but only another division of home."

Visitors to the great island continent had not always been treated to such a celebratory welcome. Australia, like America, was very much a land of interlopers—migrants, colonists, rogues, and laborers—drawn, sometimes against their will, to a place of outsized possibility. Aboriginal mythology tells of ancestors who arrived in a timeless time—the Dream Time—from lands of mysterious origin; archaeological evidence suggests that first human habitation came as many as sixty thousand years ago. A later visitation, by Captain Cook, marks the opening of what has generally been understood to be Australia's modern history. Cook arrived at Botany Bay, just south of present-day Sydney, in 1770 and claimed the land he found for king and country. This new dominion along Australia's southeast coast—he called it New South Wales— proved a convenient dumping ground for the criminal class of Cook's home country, not to mention a useful source of raw material, a strategic commercial and military base in the South Pacific, and a handy substitute for the recently lost American colonies. And so Cook was followed, in January 1788, by another British sea captain, Arthur Phillip, who arrived at Port Jackson (Sydney Harbor) with an eleven-ship convoy carrying nearly eight hundred convicts and four marine companies to control them.

A hundred years later, Spalding and his men arrived in that same port on a Friday evening, with the entire city out and in a mood for revelry. These were good days for Sydney. The New South Wales economy, driven by the export of gold and wool, was thriving. Politically, the colony had considerable autonomy from Britain. (The six Australian "Crown colonies"—Victoria, Queensland, Western Australia, South Australia, Tasmania, and New South Wales—were at the time separate and highly competitive entities; they did not form a federation until 1901.) To mark its centennial, Sydney was engaged in a year-long celebration of itself. A handsome new public park, Centennial Park, was opened to great fanfare. New office buildings reached for the sky in the commercial center. Ranges of gleaming white terrace houses and great mansions of brick and stone filled in its neighborhoods. Wealth had spread so widely and so quickly that the city's infrastructure, egregiously mismanaged, could not keep up, resulting in water shortages and open sewage in the handsome new streets—what one historian has called "a self-conscious mixture of dirt and dignity, effluvium and elegance, garbage and grandeur."

Spalding's group had been booked into two hotels, the Chicagos at the Oxford and the All-Americas at the Grosvenor, and it was to the former that the group in its entirety was taken from the harbor. When their carriages pulled up in front of the hotel's portico, they found that it had been covered over with flags and flowers in their honor. Inside, the United States consul, G. W. Griffin, was waiting with members of the sporting press. Champagne was uncorked, toasts were made, and the Australian reporters got their first look at the American ballplayers. They found Albert Spalding, the great impresario, particularly inspiring. "No wonder Spalding has made a huge fortune," reported one Sydney paper. "He's got grit and go, while his daring is proved by this undertaking."

In the evening, the tourists were treated to a night of entertainment at the Royal Theater, courtesy of Jimmy Williamson, an expatriate American who had transformed himself into Australia's leading theatrical producer. Born in Pennsylvania in 1843, he had bounced around as an actor on the American circuit before purchasing, for one hundred dollars, the rights to a promising melodrama provisionally entitled *The German Recruit*. Renamed *Struck Oil*, the show became a hit with Williamson and his wife, Maggie Moore, as its stars. Williamson traveled the show to Australia in 1874, and its success, combined with his savvy decision to acquire the Australian rights to the Gilbert and Sullivan musicals *H.M.S. Pinafore* and, later, *The Pirates of Penzance*, established Williamson as the king of the Australian stage, a position he consolidated with the formation of Williamson, Garner, and Musgrove, a theatrical syndicate known alternately as "the Triumvirate" and "the Firm."

Williamson was especially pleased to welcome a contingent of fellow Americans to his theater, and arranged for a series of boxes in the dress circle to be draped with bunting in their honor. The bill for the evening was a double feature, the first show being his old chestnut, *Struck Oil*, with Williamson and Moore in their customary lead roles. After the curtain, Spalding and his men were brought down onto the stage to receive their own ovation from the audience. When Spalding was tossed a pair of small flags to wave, one American and one of New South Wales, the orchestra roared in approval. The evening concluded with a performance of *The Chinese Question*, a comic sop on a subject as loaded in Australia as it was in California. The roots of this xenophobia were the same—workers feared competition from cheap labor, moralists feared the depravity of the godless Chinese, or "Celestial" (China was the "Celestial Empire") and racists feared miscegenation—but here on the other side of the world, the threat seemed that much closer at hand. This animosity had on occasion resulted in civic unrest and violence. Just a few months before the arrival of the tourists, in the spring of 1888, a Hong Kong trading vessel, the *Afghan*, carrying a large number of Chinese workers, was turned away first in Melbourne and then in Sydney by the threat of mob action. Later in the year, new anti-immigration policies were enacted against the Chinese as part of a broader "Australia for Australians" campaign. But on this night, such unpleasantness was whitewashed by Williamson's light comedy. If anyone saw a bit of irony in an anti-immigration play put on by an immigrant in honor of men hoping to introduce a foreign game, they kept it to themselves.

───※───

Festivities continued the next morning with a reception at Town Hall, a study in Victorian grandiosity with bulging Second Empire forms of yellow sandstone and a clock tower surmounted by a domed lantern. The host was Sydney's mayor, John Harris, a gregarious man in a purple robe of silk and ermine, and the reception took place in his council chamber, which had been set with a linen-draped table manned by a dozen butlers and spread over with champagne—Clicquot, Mumm's, and Pommery. When it came time for toasts, Harris happily suggested that his Australian brethren were sure to pick up baseball, and that it wouldn't be long before a touring team of Aussies would be heading back across the

Pacific to challenge the Americans at their own national game. This pronouncement was received with good cheer, though the biggest hand was given over to Ned Hanlan—the champion Canadian sculler then considered one of the great athletes of the day, and not to be confused with the All-America outfielder Ned Hanlon. Though small of stature, Hanlan had a fluid style and a cocky bravado that made him a popular, if somewhat controversial figure. (It had been his habit, when racing, to build a wide lead only to pull up and wait for his opponents to catch up before taking off once again—a practice that quite understandably did not endear him to his rivals.) Hanlan set his first time record in 1876, and then in 1880 took the world championship from Australian Edward Trickett in a match race on the Thames. It was estimated that some five hundred thousand dollars—a sum comparable to what is now bet on the Super Bowl—was laid on the race. Hanlan had since lost his title (to Australian William Beach, in 1884), but nevertheless remained a glamorous sportsman, and one who could speak from his own personal history about the athletic prowess of the Australian people. His message to the tourists, like Harris's, was to beware of teaching the people from Down Under the American game too well.

This, of course, was a risk Spalding and his men were happy to take. After returning to their hotels, they changed into their baseball togs in preparation for their first game on Australian soil. This time—finally— they would be playing as scheduled on a Saturday afternoon, and consequently a large crowd was anticipated at the Australian Association Cricket Grounds.

The twenty-minute ride out to the field took them through some of the prettier scenery Sydney had to offer, and when they finally arrived they found a manicured playing surface as "level as a floor" and with a "velvety" turf that put to shame the rough urban ball fields Spalding and his men were used to back home. "In whatever other respects the Colonies might be inferior to the United States," wrote Palmer, "they certainly possessed grounds so far superior in point of equipment and condition to anything we had in the United States that there was no room whatever for comparison." The lush green oval was enclosed by a whitewashed picket fence, with home plate placed before a grandstand filled to its capacity. The better classes were seated in reserved sections in front of the Australian Cricket Association's two-story clubhouse and a separate "ladies cottage" for unescorted women, a group that made up a sizable portion of a crowd estimated at somewhere between six and ten thousand.

Those in attendance were treated to what was universally described as a fine game, though the extent to which the Australian audience actually understood what they were witnessing was something of an open question. "The game itself was one that brought out all the beauties of play and would have set an American crowd wild, but it was too fast for Sydneyites," wrote Ward. "Not being acquainted with the points of play they were unable to follow such quick work." Spalding had anticipated this problem, and had indeed taken steps to prevent it. As in New Zealand, explanatory stories were planted in the Australian papers. (This became a bit awkward the following week when the *Melbourne Leader* and the *Age of Melbourne* ran the same story—"The American Game of Baseball and How to Play It"—word for word, on the same day.) In addition, before leaving the United States, Spalding had commissioned Harry Palmer to author a pamphlet with condensed profiles of the players on the tour and an outline of the rules of the game, in hopes that this would be a help to the foreign fans. But written descriptions could only do so much; to the uninitiated, a baseball game can seem about as straightforward as a German grammar lesson, and this was precisely the problem experienced by a columnist for the *Sydney Herald*, who sarcastically described the sport as "a game of such wonderfully abstruse character that it takes a man half his life to learn it, and its complications are so extraordinary that no two games are ever played in anything like the same way. The pleasure derived from watching the players arises from the tax on the ingenuity to divine what it all means."

Suspicion that the proceedings might not be fully appreciated for their character alone was no doubt reinforced after the fifth inning, when the game, then tied 4–4, was halted so the players might have an audience with Lord Carrington, the governor of New South Wales. After the usual round of introductions, Lord Carrington offered a brief champagne toast, telling the assembled he was happy to witness the

The tourists photographed in Sydney. Top row: Tom Burns, Tom Daly, Robert Pettit, Marty Sullivan, Mark Baldwin, John Tener, John Healy, Fred Carroll, George Wood, Tom Brown, Jim Manning. Middle row: Ned Williamson, Fred Pfeffer, Adrian Anson, Albert Spalding, John Ward, Jim Fogarty, Harry Simpson. Front row: Clarence Duval, George Wright, Ned Hanlon, Billy Earle. Ed "Cannonball" Crane, who was nursing a hangover, is notably absent.

contest not so much out of a curiosity about the American game, but to "give a proper and hardy welcome to our friends from across the sea." With that, the boys retook the field, and for the next three innings, perhaps owing to the champagne, were unable to score. The All-Americas managed to break through in the top of the ninth when James Fogarty reached on a single, stole second, stole third, and finally came home on a wild pitch by a clearly rattled John Tener. It was not to be the future Pennsylvania governor's day. In the bottom half of the inning, now down by a run and with two outs, Tener stepped to the plate with two men on base and a chance at redemption. All he could muster was a weak grounder to first base.

With the evening open and no further games on their docket until Monday, the tourists were free to explore the Sydney nightlife. Jimmy Williamson had extended an open invitation to the members of the party, and several returned for a second night of entertainment at his Royal Theater. Ward and Palmer teamed up with the oarsman Ned Hanlan and a couple of Sydney sportswriters to review a night of boxing at a local gym—an eight-round fight of middle-weights was the featured bout. Later in the evening the men availed themselves of Sydney's wide selection of establishments devoted to the arts of drinking and merriment. Of these, none was more spectacular than the Marble Bar at the Adams Hotel, a showpiece of material excess that had opened in 1873 and was named for the seven types of marble—not to mention the gilt, tile, bronze, mirrors, and decorative stucco—that covered its every surface. The players, however, seemed focused on interior decoration of a slightly different order. "Not a few us became students of that not uninteresting colonial institution, the Australian barmaid, with which no Australian café or drinking resort is unprovided," wrote Palmer. "In most cases they are pretty, in every instance smart, and combining with these qualities an excellent knowledge of mankind and his weaknesses, they are more valuable to the Australian liquor dealer than our most expert beverage mixers." Fortunately for all, they would have Sunday to recuperate from their studies. For Cannonball Crane, whose drinking had already forced him out of the lineup in San Francisco, that would not be time enough.

The tourists returned to the field on Monday morning to try their hands at a game that would be, at least theoretically, more familiar to the Australian public: cricket. They were down a man, however. Crane, still feeling the effects of his Saturday night debauch, excused himself on account of the heat. Anson, on the other hand, had been looking forward to the event for weeks. Indeed, he had taken it upon himself to deliver a series of impromptu lectures on the finer points of the English game to his fellow travelers. What's more, he had made several wagers on the outcome of his performance. No one had put in more time practicing the unfamiliar sport in the *Alameda*'s batting cage than Anson, and he planned on cashing in on that work now. But it was not to be. Anson strolled up to the wicket full of confidence, but on the first ball that was bowled to him he lofted a harmless pop fly to James Fogarty, who promptly put him out. Fuming, the captain walked off the field "as red as a gobbler and followed by the unmerciful guying of the boys." In a far corner, he recruited his old nemesis, Clarence Duval, to throw a bit of batting practice, which elicited even further derision from his charges. When Chicago third baseman Tommy Burns, who was known for his affable demeanor, asked provocatively whether Anson found Duval's delivery "very speedy," the two men had to be separated. The game concluded after one innings (in cricket, the term is always plural) with the score 67–33 in favor of the All-Americas. This was followed, in the afternoon, by a rematch at baseball, which was also won by the All-Americas 7–5. Professor Bartholomew, who had been scheduled to perform, was again forced to cancel because of high winds.

The next morning Spalding and his crew returned to the field for a doubleheader, the first game being another cricket match, this time between the tourists and a contingent of Australian cricketers who generously allowed the Americans to field seventeen men to their own eleven. Even with this handicap it was not much of a contest; the Australians were up by twenty-eight runs, 115 to 87, and were still batting away when the game was called at four o'clock. In the second half of the twin bill, the All-Americas once again defeated Chicago, this time 6–2, in a listless affair that left Anson's club 0-for-Australia and a disturbing four games back (eight games to twelve) in the series with the All-Americas.

The second game was cut short after five innings—perhaps Anson used this as an excuse for the loss—as the tourists had a dinner engagement that evening, and lateness was not an option. The venue was, once again, Town Hall, and the host, again, Mayor Harris. But unlike their first meeting, this would be a formal event, a "Complimentary Banquet & Social Evening," according to the handsome invitations printed for the occasion. The setting was the building's reception hall, a cavernous space with stained-glass windows and a domed ceiling from which was suspended a massive chandelier animated by a bubbling froth of gaslight globes. Two hundred places had been reserved for the event, and every one was occupied. Flags and flowers were everywhere.

The dinner began with oysters *au naturel* and in aspic, and proceeded through six additional courses and more than thirty dishes—"every delicacy the chef's deft fingers could prepare," wrote Palmer. Toasts were raised to Queen Victoria, American President Harrison, Lord Carrington, the assembled guests, the ladies present, and the members of the press. A band provided musical accompaniment throughout the event on a stage that had been constructed at the head of the room, and when the speeches were over the diners were treated to Frank Lincoln's comic stylings—his ever-popular "cocktail" routine scored yet again—and a concert by cornet virtuoso Anna Berger. The festivities closed with her stirring rendition of "The Star Spangled Banner"; upon its completion Spalding's patriotic charges pulled the flowers from the table arrangements and tossed them at her feet.

The next day was the tourists' last in Sydney—they would be moving on by rail to Melbourne, the capital of Victoria, on Australia's southern coast—and with no game scheduled they traveled about as a group shopping for knickknacks. Out of solidarity and a sense of native pride they purchased straw boaters with bands of red, white, and blue. Moved by the show of patriotism, an expatriate salesman presented each man with a lapel pin of the Stars and Stripes. In the evening, as they packed their trunks, they could reflect on what had been, despite the fanfare, a mixed reception in New South Wales. "The people of Sydney gave us every sort of welcome that hospitality could suggest," wrote MacMillan, "but they did not embrace the game of baseball with the arms of approval." At least Spalding and his men could take comfort in the knowledge that they had done everything possible to convince the Sydneysiders of the merits of the American game. "Nothing could have been better advertised, nothing better managed, nothing more totally attractive to the eye, or fuller of thrilling interest," observed a local columnist. If they were the butt of a few jokes, the men seemed unconcerned. As MacMillan wrote: "Some of the wits of the press turned loose upon us, but they did very little harm, because, after all, they were not very funny. Sydney wit is English wit, and, therefore, rather heavy."

⸺ ⸺

Though the tourists were happy to put Sydney behind them, the means of conveyance by which they were to do so was hardly to their liking. The government of New South Wales, in a final gesture of friendship, had arranged for a private train to carry Spalding and his men out of the colony. This came as good news right up until the moment the players saw the train: a "dingy old-fashioned affair," according to MacMillan, on a narrow-gauge track. Accustomed to the modern comforts and conveniences of the Pullman sleeper, the Americans were unimpressed by an aging colonial conveyance with no bathroom facilities and, worse still, no saloon. A group of players was overheard joking as they reviewed one of the train's shabby compartments, "How long are you in for?" and "Can't you get bail?" The cracks may have briefly lightened the mood, but the cramped conditions and summer heat made sleep on the six-hundred-mile overnight journey to Melbourne all but impossible. The only form of sustenance was a bottle of Kentucky whiskey gingerly passed from cabin to cabin on a string.

When the tourists finally pulled into Melbourne's Spencer Street Station the next morning, Albert Spalding was the first to step off the train, perhaps a bit weary from the lack of sleep but no doubt hopeful that the citizens of Victoria might be more receptive to his overtures than the people of New South Wales. In this he would not be disappointed, as was suggested by the crowd of five hundred flag-waving baseball enthusiasts waiting to greet him on the platform. In all things, Melbourne aimed not just to equal but to outdo Sydney, its great rival to the northeast, and a grand welcome to a group of distinguished visitors, not to mention their eagerness to adopt a modern sport, fit this mold.

The reception began with a parade up Collins Street from the station to Melbourne's Town Hall, an imposing Mansard-roofed edifice with an enormous columned portico. Still exhausted from their journey, the players made their way past a crowd of some three thousand well-wishers and into the main hall of the building, where they were greeted by the

euphoniously named Jewish mayor, Benjamin Benjamin, and then serenaded by the city organist, David Lee, on his ten-thousand-pipe instru-
ment, said to be the largest in the hemisphere, and certainly bigger than
anything in Sydney. With the musical program complete, the party retired
to Benjamin's office for champagne and a series of toasts. Samuel Perkins
Lord, an expatriate American sea merchant who claimed to have brought
the game of baseball to Australia back in 1853, wished the men good
luck in their mission. Spalding, perhaps having learned a lesson from
some of the reactionary press in Sydney, assured those assembled that his
intention was simply to introduce Australians to the pleasures of America's native game, and not to "supplant" cricket. The event concluded
with Frank Lincoln's cocktail shtick, which must now have been becoming irritating, at least for the travelers.

From Town Hall, the tourists were taken to their hotel, the Grand, yet
another masterwork of Victorian splendor (still in operation, but now as
the Windsor). Designed by Charles Webb and officially opened in 1883,
the five-story hotel boasted more than one hundred and eighty rooms.
This vast oasis of luxury sat majestically on Spring Street, its central
pavilion flanked by a pair of ornamental towers and two long bays with
open arcades running across the bottom three floors. For all its would-be
opulence, however, the rooms in the hotel were still lit by candles. More
aggravating still was that the hotel had recently been purchased by a temperance advocate, James Munro, who had transformed it into what the
Australians called a "coffee palace"—which was a grand way of saying
that it served no alcohol.

With an open date on their schedule, the tourists had the following
day to explore the city, and at a propitious moment in its history. Established at the mouth of the Yarra River as a minor colonial port in the
1830s, Melbourne had been transformed in the wake of the Australian
Gold Rush of the 1850s into a fully cosmopolitan commercial center. "I
believe that no city has ever attained so great a size with such rapidity,"
wrote Anthony Trollope, who visited in 1873. "Forty years ago from the
present date the foot of no white man had trodden the ground on which
Melbourne now stands. Nevertheless the internal appearance of the city
is certainly magnificent." At the time Trollope penned those words,

Melbourne's population was barely over two hundred thousand. By 1888 that number was closer to a half million, and it had taken on the sobriquet "Marvellous Melbourne"; the name was the gift of yet another British visitor, George Augustus Sala, a columnist for the *London Daily Telegraph*. The city naturally drew comparisons with that great American metropolis on the make, Chicago, from where Spalding and his men had come. "It is the most American of Australian cities," wrote MacMillan. "It has fine, wide streets, rectangular blocks, nine-story buildings, and a dash which makes a Yankee feel quite at home."

The Grand was well situated as a base for a tour of the booming capital. Victoria's Parliament Building, with its imposing Doric colonnade, was directly across Spring Street, and such busy thoroughfares as Swanston, Bourke, Flinders, and Collins, each lined with handsome new buildings and bustling with their daily traffic of carriages and trolleys, were only blocks away. But the highlight of highlights was the Melbourne Centennial Exhibition, one of the several nineteenth-century international trade fairs that were together propelling the nations of the world into an industrialized and commercialized modernity.

For the Australian colonies, so isolated from Europe and North America, the international exposition was a particularly useful tool for showing off the fruits of their own budding economies while bringing in the most advanced products from the great Western powers. The first Australian fair opened in Sydney in 1879. (The spectacular Garden Palace, where it was held, burned in 1882.) Melbourne, in its continuing efforts to upstage its rival city, opened a fair of its own in 1880—the timing allowed foreign exhibitors to remain on the continent and continue on to Victoria, getting a second return on their investments before traveling the long way home. The setting for Melbourne's fair was surely as spectacular as Sydney's: the Royal Exhibition Building, a resplendent twenty-two-acre Italian Gothic shed designed by Joseph Reed. That initial fair was such a success that in 1888 the city opened another, the Melbourne Centennial Exhibition, in the same building. (It still stands, and is a listed World Heritage landmark.)

Frank McCoppin, chief commissioner of the American delegation to the fair, was only too pleased to escort the delegation of ballplayers

JAMES RYAN,
CENTRE-FIELDER - CHICAGO.

JAS·H·FOGARTY,
RIGHT FIELDER - PHILADELPHIA.

James Ryan, Chicago outfielder, recorded the high jinks of his touring companions in a diary he kept during the trip. No one provided more fodder than the All-America's James Fogarty, the tour's irrepressible jokester.

through the exhibits from their homeland; they were located at the northern end of the Exhibition Building's Grand Avenue of Nations. Among the featured displays were a scaled-down facsimile of an Anheuser-Busch brewery, Colgate soap, Armour packed meat, Bissell carpet sweepers, Winchester rifles, Singer sewing machines, "galvanic belts" from the Pacific Electric Company, and Allen & Ginter cigarettes, the last packed with a new promotional gimmick: trading cards featuring such prominent American baseball players as Adrian Anson, John Ward, James Fogarty, and Jimmy Ryan.

The tourists' first demonstration in Victoria of the American game took place the next afternoon at the Melbourne Cricket Club, and Spalding had every reason to be delighted with the result. "Our professional debut in Victoria could scarcely have been a more brilliant and auspicious one," Palmer wrote. The group arrived an hour early for the scheduled three o'clock start, in time for a round of champagne toasts with the club's officials before Duval marched them out onto the field to the brass-band accompaniment of "Yankee Doodle." Some ten thousand Melbourners had come out for the event; the grandstand was packed, and spectators were lined up thirty and forty deep before the picket fence that bounded the club's pristine field. The American athletes, described in the *Melbourne Evening Herald* as "a really magnificent body of men," once again seemed particularly attractive to the women of Australia, who attended in large numbers, attired in their finest summer dresses.

The game itself was one of "brilliant order" according to Palmer. "The snap and ginger of the players awoke the warmest admiration," wrote Simon Goodfriend. Pitching for the Chicagos, Mark Baldwin allowed just seven hits and also brought home the winning run in the seventh with a line-drive single into the groin of the All-America pitcher, Cannonball Crane. Cannonball stayed in the game, but apparently was not fully recovered when Anson stepped to the plate in the following inning. Though his team was ahead, the Chicago captain was hitless and undoubtedly still smarting from his poor cricket performance in Sydney the previous week. Between the slumping batter and the injured pitcher, something had to give.

Anson, with his bat cocked, glared menacingly at Crane, who responded with two balls well out of the strike zone. This left Anson even testier—he wanted to hit, after all—and on the next pitch Crane obliged him with a high ball over the heart of the plate. The *Melbourne Sportsman* recorded the events that followed: "The sphere must have smiled when it came toward him, for Old Anse drew his mighty form three inches into the air, and sent his black-tipped stick against that piece of horse hide with a sound like that unto a Georgia mule putting its off heel through the top of a strawberry crate." Anson first stood watching as the orb flew off toward the Yarra as if it were "Prof. Bartholomew's balloon," and then began to lumber around the bases in his typically inelegant way. By the time he had reached third, All-America right-fielder Tom Brown had chased down the bounding ball and then returned it to Ned Hanlon, the cutoff in short center. Anson, however, either would not or could not be held. He ran right through Tom Burns's stop sign and "launched his aggregation of Marshalltown bone and muscle into the air, and struck the rubber all in a heap." Unfortunately, Hanlon's throw had long since preceded him to the plate. Catcher Billie Earle applied the tag, and Anson was out yet again. At least Chicago had won, 5–3.

"An almost perfect demonstration of their country's national pastime," was the *Sportsman*'s verdict. If there was any disappointment, it was that the game, which took all of an hour and twenty minutes, had passed much too quickly—these fans were used to cricket, after all, in which a match could last several days. So for a bit of extra entertainment, the players gave an impromptu lesson in the finer points of the American game to a team of Australian cricketers. (Baldwin, perhaps unfairly, struck out seven of the fourteen novice batters who stepped up to the plate.)

The Australian press appreciated the quick pace of the American sport; much like Americans, they viewed the game as one more fitting to the busy urban lifestyle of their industrialized modern society. "An excellent game and over and done with in a couple of hours!" noted *Punch*. The *Melbourne Argus* was even more effusive in its praise, noting that "cricket, if not still on the wane, is at any rate at a standstill" and that baseball is "well adapted to our climate and the disposition of our youth." The greatest endorsement came from Major Wardill, the secretary of the Melbourne Cricket Club, who, according to Palmer, had "become a most enthusiastic admirer of the sport and freely admits it is a better game for Australians than any now in vogue."

Still basking in the glow of this triumph, the next morning Spalding gathered his charges in the Grand Hotel's reading room to formally announce his intention to bring the tour fully around the globe. This news, to the extent that it was news at all, was received by enthusiastic applause and a round of cheers. Word of the dramatic changes to the National League's labor policy, news that might well have sent Ward and his

Brotherhood confreres heading for the nearest steamer agent and the first ship back to the States, had yet to catch up with the tour. Instead, there was backslapping. When that was over, Spalding, like a concerned parent, advised the men that they would be "going to strange countries, and among strange peoples," and that they would have to be discreet in their habits. The reputations of both the country and the great game of baseball were at stake. *His* reputation was at stake. As to exactly which strange countries and peoples they would be seeing—well, those details were at the moment unresolved, though a redemptive trip to England was certainly on the itinerary. That very morning Spalding had dispatched Will Lynch, who had come with the party from Auckland, to investigate the possibility of playing in Calcutta, and from there traveling overland to Bombay and continuing on to Egypt and then Europe. Lynch was to scout that terrain, and then have a telegraph waiting with instructions on how Spalding should proceed at Colombo, on the west coast of the island of Ceylon (now Sri Lanka), the tear-shaped island just off the southern tip of the Indian subcontinent. That city was the first port of call for any ship traveling to Europe from Australia.

The tourists left Melbourne for Adelaide, capital of colonial South Australia, on December 25, having in the interim played another well-received game—the All-Americas won, 16–13, before a crowd of six thousand—and having celebrated Christmas Eve with a special performance in their honor at the St. George's Theater. They knew, in any case, that they would be returning to Melbourne for another week before departing across the Indian Ocean for points east.

The Adelaide trip, another overnight journey, brought the tourists roughly 750 miles northwest up the Australian coast. The good news was that they could relax in comfort during the ride, this thanks to the handsome new rolling stock of the Victorian Railway, which had been imported from the United States. These cars, built by Mann's Boudoir Car Company, had private compartments along a central corridor, toilets, and even a rudimentary air-conditioning system. The men owed their comfort to Colonel William D'Alton Mann, a Union hero at Gettysburg

who had carpet-bagged to Alabama after the war to become an industri-
alist, newspaper publisher, congressman, and rail-road entrepreneur. The
design of luxury coaches was one of his very many professional activities. (Though he was never able to break George Pullman's monopoly on
the American market, his cars were popular in Europe, and were used on
the Orient Express.) In his later career he published a society column,
"Town Topics," that so scandalized Gilded Aged plutocrats that many of
the biggest names of the era—J. P. Morgan and Charles Schwab, were
two—offered him "loans" so as not to be included.

When the tourists finally arrived in Adelaide on the morning of the
twenty-sixth, they found a city possessed of both a physical and emo-
tional dignity that separated it from its larger and more cosmopolitan rivals. Unlike New South Wales and Victoria, the colony of South
Australia was not burdened by the stigma of a convict history. South Australians could also boast of their capital's commodious town plan—a
grid generously interspersed with green spaces—not to mention an oper-
ational sewer system that was the envy of Sydney and "Marvellous
Smellbourne."

After the now-obligatory champagne-fueled meet-and-greet with the
mayor and a brief stop to freshen up at their hotels—the group was split
between the York, the Prince Alfred, and the South Australian—the
tourists were driven to the local cricket grounds, the Adelaide Oval, for
the first of the three exhibition games they would play in their three days
in the city. Attendance was poor for this first game, around two thousand, largely owing to the fact that it was Boxing Day, the day after
Christmas, when Australians traditionally exchanged their gifts. The
game, won 19–14 by the All-Americas, was not well played. "It is certain
that the banqueting and the weather are proving too much for the boys,"
Palmer wrote in his syndicated report.

The following day's game, a late-afternoon start, was preceded by a
morning excursion to the winery of Thomas Hardy & Sons (still one of
Australia's biggest wine producers) and then a trip to Henley Beach for
lunch and beers. Given the general level of intoxication upon their return,
it was no surprise that this second game in Adelaide was of a similar character to the first. (Chicago won 12–9.) In any case, the primary attraction

of the day was the ascension of Professor Bartholomew, who was busily readying his balloon for inflation at the southwest corner of the oval when the final out was made. Crowds had in fact been building throughout the game in anticipation of his performance, both on the grounds itself and also on the banks of Torrens Lake and Montefiore Hill.

Bartholomew's flight preparation required the digging of a trench roughly four feet in diameter and as many feet deep, which he then filled with coal and kindling. A flue, jerry-rigged from bricks and a metal barrel, was then connected to the mouth of the balloon, an oblong bulb of light canvas that lay collapsed on the ground, surrounded by a tangle of rigging. When fully inflated it would reach sixty feet into the air and run forty-four feet across at its widest point.

At ten minutes before six o'clock, with the game now complete, the professor doused the kindling with kerosene, lit a fire, and in short order the balloon was filling with hot air and smoke. Twenty minutes later, it was all a group of the ballplayers could do to hold the great balloon down. This was a task to be undertaken with caution: At one of Bartholomew's exhibitions in Detroit just a few months earlier, a careless attendant had become entangled in Bartholomew's rigging and had been dragged upside-down some fifteen hundred feet into the air before the professor was able to bring the balloon and its alarmed passenger safely down to earth.

Bartholomew may have appeared somewhat effeminate to the crowd in Auckland, but now, covered in soot from the fire and in his black leotard, he appeared positively "Mephistophelian" according to the *South Australia Register*. Seeing that all was ready, he took up a position on the bar of the trapeze, grabbed hold of the rigging to steady himself, and signaled the ballplayers to release the balloon. "Instantly the huge sphere shot swiftly up in the air, the intrepid man hanging on," wrote the *Register*. The professor, soon some two thousand feet above the ground—he claimed to have reached altitudes of over three miles in the past—doffed his cap, and began his performance, a series of tumbles and gyrations that left him hanging by his feet from the trapeze. Below, the crowd was breathless. After a few more twists and turns, the professor completed his routine, and, pulling himself back into a seated position on the bar, he took hold of a second trapeze, suspended beneath his parachute, which itself hung limply from the side of the balloon. With little ceremony, he jumped. It was a good hundred feet—Bartholomew claimed three hundred—before the chute, yanked loose from the balloon by his weight, fully opened; once it did, he continued his gymnastics until coming to a safe landing on his feet a hundred yards behind the oval, where the crowd, now cheering wildly, rushed to greet him.

Meanwhile, the balloon, which had been weighted at its top with a small bag of sand, flipped over and began a rapid deflation, bleeding an exhaust of smoke and hot air as it snaked its way back to earth. When it finally landed, Bartholomew packed it up and headed off to his hotel in a cab—but not before granting an interview to the *Register*. "Professor Bartholomew appears to treat his perilous performance very lightly," the paper wrote. "It seems comparatively little to him, however much it may astonish the spectators. He says it does not make him giddy, nor does the rapid descent before the parachute expands take his breath away. The performance was a complete success and sensational in all conscience, but the Professor considers it safe." Before long Bartholomew would have to reconsider that assessment.

The tourists' final day in Adelaide was yet another holiday, the fifty-second anniversary of the founding of South Australia, and for some reason the town fathers felt that an exhibition of the American national game would be an appropriate way to commemorate the momentous occasion. (Saturdays were already half-days in Australia, whereas the United States still had a six-day work week.) To those coming from America, with its Calvinist devotion to work and its industrial demand for labor, the Australian penchant for leisure seemed almost criminal, and prompted a derisive response from Simon Goodfriend, who offered readers of the *New York Sun* a comparison of the two countries clearly indebted to Mark Twain: "Holidays are frequent in Australia. They occur on all possible and impossible pretexts. One runs upon them unexpectedly in the calendar, not knowing whence they come or whither they go. In America it is business before pleasure; in

Australia pleasure before business. When a day has no possible use here it is erected into a holiday."

One of the many benefits of those holidays was time to both watch and participate in sports. On this day, that translated into a crowd of nearly five thousand for a game won by the Chicagos 12–9. But it also boded well for the future of baseball on Australian soil. Indeed, just two months after Spalding and his men departed South Australia, the *New York Times* ran an item that it had picked up from the Adelaide *Register*: "There seems little doubt but that the American national game of baseball, so successfully introduced into Australia by Spalding's team of baseballers, will become a popular outdoor game. Already, although it is only a few weeks since the game was first played here, several clubs have been started, and one of the city teams numbers 25 members." After so much controversy and after so many miles, incontrovertible evidence was starting to accumulate; Spalding's tour was beginning to look as though it just might be the success that he had been promising all along.

———

The players departed Adelaide that afternoon at four o'clock and arrived early the next morning at Ballarat, a mining town along the return route to Melbourne, some 50 miles to the west of that city. This brief stopover took the tourists as close as they would come to the romantic Australian void known alternately as the Outback and the Never Never. Though in truth Ballarat was not that remote, and certainly not that wild, a fact Anson lamented. "If we could have shot a kangaroo or two before our departure and run up against a party of bushrangers, black-bearded and daring, even though they had managed to relieve us of a few our valuables, we should have been made happy," he wrote. "Alas! the bushrangers, like the bad men of our own glorious West, had been wiped out by the march of civilization, and even the kangaroo had taken to the woods."

Ballarat had been settled in the 1830s as an agrarian center, but its character was changed dramatically in August of 1851 with the discovery of gold at Poverty Point. Within two years, more than twenty thousand prospectors could be found working Ballarat's rich gold fields. By the time Spalding and his men arrived, at the close of 1888, the city's easily tapped reserves had been depleted, but mining operations continued deep underground.

The arrival of so many American celebrities in this provincial city was treated as a significant occasion. The tourists might have preferred to spend the morning catching up on their sleep, but their proud hosts had planned a full day of activities, and were not to be put off. The events began with a quick stop at Craig's Royal Hotel for a light snack: sandwiches, coffee, and that classic Victorian pick-me-up, the brandy and soda. Then it was off to the botanical gardens ("Well worth a visit," according to Anson) and a dip at the Ballarat Swimming Aquarium before returning to the Craig for a formal breakfast. No sooner was that complete than they were back out beating a touristic path to the Barton Gold Mines, where they donned overalls and slouch hats and in small groups descended 1,280 feet down to the floor of the shaft, which was uniformly found to be wet, dark, and unappealing.

The itinerary continued with not one but two civic receptions, for Ballarat was cleaved into a pair of separate entities—conveniently labeled East Ballarat and West Ballarat—and the two were not on speaking terms. Mayor Macdonald, of West Ballarat, offered the usual feast of champagne and hors d'oeuvres. Mayor Ellsworth, of East Ballarat, countered with a similar spread and then one-upped his rival by convincing the tourists to join him on a visit to the local orphanage—the sort of trip no ballplayer has ever refused. Spalding, impressed by the mayor's energy and always a sucker for children, invited all of the boys and girls to that afternoon's game, to be played at the town's Eastern Oval.

The All-Americas won that contest 11–7 behind the pitching of John Healy and a home run by John Ward. But it was not baseball that the Eastern Oval crowd of five thousand, including some two hundred orphan children, would remember most. That distinction would once again belong to Professor Bartholomew.

Following the game, the ballplayers took up their positions around the professor's deflated contraption. Dressed in his devilish outfit, Bartholomew fanned the inflating fire, and the men grabbed tighter and tighter hold of their ropes as the balloon expanded to its full size, whereupon the aeronaut mounted the trapeze. With the rather uninspired call of "Let go!" the balloon was released, and Bartholomew began performing his carnival tricks. That a southerly wind was gently pushing the balloon toward Ballarat's central business district might have been cause for concern, though few of the spectators mentioned it; in any case, once aloft there was not much that could be done.

When the routine was complete, Bartholomew reached over to the trapeze beneath his parachute, took hold, and dropped free of the balloon. On this occasion, however, it seemed to take an even longer time for the chute to open, and when it finally did the professor found himself dropping at a rapid rate and on an undesirable trajectory. Out of control, he smacked first into the chimney and then the iron coping along the roof of the Buck's Head Hotel. From there, he fell unceremoniously into the back yard of one J. K. Baird. (The balloon, for the record, touched down in Morey's Machinery Yard, on Lydiard Street.) The professor was immediately transported to the local hospital, where it was found that, by some miracle, the only serious injury he had sustained was a deep gash below his left knee. This would be enough to sideline him for at least a month, but he was apparently undaunted. In an interview from his bed at the Craig, he offered an explanation for his mishap to a local reporter: "The air in Australia offers much less resistance than in other countries." But apparently not that much less. The following June, at an exhibition at the Elmira, New York fair grounds, the professor's parachute again failed to deploy properly, and he dropped onto a fence, breaking a leg.

The tourists' final week in Melbourne passed in a fairly desultory manner as a result of their makeshift itinerary. They did have a chance to take in an Australian-rules football match between the Carleton and St. Kilda clubs, and, in the game's aftermath, had even agreed to participate in an exhibition contest in that sport against the bruising St. Kilda team. To the great fortune of the ballplayers, who watched the rough-and-tumble first match with some alarm, the second game was rained out. "Our boys realized we could make little show against the Australians," Palmer noted dryly.

New Year's Eve was spent on the town, none of the tourists being dissuaded from their revelries by the prospect of a game scheduled for the next morning at eleven o'clock. A small and no-doubt hungover crowd watched the players loaf through a 14–7 game won by the Chicagos. Primary entertainment of the day came that afternoon, with an exhibition of boomerang throwing and rope skipping by a team of Aboriginal performers. "The degree of skill attained by the black-faced, bushy-haired Queenslanders in the use of the boomerang is certainly remarkable," Palmer wrote. "A dozen big fellows performed feats with the peculiar Australian weapon which our party had frequently read of, but had never before credited."

The Americans' final games in Australia took place on January 5, a warm and sunny Saturday afternoon. Good weather and a solid week of promotional work begat the largest audience they had played before since their first game in San Francisco, a crowd some seventeen thousand strong. Festivities began at three o'clock, with a two-inning exhibition match between the All-Americas and a team of local expatriate Americans, who put up a spirited show but nevertheless fell to the pros by a 20–3 count. This was followed by an Australian-rules football match between the Carleton and Port Melbourne clubs, and then the headline event, a five-inning game between the Chicagos and the All-Americas. Mark Baldwin, the dapper Chicago pitcher, stole the show, tossing a one-hit shutout sealed, on the last play of the game, with a spectacular running grab in right field by Robert Pettit. By winning four of the final five games on the island continent, Anson's Chicagos closed the All-Americas' series lead to just two games, with the tally at 15–13.

The day concluded with a long-distance throwing contest, the stake being the Australian record of 126 yards, 3 inches. As an added incentive, Spalding offered a hundred-dollar prize to anyone who could break the mark. First up was Ned Williamson, the burly Chicago shortstop, whose heave came up two yards short. Next was Fred Pfeffer, but he could do no better than his fellow Chicago stalwart. Thus it was left to Cannonball Crane, who stepped to the line and with a nod to the grandstand demonstrated just how he had earned his nickname. When his majestic toss finally landed, the ball was 128 yards and 10 inches from where Crane had released it, and the New Yorker was one hundred dollars richer.

———————

With one last day before departing across the Indian Ocean, Spalding and his men had time to do a bit of trinket shopping for their families and friends. Indeed, the "rampant rage for foreign curios," according to Ward, depleted the cash reserves of several members of the party. Emu eggs were one of the more popular souvenirs. John Tener bought a rug made by Aboriginals, which he shipped back home to his Aunt Maud in Pennsylvania.

Albert Spalding departed with something more precious than any bauble: the knowledge that, despite dire predictions and lackluster early returns, his grand tour had already proved itself a substantial success. The traveling ballplayers had been treated as conquering heroes in each of the cities they had visited, and there was every evidence that the sport-loving people of Australia—or at least those resident outside Sydney— were genuinely interested in the American game. The Australian press had taken to the athletes, to their game, and to the indefatigable man who had brought them together. "The enterprising spirit invariably displayed by the average American in anything he undertakes is as undeniable as it is proverbial," read one Melbourne paper's paean to Spalding. "No project is too deep for his conception, nor can its magnitude be sufficiently great to make him hesitate or falter, and perhaps the most admirable of all the national characteristics of an American is his prompt decisiveness in action, even in matters of the weightiest importance." The *Melbourne Herald* expressed its enthusiasm in poetic form:

> *Let football find its votaries,*
> *And cricket do the same,*
> *In days sensational such as these*
> *It's baseball is the game!*

Back in the United States, the banner headline that ran over Palmer's final dispatch from the Antipodes read, "Baseball Takes Hold: Now

Firmly Rooted in Australia." So overwhelming was the Australian response that Harry Simpson, Spalding's traveling secretary, agreed to stay on in Melbourne—at his own initiative and cost—to help build the sport and to act as a representative for Spalding's sporting-goods concern. In just a few months, he had clubs organized in all three colonies and outlets for Spalding sporting goods in Sydney, Melbourne, and Adelaide.

Australia, however, was wide-open territory, a sport-loving country with a history similar to the United States' and no special game to call its own. Just how Spalding and his men would be received in lands where the cultures, not to mention the athletic traditions, were far different and much better established was an open question, one that would soon be resolved.

CHAPTER 7

RICKSHAWS AND PYRAMIDS

B Y THE LATE NINETEENTH CENTURY, AS SPALDING AND HIS group of merry excursionists were making their way around the globe, the American tourist, though still a young breed, had already become a well-established figure of caricature and derision. Americans, for that matter, were often their own harshest critics. "There is but one word to use in regard to [them]—vulgar; vulgar, vulgar," Henry James wrote in a letter to his mother from Italy in 1869. "Their ignorance—their stingy, grungy, defiant attitude—their perpetual reference of all things to some American reference or precedent which exists only in their own unscrupulous wind-bags—and then our unhappy poverty of voice, speech, of physiognomy—these things glare at you hideously. It's the absolute and incredible lack of culture that strikes you in common travelling Americans." A somewhat less bitter description of the American tourist was published in that same year: Mark Twain's *The Innocents Abroad*, the comic account of the passengers of the *Quaker City* on the first-ever packaged cruise—"pleasure excursion" was Twain's phrase—from the United States to Europe and the Holy Land.

It was perhaps a measure of Spalding's audacity that he felt his touring ballplayers might somehow offer a corrective to the unfortunate, if not altogether inaccurate, stereotyping of traveling Americans as ill-mannered and uncultured buffoons. From the outset he advertised them as exponents not just of America's national game but of America itself;

men specifically chosen—or at least theoretically chosen—so they might "reflect credit on the country." The enormity of this project became readily apparent just as soon as Spalding and his men boarded the steamer S.S. *Salier*, of the Lloyd Line, which was to take them across the Indian Ocean. Awaiting them on the ship's broad quarterdeck was a man who, to their horror, had set out some years earlier on a globe-trotting mission that was, minus the baseball, quite similar to their own. Seeing the handsome party on board for the first time, he was quick to introduce himself: "Theophilus Green, Representative American."

Bald, pink, plump, newly rich, and irredeemably obnoxious, Green was the very avatar of the stereotype Spalding hoped to combat and, perhaps not coincidentally, a funhouse reflection of the magnate himself. For the unsuspecting player, seated innocently enough on deck and minding his own business, there was no greater danger than the surreptitious approach of the ever-voluble Green, who, like General Strange before him, enjoyed nothing better than an audience. But where the general impressed the tourists as a romantic figure of benign and dignified authority, Green was an aggressive, supercilious nuisance. And though he was undeniably well traveled, he apparently had developed little sympathy for the peoples and customs encountered on his many peregrinations. "In the midst of an interesting description of Cairo, or Jerusalem and its people," wrote Palmer, "he would suddenly break off and tell how smart he had been in evading the thieving and bulldozing propensities of an Egyptian cabman, or a Syrian inn-keeper; and laying his finger on the side of his nose, would devote five minutes perhaps to telling how vastly superior was his own cunning to that of the Cingalese, Neapolitan, or Muscovite beggars who had so often appealed to him for alms."

The attitudes Palmer and his fellow tourists had thus far evinced when confronted with other cultures suggest that it was not the content of Green's commentary that offended so much as Green himself. Even still, there seemed to be a genuine feeling of upset that they would not be able to undo the damage this man had wrought. As Palmer noted, "My chief regret was that our party of magnificent-looking fellows, with their liberal ideas, their love of fun, their fine physiques, and their genial, happy natures, were not going to some of the countries Mr. Green had visited, so that, in the matter of representative Americans we might have shown those people the difference." That their own behavior might not always be seen as endearing or culturally sensitive didn't seem to cross their minds.

The Spalding tourists found more pleasant company in the brothers George and Bob Wilson, a pair of broad-shouldered Australian adventurers traveling in the *Salier*'s second-class compartments. Carrying a formidable arsenal of weaponry and, by their own account, an "unlimited supply of ammunition," the two were on their way to the slave-trading capital of Zanzibar, from whence they would cross into what was then German East Africa on a hunting expedition deep into the interior of the "Dark Continent." These were the kind of men worthy of the baseballers' admiration. "Think of it!" wrote Palmer. "To be cut off from all connection of any and every kind with civilization; to take their lives in their hands among savage tribes, who would as likely to murder them for their weapons as not; to face the dangers of climate and poisonous reptiles, and all for their love of adventure and their desire to slay the King of the Beasts in his native lair." Spalding arranged for a champagne reception to wish the duo good luck before they left the ship at Aden, on the southwestern coast of the Arabian peninsula. The hunters promised to keep their new friends apprised of their travels, but were never heard from again.

<hr />

It would be a long and uncomfortable month before the *Salier* would reach Aden. (With its engines set to full steam, the *Salier* could make all of 12 knots—less than 14 miles per hour.) The journey from Melbourne, which had begun in the cooling waters of the Australian Bight, had taken them west and north as they skirted the Australian continent and steamed into the placid Indian Ocean. Here the travelers once again found themselves suffering in tropical heat, and they would be so afflicted for some time. Colombo, the next stop on their itinerary, was well over four thousand miles away. "There were days when the sun beat down so fiercely on the deck that the boys lay in their bunks panting like lizards," John Ward wrote in a dispatch to the *Chicago Tribune*. Worst affected was Cannonball Crane, whose fragile disposition always left him vulnerable. "His mental condition was such that it was not safe to approach him," the All-America shortstop noted. Jimmy Ryan's perfunctory diary entries convey something of the wearying effect of the unremitting heat:

> *Saturday, January 19th*
> Saw a sail today but was too far away to make her known. The heat was relieved by a heavy shower.
>
> *Sunday, January 20th*
> Nothing to do to-day. Some of the boys climb to the masthead and endeavor to get a cool breeze.
>
> *Monday, January 21st*
> Sea like glass and awful hot.

The indolence naturally inspired a sense of melancholy and longing among the tourists, who had now been absent from their families and friends for nearly three months. "There is no denying that we are, at times, a bit homesick—though no one is sorry he came or would shorten the trip a single day," Ward wrote. John Tener echoed that sentiment in a letter to his aunt Maud back in Pennsylvania: "I am very glad that each day's journey brings me a little nearer home, for I know that the [most] pleasant feature of this long trip will be my return home to find you all well."

In the meantime, they spent their days on the *Salier*'s wood-planked quarterdeck, indulging themselves in such classic cruise pastimes as shuffleboard, ring-toss ("quoits"), and cards. At night they slept outdoors in their pajamas, just as they had on the *Alameda*. A game of draw poker ran at all hours in the open smoking area that came to be known as "Little Monte Carlo." Duval taught the men craps. The one activity they did not attempt was cricket; after their unimpressive showing in Sydney, no one—Anson in particular—seemed to have any interest in taking up that sport again.

They did, on the other hand, have plenty of time to discuss the rules of baseball, and how they might be improved. The general consensus was that pitchers had too great an advantage over batters (not a surprising conclusion, given the batter-to-pitcher ratio among the travelers), and that some action was required to find an appropriate balance. The obvious solution, which would actually be adopted for the 1889 season, was to reduce the number of balls required for a walk from five to four, where it has remained to this day (as recently as 1883 it had been eight). Another proposal was to move the rubber back five feet. An impromptu vote came out 10–2 in favor of this arrangement (the two naysayers were—no surprise—the pitchers Healy and Crane).

Anson had an even more aggressive scheme, one that left the rest of the tourists sitting in stupefied silence: Right-handed batters, he suggested, should have the option to circle the bases clockwise. The idea was to remove any advantage left-handers might have by virtue of hitting from the side of home plate closest to first base, saving them a step out of the batter's box. An interesting idea, maybe, but Anson had not considered what would happen when two players moving in opposite directions came upon each other on the base paths. Perhaps he had been affected by the heat.

A bit of excitement did come when Wood and Fogarty noticed a broad streak tailing the ship, its dorsal fin now and again breaking the surface. The men summoned the first mate, who informed them that it was "a shark of the man-eating variety," and that they had best steer clear of the ship's rail, for "sea wolves" such as these were known to feast on the occasional inattentive passenger. He was surely kidding, but it was noted that Wood and Fogarty were not seen again on deck for four days. Several of their more daring teammates, however, thought they might dispatch the creature with their revolvers. When this failed, Anson suggested that Duval be used as bait, a recommendation the ship's captain rejected in favor of a chunk of salt-pork fastened to a chain rope. When the shark was subsequently hauled onto deck and bludgeoned by the crew, Anson was allegedly seen cowering near the mizzenmast.

The incident signaled a sad reduction in status for Duval, who had performed his minstrel act onstage in Australia to general acclaim, especially among women. "His queer antics made him quite a favorite with the ladies," wrote Goodfriend. "He is a born comedian, and the sidesplitting capers which he so frequently indulges in are all the more humorous because they are done spontaneously." On the *Salier*, he attempted an imitation of Professor Bartholomew's parachute descent, jumping with an umbrella from the ship's rigging onto the canvas awning over the quarterdeck. (He landed with a thump and the umbrella was destroyed, but no one was hurt.) Nellie Williamson, wife of the Chicago shortstop, had started Duval, who was apparently illiterate, on reading lessons. The largely German crew of the *Salier*, meanwhile, had mistaken his drum major's outfit for some kind of royal costume, and were treating him to every possible luxury, much to the amusement of the ballplayers. With the situation taking a turn toward farce, Spalding felt compelled to do something to regain control, and turned Duval over to the ship's captain as an added hand. For the remainder of the journey, he could be found in the ship's dining room working a punka rope, which kept the room's ceiling fans in constant motion. Not every member of the party was considered a representative American.

The meals served in the wood-paneled dining compartment were leaden German affairs with an emphasis on roasted meats and root vegetables. That the waiters spoke little English didn't make matters any easier. When the chief steward attempted pancakes—"vheat ghakes"—as a gesture of good will, the results were, according to Newton MacMillan, "impregnable to the knife." Fogarty picked up five of the card-like flapjacks, shuffled them in his hands, and tossed a stack back down on the table. "Give me three cards," he said. So much for appreciation. Fogarty and the steward had to be separated.

Exploration of the iron-hulled ship proved to be the tourists' most reliable break from the tedium of their journey. Longer than a football field, the *Salier* had a single funnel amidships that marked the division between accommodations for first- and second-class passengers (in the after portion of the boat), and those traveling in steerage (in the forward sections)—a reversal of the standard arrangement. Noah himself would have been impressed by the *Salier*'s stock pens, which occupied the forward deck and housed of a pair of milk cows in addition to steer, sheep, calves, pigs, pheasants, chickens, quail, and various other creatures destined for the ship's handsome dining room.

As interesting as the *Salier*'s menagerie were its hundred and fifty steerage passengers, a population that included Germans, Italians, Chinese, Singhalese, Turks, and "Hindoos," the last being a diverse group that self-segregated according to caste and would not eat the ship's food (they slaughtered their own animals and cooked for themselves on deck). "It was indeed interesting to take a walk through their quarters, and listen to the babble of tongues," Palmer wrote. Expeditions through these realms were generally led by James Fogarty, would-be ethnographer, who took to calling the combined forward reaches of the ship "the zoo." With a small group of players in tow, the All-America outfielder would discourse on the origins and behavioral characteristics of the various inhabitants encountered, human and otherwise.

If these field trips put to rest Palmer's notions about the players' "liberal ideas," they are telling of a broader fascination with scientific classification that was typical of the period, a skewed application of the Darwinian project that would somehow allow the Occidental observer to render his Oriental subject separate, inferior, and harmless. The sad irony in this instance was that the players themselves were predominantly first- and second-generation emigrants—several had made the journey to America in steerage themselves. But sympathy for these other strivers seemed to elude the men.

Arrival at Ceylon came on Friday, January 25, after eighteen days at sea. Its gentle landscape of yellow sand beaches and waving coconut palms was spotted at noon from the deck of the *Salier*, and some four hours later the ship pulled into the raucous port of Colombo, capital of the British colony. (Ceylon became an independent member of the British Commonwealth in 1948, and the Republic of Sri Lanka in 1972.) Indoctrination into the ways of the subcontinent came almost immediately, as the ship was swarmed by natives who paddled out in catamarans, climbed aboard, and offered the tourists trinkets of all kinds. Meanwhile, four "coffee colored" Tamil children on a loosely constructed bamboo raft dove for change tossed into the sea by the liner's passengers.

When the ship arrived, Spalding was still unsure of the future course of the tour. For the *Salier*, Colombo was merely a coaling station on the route to Europe through the Suez Canal, open since 1869. Spalding's hope was to depart Colombo on a different vessel, head for the port city of Calcutta, and then travel by rail across India to Bombay, on India's west coast. From there, the tourists would resume their trip west across the Arabian Sea to Egypt, whence they would depart for Europe. With this in mind, Spalding boarded a small boat that took him into the port, where he expected a telegraphed message from Will Lynch, the advance agent he had sent along from Australia, to be waiting for him with instructions on just how to proceed.

When Spalding walked into the Lloyd's Line office he was dripping wet from a slashing rain that had suddenly drenched the harbor. His mood did not improve when he got hold of the missive from Lynch, which was cryptic to the point of uselessness. The communiqué, sent from Bombay, simply said the tour should meet up with Lynch in Aden, on the coast of the Arabian peninsula (in present-day Yemen), but with no suggestion as to how exactly it should get there.

Now both damp and frustrated, Spalding booked the tour into the Grand Oriental Hotel, the poshest in town and conveniently situated by the waterfront, and set off for the American consulate, where he could at least review his options with hands familiar with the territory. Here, he was faced with the dismaying reality that venturing on through India would be a foolhardy and costly enterprise. The Calcutta–Bombay route was more than fourteen hundred miles long and would require a bare minimum of seventy hours in the extremely uncomfortable British rail cars that had already caused the travelers so much discomfort in Australia. The trip would also set him back some fourteen pounds sterling per person just for the passage. This problem was compounded by a general lack of fenced-in grounds in India, meaning it would be impossible for Spalding to charge admission to his exhibitions and thereby offset his added expenditure. Rumor of a cholera epidemic on the mainland settled matters: there would be no stopping in India.

Faced with the diminution of his tour, Spalding returned to the Lloyd's Line office prepared to bargain. As his men sat down to a comfortable dinner at the Grand Oriental—capon, curry, bananas, *café noir*, and cigarettes were on the menu—Spalding was busy convincing the local agents to delay the departure of the *Salier* to the next afternoon so that his baseballists might at least play one game in the region, for the sake of posterity and publicity. The prospect of thirty additional fares was enticement enough to hold the ship's departure for half a day.

If the change in itinerary caused any disappointment among the players, it was dispelled in a wild night of rickshaw racing through the streets of Colombo. "People who have been at sea for twenty-three days [sic] can understand how coltish a man feels when he gets on land," Ryan wrote in his diary from the comfort of the hotel. For one night, at least, the tourists would sleep in luxury, with a cooling breeze blowing in across the hotel's marble floors. Each room had a latticed balcony and was equipped with a daybed and a discreetly placed sign bearing the curious message "Please Do Not Kick the Servants."

Harriet Spalding, dignified matron that she was, could not help but wonder what passed for acceptable manners in this part of the world, and sought her magnate son's guidance. "I don't know what it means," he replied, "but I guess we will if we stay here long enough." The answer was revealed the following morning, when Harriet opened her door and nearly tripped on a porter in a white dhoti who lay asleep on her doorstep. Awakened by her presence, he jumped to attention. "Good lady, is there anything you want?" She had come a long way from Byron, Illinois.

<hr />

No one better described the intellectual discomfort of the traveler than Henry James. "There is something heartless in stepping forth into the streets of a foreign town to feast upon novelty when the novelty consists of the slightly different costume in which hunger and labour present themselves," he wrote. "Our observation in any foreign land is extremely superficial." Spalding and his men didn't seem troubled by such attitudes; if anything, they were happy to reduce foreign peoples and places to stereotypes, and could do so in astonishingly short periods of time.

"One day in Ceylon is to the untravelled American a liberal education in Orientalism compressed into a single lesson," wrote MacMillan. After twenty-four hours of observation, Ward felt free to describe Colombo as "a queer sort of a place inhabited by a queer sort of people," to the readers of the *Tribune*. For *Sun* readers, Simon Goodfriend wrote that the faces of the local men were "weak and effeminate looking." The women, on the other hand, had "big, soft black eyes, which they use to best advantage as we pass." Such were the clichés of the Western tourist, predictable if uncomfortable. The short stay all but guaranteed there would be nothing more complex. However much they may have derided Theophilus Green, they too seemed incapable of seeing through the veil of their own preconceived notions.

In the Orient, the first stop on the tourist's beaten path is inevitably the bazaar, where a cloud of hawkers and supplicants engulf the nonplused innocent. This, by their own account, was the situation in which Harry Palmer and Jimmy Ryan found themselves as they set out on a shopping expedition to Colombo's once-fortified Portuguese district, which had since become its commercial center. (The British had taken over from those first European colonists in 1796.) From sandalwood boxes to carved statuettes and ivory trinkets, the offerings haven't changed much over the years. "The dusky inhabitants were thicker even than the Chinese in Chinatown, San Francisco, and their incessant chattering, mingling with the yells of the bullock-cart drivers, made the neighborhood a Bedlam," wrote Palmer. The chaos did not prevent the two from purchasing several summer-weight suits from a local tailor for just seven rupees apiece, and these they accessorized with frilly red-silk cummerbunds that gave them a suitably "Oriental appearance." On the return to the hotel they stopped for a performance by a snake charmer— no trip to this part of the world would be complete without one.

While that intrepid pair was off on their expedition into the heart of the city, a larger group traveled to the Kelaniya Temple, a Buddhist shrine roughly seven miles from central Colombo. The party, carried in a fleet of rickshaws, bullock carts, and a horse-drawn wagon, traversed a pontoon bridge and continued along a winding road bordered by coconut, banana, and bamboo trees. After a bumpy hour they arrived at the temple, a hive-shaped stupa capped by a spike. For a small price, the local priests were happy to provide a tour of the site, which dated from the third century B.C. and was said to have been visited by the Buddha himself. MacMillan, however, was not impressed and took the opportunity to poke fun not only at the locals but the adherents of a certain esoteric, spiritualist group that had been growing in popularity in the United States. "It may interest those intellectual persons in Boston and New York who affect Theosophism," he wrote, "to learn that these priests wore dirty brown robes, went barefooted, and chewed the disgusting betel nut; that their hands were dirty, their nails black, and their faces unwashed, and that they did not disdain, but rather solicited a rupee all around (including their high priest) as a return for their services." Little did he realize that the man who would become Theosophy's most visible American benefactor was standing just a few feet away: Albert Spalding.

Back at the hotel later that afternoon, the reconvened tourists had an opportunity to trade tales of their adventures over a tiffin lunch of curry, jackfruit, tamarind, and coconut. In the shaded cool of the dining room, Jimmy Ryan explained the snake-charmer's art to his peers. "The mode of charming is to squat down before his snakeship and from a sort of reed, produce a sort of music which renders him perfectly docile." He said this with the confidence of an expert, and then added a dash of drama: "It is of frequent occurrence, though, that the cobra turns upon his owner and stings him to death." It was Palmer who got the laugh, however. "Ryan and I took good care to stand a safe distance from the charmer and his pet," he said.

Lunch was followed by a tour of the American warship U.S.S. *Essex*, a corvette en route back to the States after a two-year tour of duty monitoring the treaty ports along the Chinese coast. The American sailors, baseball fans all, were happy to receive the players and looked forward to the afternoon's matchup. Ed Cannonball Crane received a pet Japanese monkey as a gift from one of the men, and after Clarence Duval performed one of his "plantation shakedowns" and Anna Berger knocked out "The Star-Spangled Banner" on her cornet, the sailors rowed the tourists from the *Essex* over to the *Salier*, where they picked up their baseball uniforms. From there, they returned to the Grand Oriental to ready themselves for action of the hardball variety.

The ceremonial trip from the hotel up York Street to Galle Face Green, where the game was to be played, surpassed any of the tour's previous parades. "Such a scene as the road from the hotel to the cricket ground I have never seen before or since," wrote Palmer. "There were hundreds of howling, chattering, grotesquely-arrayed natives, with their red, white, green, blue, and orange turbans and jackets; odd-looking, heavy-wheel carts drawn by ambling hump-backed little bulls, not bigger than an American calf; bare-legged Cingalese darting among the carts with their jinrickshaws; peddlers and beggars without number, and, in short, a state of wild confusion that was as laughable as it was novel to our party."

The field itself was a picturesque vision of colonial enterprise. Galle Face had been laid out in 1859 by the British governor at the time, Henry Ward, as a long, green swath of parkland with the sea on one side and a stand of coconut palms on the other. The clubhouse, now packed with a handsomely dressed crowd that included the crew of the *Essex*, looked out over a lawn inscribed with a baseball diamond. A military band performed from a balcony, and between innings a company of Scotch Highlanders squeezed out tunes on their bagpipes. Natives, kept from the clubhouse, gathered along the foul lines to watch the action, for the field was unenclosed and therefore no admission was charged. The game began at four o'clock, and before the ballplayers were forced to return to the *Salier* two hours later so as not to be left behind, they had played five innings. Neither team could claim the historic game, however; it ended with the score knotted at three.

The colonial establishment was impressed by the American pastime and its practitioners. "It is a slugging game calculated to rend the lungs and make hair grow on the baldest head in thirty minutes," one spectator told the *Ceylon Independent*. "If baseball has anything to do with the building up of such physiques, then it is certainly a game worthy of encouragement," echoed the *Ceylon Observer*. As for the response of the native islanders, we have only MacMillan's record: "They regarded the whole thing as a joke, for to the Indian mind nothing is more absurd than athletics. To the Oriental, perfect repose is the ideal state. The chasing of a fly ball to him is the sheerest folly."

———◆———

After the chaos and tumult of Colombo, Spalding and his men were happy for a return to normalcy aboard the *Salier*. That tranquillity was short-lived, however. Early on the morning after their departure, the party was driven from their beds by a pair of cannon shots. The ceremonial blasts were in honor of the birthday of the German emperor, Kaiser Wilhelm, a fact that Fogarty, who was up on deck for the first report, learned from one of the crewmen. This news did not keep him from charging through the first-class hallway hollering, "Pirates, boys, Pirates! Everybody up! We are attacked by pirates!" A wholesale panic among the passengers followed. Spalding locked himself in a closet. Anson stuffed his wife's jewelry into his mouth and took up a post at his door with a bat (a Spalding model, naturally). "The most remarkable thing was that everyone believed that we were attacked, yet no one thought of a gun," wrote Ward in the aftermath. "If there really had been pirates, it is to be feared they would have found easy work." Fogarty, on the other hand, was lucky to escape being hung from the *Salier*'s yardarm.

There was little more excitement on the ship over the next week, at least until daybreak on the morning of February 1, when the Socotra islands, a volcanic archipelago off the tip of the Horn of Africa, were spotted off the starboard bow. By noon, the island chain had been left astern, and the rugged and forbidding bluffs of Somaliland were in view. Soon after, the *Salier* turned north to round Cape Guardafui and enter the Gulf of Aden.

The *Salier* dropped anchor at Aden the next evening, but it was to be the briefest of stops, with only a ceremonial touchdown on land. Three small boats carried the tourists to shore, where they spent an hour shopping for curios from the merchants at Steamer Point; there was not even time for the men to venture into the city proper. "The Arabs and Africans dress very scantily, and beggars abound everywhere," Ryan wrote in his diary after returning to the *Salier*. If a cursory impression was all they were allowed, so be it. As soon as the men were back on the ship, the liner pulled back out into the gulf and pressed on through the night toward Suez.

By morning the *Salier* had arrived at the mouth of the Bab-el Mandeb (Gate of Tears), the treacherous strait connecting the Gulf of Aden to the Red Sea. Two channels pass through these waters, and all hands were on deck when the *Salier* took the narrower of the pair, the Bab Iskender (Gate of Alexander), just two miles across at its widest point. Off the port bow the men could see the island of Perim, to the right was the Arabian shore, and straight ahead was a deadly formation known as the Twelve Apostles, the ruin of many an unfortunate ship. The *Salier* managed to glide through this obstacle course and enter the Red Sea.

Four days later, with the port of Suez peering out across the water, Spalding and his men gathered on the *Salier*'s canopied quarterdeck for the last time, anxious to put their days at sea behind them, at least for the moment. It had been more than a month since their departure from Melbourne, and in that time they had spent barely twenty-four hours on terra firma. With the harbor in sight, their anticipation was almost palpable; an energized buzz coursed through the group as they stood chattering about the adventure to come: Cairo, the pyramids, perhaps even an audience with the khedive himself. Few of the men had slept much over the last few days. The previous night they had drifted past the burnt-red peak of what they presumed to be Mount Sinai. Now, the desert sands of the Egyptian coast slipped endlessly into a distance that seemed to reach all the way back to the time of the pharaohs. "Everything about reminds us that we have come from one of the newest to the oldest civilization on earth," wrote MacMillan.

If Spalding and his men harbored visions of a romantic Arabia of indolent lassitude, the initial trip through Suez brought a swift dose of reality. As in Colombo and Aden, the colonial port was a scene of chaos. "Hardly had we set our feet on the shores of Egypt before we were besieged by swarms of Arabian and Egyptian donkey-boys in loose-fitting robes—black, white, and blue—driving before them troops of long-eared donkeys," Anson recalled. Somehow, amid this excitement, Spalding managed to organize the services of a mule train for the five-block ride across town to the railroad depot on rue Colmar.

What Spalding and his party found on their brief trip through town was a rather seedy outpost of the British colonial system. The city's prominence dated to the 1840s, when Britain began moving troops back and forth to India through Egypt. With the opening of the great canal in 1869, Suez became internationally famous but hardly better off. Profits from the engineering marvel were funneled back to Europe, and Suez was left to a period of prolonged decline. "Of all the tumble-down, ramshackle, dilapidated-looking structures we saw during the trip, those of Suez take the palm," Palmer wrote. "If dirt and general shiftlessness are evidences of antiquity, then surely Suez and its people are the most thoroughly antique of all the antiquities of this nineteenth century. It was a relief to each and every one of us when the train pulled from the station."

From the windows of that train's compartments, the sweeping desert vista the tourists had seen from the decks of the *Salier* revealed itself to be a mirage. In place of the romantic landscape of shifting sands and antique ruins they had imagined from a distance, they found a hardscrabble terrain dotted with earthen huts. Whether Egyptians were too poor or too attached to these quarters to replace them with "more comfortable or modern dwellings" was a question Palmer could not answer.

After two hours of slow travel parallel to the canal, the tracks cut west toward Cairo and into the fertile valley of the Nile, and the rough landscape gradually gave way to farmland that was lush and green. "Great fields of grain and clover, with here and there a grove of imposing palms or acacias, stretched away from each side of the tracks," wrote Palmer. "Flocks of sheep and goats became a common sight, along the roadways of the irrigating canals, which overspread the valley like an immense net." Cotton was the principal crop they saw as they rolled along; it had been the engine of the Egyptian economy since the 1860s, when the American Civil War forced the powers of Europe to develop alternate sources for that indispensable product. Egypt, just across the Mediterranean, was a logical choice, and in short order Europe's militarily backed commercial interests forced the Egyptian state into a position of utter subservience. The train ride from Suez to Cairo brought Spalding and his men directly through the landmarks of this contested territory, including Tel el-Kebir, where in 1882 the British had put down a bloody rebellion to solidify their hold on the country, and some twenty miles later Zagazig, a small industrial city that was the center of Egyptian cotton production.

At each station stop along this route, the train was besieged by *fellaheen*—Egyptian peasants—begging for alms and selling fruit and sweets and jugs of cool water to the passengers in their cramped and dusty compartments. A mutual curiosity seemed at work at these stops, though it soon became apparent that it was not Spalding's virile athletes that interested the Egyptians so much as the pet monkey Crane had received as a gift on the *Essex*. And it was actually not so much the monkey that was attracting attention, but its strange costume—a scarlet organ-grinder's outfit. When Jimmy Ryan noted its similarity to Duval's drum-major's getup, the stage was set for trouble.

When the tourists pulled into the next station, Duval was dressed in his uniform, now accessorized with a catcher's mask and with a rope leash tied around his waist. Palmer provides a vivid description of the ensuing events:

> Clarence sprang through the doorway into a score of Egyptians, waddling and chattering like an angry monkey. Women screamed and men fell over each other in a wild effort to get out of reach of the terrible looking ape which Ryan, apparently with the exertion of great strength, held with difficulty, and finally forced back into the carriage. Then Clarence sat at the window, chattering and making faces as long as we remained at the station, and not a native would come within twenty feet of our coach. One could scarcely blame them, for could a disciple of Darwin have seen the mascot in his impromptu make-up, his heart would have bounded with delightful visions of the missing link.

Ryan, for his part, made no mention of the episode in his diary. Perhaps, looking back on the day's events, he felt it was not his finest moment, and certainly not one worth recording for posterity. Or maybe, given what was to come, he had simply forgotten all about it.

Spalding and his team were now accustomed to an enthusiastic welcome upon their arrival in a foreign city, and the reception they received when they pulled into Cairo was as boisterous as any. It was not, however, scripted. The platform at Cairo was so dense with humanity that their step down from the train amounted to a leap of faith. The only recognizable face was that of Will Lynch, who had arrived a few days earlier from Bombay. He had a series of carriages waiting for the group, but it looked as though reaching them through the pressure of the importunate crowd was going to be all but impossible. A solution presented itself when Fogarty noticed the natives were in bare feet. "Step on their trotters, boys, they

Fred "Dandelion" Pfeffer, firebrand second baseman of Chicago's great Stone Wall infield, smoked four cigars before every game to help improve his hitting, and then penned a book, Scientific Ball, *that stressed appropriate training habits.*

Ned Hanlon, outfielder for the All-Americas, would become one of the game's most influential figures as manager of the rough-and-tumble Baltimore Orioles of the 1890s.

can't stand that!" he shouted. Though this was probably not the best way to make a good first impression, it was nevertheless effective, and soon enough the players had opened a space in the crowd to gather their belongings and set off across town for their lodgings at the Orient Hotel.

It was in the lobby of this oasis of colonial luxury that the tourists got their first look at an American newspaper that postdated their departure from San Francisco. Fred Pfeffer held the tabloid in question, but he was surrounded by curious teammates peering over his shoulder, anxious for news from home. What they saw came as a shock. Instead of happy reminders of life back in America, they found a report about the "Brush Plan," the draconian new labor policy the National League's owners had imposed back in November, when the tourists were still steaming across the Pacific toward Hawaii. Details were vague, but it was clear that the system would bring to a new low the already fraught relationship between the men who played the game and those who paid them to do so.

The touring players' first response was outrage, followed almost immediately by an intense concern for their own well-being. "It can be readily imagined how anxious the players are to learn where they stand, if such an innovation has been made, especially those who have not yet signed," Goodfriend wrote in a dispatch back to the *Sun*. Ward was dismissive of the entire plan and its controversial scheme to divide up the league's talent into five categories based on skill and comportment. "There are no two persons who would classify players alike, and no one, not even a player, could begin to do justice," he wrote.

But that was the least of it. For Ward, the president of the Brotherhood of American Base Ball Players, news of the plan came as a piercing affront, a signal that the owners had embarked on a new offensive at the very moment he had hoped to be making progress in their relationship. Indeed, one of his principal motivations for accepting Spalding's tour invitation was the opportunity it would present to address union concerns with the man understood to be not only the most powerful of the league's owners, but also a conciliatory figure sympathetic to the players' plight. Spalding, after all, had been a player himself and one of the pioneers of professionalism at that.

Primary on Ward's agenda was curtailing abuse of the "reserve" system, which had been introduced in 1879 as a means to stem salary escalation and to put a halt to the constant roster shuffling that was destabilizing the league. In its original form, the system allowed each club to retain—"reserve"—five of its players, presumably its best, for the next season. In the years following its first implementation, however, the reserve rule metastasized into a far broader and more restrictive statute, effectively locking all players into indentured servitude with whatever club first signed them to a contract.

Though even Ward acknowledged that some form of reserve rule was necessary to keep the league afloat, by 1887 application of the policy had become so onerous as to prompt his inflammatory accusation, in *Lippincott's Magazine*, that the professional ballplayer had become "a chattel." He wrote of the reserve rule: "Instead of an institution for good, it has become one for evil; instead of a measure for protection, it has been used as a handle for the manipulation of a traffic in players, a sort of speculation in live stock, by which they are bought, sold, and transferred like so many sheep. In its development it has gone on from one usurpation to another until it has grown so intolerable as to threaten the present organization of the game."

If the players hoped to seize the moral high-ground by playing to the sympathies of the game's working-class fans, the owners were only too happy to remind the public that even with the reserve in effect salaries paid to top ballplayers far exceeded the blue-collar worker's pay, about eight dollars per week—and for just six months of effort at that. Union organizers were derided as "anarchists," a particularly damaging slander in the wake of the deadly Haymarket Affair. As Spalding would later write, "Base Ball depends for results upon two interdependent divisions, the one to have absolute control and direction of the system, and the other to engage—always under the executive branch—in the actual work of production."

The stir that came in the wake of the *Lippincott's* article was followed by a period of apparent rapprochement. In late 1887, a delegation of Brotherhood representatives led by Ward extracted a few concessions from league leaders, including revisions to the standard player contract. For Ward, the simple fact that the Brotherhood was taken seriously was considered a step in the right direction, and even if the owners reneged on some of their promises, as they did, there remained a feeling that the players would at least have some small voice in league policymaking. It was in this spirit of wary goodwill, then, that Ward had departed on Spalding's adventure. But now, in Cairo, news of the league's new scheme came as a crushing blow to his aspirations and cast a shadow over the tour itself. Was the trip nothing more than a ruse to get him and his Brotherhood cohorts out of the country, leaving the league free to operate without any serious opposition? Fred Pfeffer thought as much, and speculated that such serious business would not have been transacted without Spalding's prior approval.

Spalding, notwithstanding his penchant for deception, was probably innocent of this charge—at least partially. When he had begun cooking up the All-America roster during the 1888 season, the prospect of removing Ward from the scene must have seemed like a stroke of genius. Halfway around the world, he'd be under Spalding's thumb, far away from the press and in no position to stir up trouble with the Brotherhood. In Ward's absence, league business could proceed as usual.

That being said, Spalding could not have been pleased to read about the new classification scheme that had been passed in his absence. Certainly he was no fan of the plan's progenitor, John T. Brush, a newcomer to the ranks of baseball ownership and the hardest of that hard group's hardliners. A Civil War veteran hobbled by a nervous disorder that made walking a challenge, Brush evinced little sympathy for the athletic men on his payroll, and lacked Spalding's natural charm and political agility. "One of those thin, wiry men whom nothing seems to wear out," was Spalding's rather backhanded description of him. For more than two decades, Brush would be a thorn in Spalding's side, opposing him on virtually every aspect of league business. Some of Brush's obsessions were simply ridiculous: In 1898 he would force the adoption of another regulation bearing his name, a fruitless attempt to ban foul language in the game "at any or whatever cost." In 1902, with the upstart American League challenging the National's supremacy, Brush stood as the sole owner opposed to conciliation. A few years later, he would take a leading role in an effort to combine the National League's clubs into one monopolistic corporation. Spalding was forced out of retirement to confront that scheme.

As it was, the classification plan had all the hallmarks of Brush's imperious and confrontational approach to the affairs of business. For Spalding, a master of the backroom deal whose first impulse was always to co-opt his adversaries, the draconian plan must have appeared needlessly incendiary and crude. There was, he understood, no need for such a wholesale revision to the league charter. As former National League president and longtime Spalding ally A. G. Mills wryly noted, the club manager who couldn't "handle salary with the powerful reserve rule at his command ought to have a wet nurse." It also seemed clear that the plan's leveling effect would remove some the advantage Spalding's big-city Chicago club held over such "small-market" teams as Brush's Indianapolis club. But a more immediate problem was that Spalding was faced with the fact that Ward, one of the tour's chief attractions, was now interested in an early trip home. Spalding smartly moved to appease Ward with an assurance that Brush's scheme was "not only impracticable but positively dangerous," and that matters could be satisfactorily resolved upon the tour's return to the States. After all, Spalding had always been the league's fixer.

If this was Spalding's assumption, he severely underestimated the scope of the problem facing his league. Had he been paying close attention to Ward, he might even have picked up a clue as to just what dangers might lie ahead. Back in 1887, Ward had concluded his *Lippincott's* article with a warning that unless the clubs reformed their labor practices, "the players will try to do it for them." If that threat was not taken seriously, Ward now left another in his latest dispatch back to the States: "Will they ever have done with these experiments?" he wrote. "Or will it be necessary to sweep away the entire tangled network of stupid legislation and begin all over on a new basis."

Standing in the lobby of the Orient Hotel, Ward and his peers could do little except plot for the future. And that is exactly what they decided to do.

The travelers' first full day in Cairo, a Sunday, was spent touring the city's primary sites of interest: the great Mosque of Mohammad Ali, Saladin's domed citadel, the palace and gardens of the khedive, the famous Nile-O-Meter (a ninth-century device for measuring the height of the river's floodwaters that consisted of a marble column marked off in cubits). They wandered along the Muski, the principal thoroughfare of Cairo's old city, meandering in and out of its carpet bazaars, tobacco shops, and booksellers. Several of the men took advantage of the bargains offered by local fez dealers. Everywhere, they were beseeched for alms—"*Tâlib min Allâh hakk lukme 'êsh*" ("I seek from my Lord, the price of a morsel of bread"), which their guidebooks taught them to dismiss with a curt "*Allâh ya'tîk*" ("God give thee").

The Cairo that Spalding and his men discovered was, much like Melbourne, a booming colonial capital infatuated by nothing so much as its own cosmopolitan opulence. The urbane character of the city had been shaped by Ismail, an extravagant khedive who had been educated in France in the 1860s and then returned with a vision to transform Cairo into a "Paris on the Nile." In 1867 he offered free land along the acacia-lined boulevards of the eponymous new Ismailiya quarter to anyone who would erect a house worth 30,000 francs, then a substantial sum, and would do so within eighteen months. In very short order, a city of elegant villas in a riot of styles—neoclassical, Victorian, Moorish—was born. A new opera house was built, and Giuseppe Verdi was commissioned to write *Aïda* to inaugurate it. (The theater opened on time, but Verdi was late, so *Rigoletto* was performed instead.)

The prime beneficiaries of Ismail's efforts were the city's European residents, who reaped massive profits while their governments and banking houses manipulated Egypt's immense and unrecoverable debt. In 1882, a chastened Ismail abdicated to his son, Tawfik, and the British literally foreclosed, occupying the country and installing Sir Evelyn Baring, better known to history as Lord Cromer, as consul-general.

Ismail's Cairo was as glamorous as any city the tourists would visit on their journey, and the Orient, a conservative three-story block, was an ideal base of operations from which to explore. If it did not quite reach the standard of the legendary Shepheards Hotel, just a few blocks away, the accommodations were still first-class, and centrally located in the new Ezbekiyeh district, home to a large and wealthy community of European expatriates. "One can sit at the Eldorado Café at Cairo and listen to a French opera, while around him at the tables he will hear the Arabic, Hindostanee, Greek, German, Egyptian, French, Italian, and English languages spoken simultaneously," wrote Palmer. "It may be said that on no drive in London, or even in Paris, can so much splendor be seen as here." In the evening they strolled about the gaslit city, passing through its crowded streets and stopping in its cafés, where they could drink beer, gamble, and perhaps acquire the services of a fashionable lady of pleasure, for Cairo was also a well-known center of prostitution.

Anson had more respectable, if romantic, plans; after so many days confined to quarters with the boys, he had arranged for a night out on the town with his attractive young wife. At the suggestion of a local guide, the Chicago captain had hired a carriage and directed its driver to take him and his wife out to the theater district. The ensuing tour brought the Ansons past the Opera House, the Grand Hotel, and then to a palatial building with colored canopies set in a lush, brilliantly illuminated garden. What was this? Anson asked. "The Sirdaria," said the driver—the seat of the commander-in-chief of British forces in Egypt, Major General Francis Wallace Grenfell.

The driver may have said "Sirdaria," but the Ansons heard "circus," which was precisely the form of entertainment they were looking for. The couple descended from their carriage, passed through the villa's formal garden, and walked into its grand entry hall. A band was playing. A fountain gurgled. Handsome guests paraded about in formal dress. "This is a pretty swell sort of a circus," said Anson to his wife. With typical bluster, he pulled aside a man in uniform—it turned out to be the host—and asked where he might purchase tickets for the show.

Major General Grenfell was, fortunately, amused by the Americans and their confusion. "Tickets? What tickets?"

"Why, the tickets to the circus here," answered Anson, who still hadn't caught on.

"There is no circus here, my friend," said the general magnanimously. "This is my private residence. I am commander-in-chief of the Egyptian Army, and I am simply entertaining a few friends here tonight. I would be much pleased if you would remain—"

"Don't say a word, sir," interrupted Anson. "It is my mistake and I hope you will excuse me." With that, the Ansons beat a hasty retreat to the Orient.

When they arrived, they found the following message posted prominently in the hotel lobby:

Baseball at the Pyramids.—The Chicago and All-America teams, comprising the Spalding American Baseball party, will please report in the hotel office, in uniform, promptly at ten o'clock to-morrow morning. We shall leave the hotel at that hour, camels having been provided for the All-America players and donkeys for the Chicago players, with carriages for the balance of the party. The Pyramids will be inspected, the Sphynx visited, and a game played upon the Desert near by, beginning at two o'clock.

Although Spalding's note suggested a certain degree of decorum, the scene that confronted the ballplayers the next morning as they stepped out of the Orient lobby and into the Cairo glare was anything but calm. As requested, the hotel management had arranged for a procession of donkeys and camels to carry the tourists to the pyramids, but as word spread of the impending excursion, a flood of freelancing drivers arrived with their own beasts of burden, all jockeying to land one of the prized American fares. "Donkeys brayed, camels trumpeted, donkey boys howled and fought and chattered, and scratched each other's faces and tore each other's gowns and cried big tears of vexation," wrote Palmer. Order was restored only when the local police arrived to impose discipline on the insurgent drivers with bamboo rods. A commemorative photograph taken just after matters settled down shows the ballplayers, along with a sizable cortege, saddled up in a line before the Orient's stately façade. It is a wide-angle shot taken from a distance, a fact that makes it somewhat difficult to distinguish individuals among the group. One figure, however, is unmistakable: Albert Spalding, in the center of the frame, staring out from beneath the brim of a pith helmet, the very picture of dignified authority in a world on the brink of chaos. It is, one imagines, just how he saw himself.

At ten-thirty, with the image of the gathering now committed to glass plate for posterity, the caravan got moving. The two team captains, Ward and Anson, led the way; Spalding was in a carriage toward the rear with his mother. Anson, normally such a menacing presence, cut a particularly ridiculous figure bobbing along on a donkey half his size. Crowds gathered to view this strange parade as it made its way along the Shâriá el-Maghrâbi, Cairo's Embassy Row, and toward the residence of the American consul, John Cardwell, who had established a makeshift

The tourists lined up before Cairo's Orient Hotel, after a near riot. Spalding, always unflappable, stands at the center of the frame, in pith helmet.

reviewing stand on a balcony adorned with flags and bunting. Upon arrival, the players gave Cardwell three cheers, and he reciprocated by coming down from his perch to greet Spalding, shake a few hands, and send the men on their way. With that, the party moved on across the fortified Kasr el Nil bridge, through the khedive's gardens, and then south along an acacia-lined boulevard that led to the sandy Ghizeh plain.

It wasn't long before the players were racing their donkeys and camels along the route, but the romance of these exotic beasts soon wore thin. At the village of Ghizeh the party came to an abrupt halt. At the outset of the ride, the Chicagos had been miffed at their assignment to the lowly donkeys while the All-Americas traveled by camel, and demanded there be an exchange at the halfway point. Now, having watched these "ships of the desert" jostle and jolt the All-America players for some two hours, they regretted the bargain they had negotiated. The camels, "lurching along with loads like vessels in an ocean storm," wrote Anson, "proved to be a severe tax upon the patience of their riders."

When the tourists finally arrived at the pyramids, at two o'clock, they were tired from the heat and bruised from the trip but nevertheless excited by the monumental scene before them. After a brief meal, the group made its way over to the Sphinx and climbed about the great statue in preparation for yet another ceremonial photograph. Ward and Crane took up position at the center of the frame, halfway up the Sphinx's breast. Several others players nestled up against the statue's neck. Again, Spalding commanded pride of place, standing hawklike on a massive plinth at the base of the colossus. Just beside him and to his right was his sixty-two-year-old mother, Harriet. The image, just as the one taken in front of the Orient, left no mistake: The Americans had arrived, and they had conquered.

Afterward, Spalding scouted the area and chose a site for the storied game with an eye for dramatic scenography. The Great Pyramid, Cheops, would stand as a distant backstop behind home plate, with the Sphinx down the third-base line and the sunken tombs of the Fifth Dynasty pharaohs somewhere beneath the players' feet. So decided, a diamond was hastily measured and a makeshift batter's box inscribed in the sand. Meanwhile, a crowd of roughly two hundred curious Arabs and bemused English tourists assembled along the foul lines, casually observing the preparations. Most prominent among the spectators was a rifle-toting Bedouin sheik, who, it was said, reviewed the proceedings from an elevated position aboard a white stallion.

Both sides were anxious to win what would surely be a game for the history books; Palmer wrote that the players were "out for blood," and Anson that it was a "hotly contested" affair. When balls were fouled off into the crowd, local boys scrambled to retrieve them, and only returned their trophies upon the promise of baksheesh. Ward, with a bit of artistic license, wrote that "the players plowed up sand to such an extent that they were almost buried" and that "few fly balls were caught owing to excessive difficulty of locomotion." MacMillan, too, claimed, "the fielders and base runners would have required the feet of camels to have made records on the sliding sands." A photograph of the men in action, however, shows a field quite similar to the sandlots the men were used to playing on back home in urban America. (The rifle-toting sheik is also

*The tourists playing their historic match on the plain of Ghizeh, with Cheops,
the tallest of the pyramids, as a distant backstop. Afterward, they attempted a
ball toss over the giant tomb.*

nowhere to be found.) More to the point, the record shows that the teams
combined for ten stolen bases, a considerable total.

Spalding, with his acute sense of publicity, had instructed Ward to
start backup pitcher John Healy for the All-Americas—Healy, a native of
Cairo, Illinois, was known around the league as "The Egyptian."
Chicago took advantage in the first inning, scoring twice before Anson,
perhaps daydreaming about the enigmatic ruins surrounding the field,
was picked off first base. The All-Americas countered in the second, taking a commanding lead with seven runs off Chicago pitcher John Tener.
When Healy was hit by a pitch during the rally, MacMillan wryly noted
that the Sphinx was "observed to weep" in sympathy. The hero of the day
was Chicago catcher Tom Daly, who connected for the only home run of
the contest in the fourth. Spalding, who served as umpire for the historic
match, called the game after five innings, with the final score 10–6 in favor of the All-Americas. "A triumph, in an artistic sense at least," was

The tour's correspondents gathered for a portrait at the ruins in Ghizeh. From left: John Ward, Harry Palmer, Simon Goodfriend, and Newton MacMillan. They had purchased their fez hats in Cairo's teeming bazaars.

MacMillan's take on the events, and this seemed to capture the general consensus. Professor Bartholomew, however, slept right through the game a few feet into foul territory, with his good eye closed and his glass one staring up into space.

Their official business thus complete, the players were again free to explore the monuments. Presented with the most revered of archaeological sites, Spalding's representative Americans behaved in a manner that might well have appalled even Theophilus Green. The shenanigans opened with a competition to throw a baseball over Cheops. Chicago catcher Tom Daly was dispatched to the far side of the giant tomb to receive any successful attempts. But, as Ward wrote, "he had no opportunity to distinguish himself, as the height of the pyramid"—451 feet—"made a farce of the whole proceeding."

Having witnessed the failed ball toss, Spalding and several other members of the party—including, most impressively, his mother—decided to scale the Great Pyramid. This was accomplished, as was customary, with the assistance of a trio of local attendants: one to yank on each arm and a third to push from behind. It was not a comfortable process. "Every step meant a spasmodle heave on my arms and a well meant but misapplied volley underneath," wrote Ward. Years earlier, Mark Twain had a similarly unpleasant experience: "Who shall say it is not a lively, exhilarating, lacerating, muscle-straining, bone-wrenching, and perfectly excruciating and exhausting pastime climbing the pyramids," he wrote in *The Innocents Abroad*. Harriet Spalding, appalled at the prospect of such an undignified climb, tried to dismiss the two assistants Albert had engaged for her. He would have none of this, however; dutifully concerned for her safety, he insisted that she keep both. She did, and then tipped the leader ten cents at the summit.

Ward, breathless and damp with sweat, was first to reach the top, soon to be followed by Anson, Crane, Daly, and Pfeffer. Before them was a panorama that had captivated travelers for centuries. Looking through the mist to the south, they could see the rolling sands of the desert and, on the horizon, the pyramids of Abusir, Sakkara, and Dashur. Immediately before them was the Sphinx, lying motionless in the haze not far from Chefren and the many smaller pyramids scattered across the Ghizeh plateau. To the east was the Nile, a brownish filament caught in a swath of green farmland. The citadel and minarets of Cairo were visible to the north. "There is perhaps no other prospect in the world in which life and death, fertility and desolation, are seen in so close juxtaposition and such marked contrast," noted the 1885 Baedeker guide to Egypt. But if Spalding and his men were impressed, they did not admit to it. Daly summed up his opinion with a single word: "Rats!" Pfeffer, practically embodying the stereotypical tourist described by Henry James, claimed that the Arizona desert "could give the Sahara article cards and spades and beat it on general vacuity and flatness." Ryan seemed confused by the scene in general and the pyramids in particular: "They are supposed to be about 7,000 years old and built by the Egyptians when the entire land was under water," he wrote in his diary.

The players' final engagement on the Ghizeh plateau, and one that would surely have made Henry James wince, was a last look at the

Sphinx. For Twain, this monument was awe inspiring in ways that surpassed even the pyramids. "There is that in the overshadowing majesty of
this eternal figure of stone, with its accusing memory of the deeds of all
ages, which reveals to one something of what he shall feel when he shall
stand at last in the awful presence of God," he wrote. But once again
Spalding's men were unmoved. The colossus had taken its share of abuse
over the years—Ancient Greek and Roman travelers tagged it with graf-
fiti, a militant sheik knocked off its nose in 1496, and a British army
colonel had recently bored a series of holes in its flanks to find out
whether it was hollow—and now a team of American ballplayers imposed their own indignity. One by one, they tested their throwing accuracy, hurling baseballs at the statue's right eye. Only James Fogarty
proved a successful marksman.

The tourists' next day in Cairo was their last, and they passed it visiting
several of the many landmarks that had previously eluded them. "One
could easily spend six months in Cairo and the surrounding valley of the
Nile, and then come away without having finished what must always remain one of the most interesting countries upon the globe," wrote
Palmer. Tawfik himself had sent word through the American consul that
Spalding and his men were welcome to visit him at his palace on the
bank of the Nile at Heloun, and that he was most sorry to have missed
the festivities at the pyramids. Unfortunately, there was no time for the
side-trip. Indeed, the tourists would also have to abandon their proposed
visit to Jerusalem in order to keep the schedule that had been forwarded
to Spalding by Stamford Parry, the Burlington Route agent he had long
ago dispatched to Europe from San Francisco. (This news was received
with some disappointment by the men MacMillan lampooned as "Rev.
Dr. Anson and his class of Bible scholars.")

The next morning the tourists boarded a train to Ismailia, at the midpoint of the Suez Canal, and by five o'clock in the afternoon they were
seated comfortably on a small steamer making its way north up that
channel toward Port Said. "A better opportunity for seeing the artificial
waterway could scarcely have been afforded us," wrote Palmer. The canal

may have seemed the fruit of modern science and industry, but the truth was that a navigable route joining the Mediterranean and the Red Sea had a history of several thousand years. A string of rulers—Ramesses II, Necho II, Darius I, Ptolemy II, Trajan—had driven liquid roads through the sand, depleting their treasuries and their populations in the process. A waterway had existed off and on and in various states of passage from the thirteenth century B.C. through the eighth century A.D. The modern history of the canal begins nearly a thousand years after that, with Napoleon Bonaparte abandoning a plan to bring the route back to life. It was a Frenchman who would complete the job, however; the diplomat Ferdinand de Lesseps pushed the great project forward over the course of more than a decade. When it opened, in November 1869, the eighty-seven mile route cut the traveling distance from Europe to India by more than fifty-five hundred miles. By 1889, more than three thousand ships were passing through each year.

The ballplayers' voyage through the marvel of modern engineering lasted barely more than five hours. By ten-thirty, Spalding and his men had arrived in Port Said, where they transferred to the Lloyd Line steamer *Stettin*, which would take them across the Mediterranean to Italy. Henceforth, they would be travelers in Europe, where they would be the ones considered unsophisticated, backward, and primitive. This suited the men just fine. "The manners and customs of the Orient are not to my liking," Anson wrote. "The line of demarcation between the rich and the poor is too strongly drawn and the beggars much too numerous to suit my fancy." With that, they departed for Italy.

⌒ CHAPTER 8 ⌒

ON THE CONTINENT

"WOOD—THREE! BALDWIN—ONE! BURNS—TWO!" FROM HIS perch atop a steamer trunk on the deck of the *Stettin*, and with the ramparts of Brindisi shining in the afternoon sun over his shoulder, Albert Spalding hollered out mail call to the anxious group of baseball players huddled closely around him. These were the first letters the men had received since their departure from Chicago, and they tore open the envelopes in a frenzied rush to read messages from home. John Tener was relieved to hear from his aunt Maud in Pittsburgh; Anson had a packet of letters from his young daughters back in Chicago; for Ned Hanlon there was a missive in a "neat, feminine hand," the contents of which he would not disclose but which drew a broad smile nonetheless. Aside from the usual news and gossip from lovers and family and friends, the men had other reason to grab anxiously for the mail. They were, to a man, nearly broke. The globe-circling extension of what had been planned as a round-trip excursion to Australia had left their traveling funds depleted. Now their cabled requests for money had finally been answered with letters of credit that would tide them through the rest of the trip.

Spalding, having stepped down from his perch, was left with two letters of his own. The first was from his brother Walter, who had been left to run the family business in his absence. The second, in an envelope that carried a U.S. Government seal, was from Thomas F. Bayard, the secretary of state. Spalding opened this one carefully, for he knew its contents were valuable indeed. With the expanded itinerary of the tour, Spalding thought it wise to supplement President Cleveland's endorsement of his players as exponents of America's national game with an official letter of introduction that formally requested all American consuls grant him and his party full diplomatic courtesy. Now there could be no question; Spalding and his tourists were true representative Americans, Theophilus Green be damned. Alas, the letter would prove to be somewhat less than effective in convincing anyone else of this truth.

———

The mail had arrived on board the ship along with a contingent of customs agents who cleared the *Stettin* and its passengers for entry into Brindisi. The walled city on the back heel of the Italian boot had been a rough-and-tumble gateway to the Mediterranean for centuries—the poet Virgil died there in 19 B.C. The intervening years had not always been kind, but it had recently seen something of a renaissance as a southern European terminus. One of the fruits of this new energy was the Grandes Hotel des Indes Orientales, a luxurious behemoth built just off the quay to house passengers arriving from overseas. It was here that the tourists spent their first night on European soil, after a brief walk through the town's winding lanes and a macaroni supper at which they were serenaded by a trio of local musicians.

The players were to depart promptly at nine o'clock the next morning for Naples, and would have done so were it not for a dispute at the station. To save costs and hassle, Spalding had sent most of the tourists' luggage along to Southampton, England, where it would await them until their anticipated departure from Europe back to the States. (This led the *Sporting News*, always ready to disparage the tour and its progenitor, to write that the tourists were now traveling "like emigrants," with their belongings in potato sacks.) Some items could not be checked through, however, and one of those items was Anson's heavy bag of baseball bats. When the Chicago captain tried to pass the large sack off as "hand luggage," the tourists were given their first taste of the willful Italian spirit by a pint-sized railway agent who made up for his lack of height with an obstinate nature and an outsized sense of indignation. He demanded that Anson pay a surcharge for the extra weight. At this point Anson would have done well to follow the counsel of Baedeker's *Handbook for Travellers to Southern Italy*, which revealed its Germanic roots with a decidedly condescending attitude toward the Latin character: "The equanimity of the traveler's own temper will greatly assist him if involved in a dispute or bargain, and he should pay no attention whatever to vehement gesticulations or an offensive demeanor." Anson, however, was no man to back down from an argument. He and the agent went toe to toe for several minutes, but it was never a contest. The train did not move until the captain had paid his fine.

The 241-mile trip by rail to Naples took the tourists across the heel of the Italian boot and then cut west at Metaponto, crossing the stark landscapes of the Apennines before descending to the Tyrrhenian coast. Upon their arrival in Naples, there was more trouble with Italian authorities. During the trip, Marty Sullivan, the All-America right-fielder, had absconded with the conductor's horn, and the angered official had cabled ahead at one of the intermediate stops so that when the men finally disembarked they found themselves under arrest by the Neapolitan *carabinieri*. Spalding, three interpreters, and a handful of agents engaged in a prolonged argument before it was agreed that he pay another small "fine," and the party was released.

While the *Sporting News* reported Spalding's penury, the tour had once again been booked into the finest hotel available, the Vesuvio, a luxury palace on the via Partenope with a privileged view of the Bay of Naples. Spalding had rushed to the hotel on a late train from Brindisi the previous night in order to reunite with his wife Josie and his son Keith, who were waiting in Naples with a maidservant and would henceforth accompany him on the tour. (He had returned to the station to rescue the players from incarceration.)

The Vesuvio proved an ideal setting for a reunion. Together for the first time in five months, the family gathered on the balcony of their suite with the moonlight illuminating the harbor below, Mount Vesuvius sputtering forth to the south, and the islands of Capri and Ischia sitting far off on the horizon. "Perhaps, the loveliest spot in Europe," was how

Thomas Cook's *Handbook for Southern Italy* described the city and its spectacular setting. "The universal verdict of visitors is that neither pen nor pencil ever gave any real conception of the surpassing loveliness of Naples and its Bay."

On their first night in the city, not a man among the group would have disputed the book's assertion. John Ward led off his first dispatch from the city with the old Italian saying *Vedi Napoli e poi mori.*" See Naples and die. Closer inspection revealed a city grand and grim in equal measure. As Twain quipped in *The Innocents Abroad*, seeing Naples might not kill you, but a prolonged stay just might. *Baedeker*, true to its severe origins, was downright pitiless: "The narrow, dingy streets, the high and narrow houses, with flat roofs and balconies in front of every window, are far from attractive," it proclaimed with characteristic authority. "The never-ending noise, the clatter of wheels at all hours of the day and night, the cracking of whips, braying of donkeys, and shrill shouting of hawkers, render Naples a most distasteful place, especially to those whose stay is limited."

Old as it was, Naples in 1889 was a metropolis very much in transition. Italy's most populous city, it had just five years earlier suffered through a devastating cholera epidemic. More than fourteen thousand died from that plague. Housing was squalid; sewage ran free. A traveler's 1881 account complained that "evil odours are more abundant in Naples than any other Italian city, and the warmth of the climate at once adds to their number and intensifies their quality." A program of slum clearance and civic improvement was initiated to repair these ills: An aqueduct was opened to bring fresh water from the mountains; the most egregious *fondaci* (tenements) were knocked down (along with more than sixty churches); and an elegant new avenue, the corso Umberto I, bordered by grand apartment houses, was driven through Naples' clogged heart. But the construction of this new city proved an irresistible target for the greedy and corrupt, and an unfortunate boon for the development of Naples' most notorious industry: *la cosa nostra*. The people whom the program to eradicate blight was ostensibly designed to help most—the city's poor—saw the least benefit.

It was this Naples, a city at once desperate for and resistant to modernity, that the Spalding tourists, divided into small groups, set off to explore after a good night's sleep. Palmer and Tener paired up for a walk to the famed Naples Aquarium, where they could put a finger to an electric eel and view countless other denizens of the Mediterranean deep. (Founder Anton Dohrn, a German biologist and ardent Darwinist, used the spectacular aquarium to fund the pursuits of the attached "Zoological Station," which attracted marine scientists from the world over.) In the evening, the two joined up with the rest of the party at the Teatro San Carlo, where the noted Spanish tenor Julián Gayarre headlined a production of Donizetti's *Lucrezia Borgia*. To Palmer's astonishment, the handsome crowd hummed along throughout, and after each aria rose to its feet to cheer with a "seemingly uncontrollable burst of enthusiasm" that would have impressed even the cranks at Chicago's West Side Park.

The next morning, Palmer and Tener, joined by Ward, Hanlon, Wood, and MacMillan, departed early by train for Pompeii; the petrified Roman city, buried in the Vesuvian eruption of A.D. 79, had been a must-see stop on the tourist trail for over a hundred years. Excavation work had begun in the eighteenth century and had accelerated greatly beginning in 1860, when Giuseppe Fiorelli took over the project and introduced more scientific archaeological methodologies, including the reproduction of figures by injecting plaster into voids in the hardened ash left by bodies that had since decomposed. "The cast of a dog bent almost double, the muscles convulsed, and the bronze collar still about the neck, indicates the terror and torture the poor beast must have suffered in the agonies of suffocation," wrote Palmer.

The great feature of Pompeii, then as now, is its scope, which allows the visitor a window into the quotidian life of a civilization, as energetic as our own, that has receded from common memory. "Those who visit the ruins only once should avoid occupying much of their time with minutiae, as the impression produced by the whole is thereby sacrificed, or at least diminished," cautioned *Baedeker*. To walk along its rutted streets and through its many homes and shops and public buildings is to challenge the imagination to step back some two millennia. Then as now, the tourist at Pompeii is inevitably overwhelmed by the site's magnitude, and Spalding's party of baseballists was no exception to this tradition.

No part of the ruin offered the tourists a more intriguing or personally compelling entry to a time gone by than the *amfiteatro*, an oval stadium with a seating capacity of twenty thousand. Spalding very much wanted to hold the tour's one game in Naples here, but local authorities refused the request. (The arena, with a playing surface barely a hundred feet wide at its midpoint, would not have made for a pitcher-friendly park.) Worse still, upon arriving at the Vesuvio, Spalding found a message from Stamford Parry, his advance agent, with news that his attempts to put on a game at the Coliseum in Rome had also been shot down, this despite an offer of five thousand dollars up-front to the local authority and a pledge to donate half the proceeds to charity. Spalding seemed uncharacteristically oblivious to the absurdity of this proposal; the floor of the Coliseum encompassed an open archaeological site, and was hallowed ground at that. The faux pas didn't elicit much comment among Romans, though certain members of the American diplomatic contingent were not at all amused by what they clearly considered a vulgar request.

<hr />

It has now been more than a half century since the last eruption of Vesuvius, and though the volcano is still considered active, we have perhaps been lulled into a sense of complacency as to its terrible power. This was most assuredly not the case when James Fogarty and Fred Carroll arrived at its base. On the same day that Palmer and Tener took in the city of Pompeii, their traveling companions ventured to the summit of the mountain that had buried it. Vesuvius had erupted eight times in the nineteenth century, most recently in 1872, and it had been spewing out lava and ash on a fairly constant basis ever since. Its activity was little understood, despite the presence of a seismological observatory on its shoulder. Contemporary vulcanologists—the term itself was new— thought the eruptions were generated by steam heat created by the mixture of sea water and, as *Baedeker* dramatically put it, the "burning liquids of the interior of the earth."

Danger had never been a deterrent to visitors, however. The frisson of risk, the beautiful view from the summit, and a certain sense of historical communion had been drawing travelers for millennia. Fogarty and Manning began their journey at Resina, where they hired guides for six lira apiece and prepared for their climb up the mountain, then nearly four thousand feet and growing daily. Had they arrived either a few years earlier or later they would have had the option to ascend much of this distance via a funicular railway, built in 1880. Unfortunately, a suspicious fire—reputedly set by local guides who found it to be a drain on their business—had left it temporarily out of order.

So the two All-Americas started up the mountain on foot, climbing and sweating and occasionally stopping to gaze out at the Bay of Naples below. By comparison, their trip to the top of Cheops was a mere trifle. Eventually they found themselves trudging through ash and dust and cinders that came up to their ankles, and they could feel the mountain's power beneath their feet: a slow, dull tremble that throbbed like the screw of an ocean steamer, but with a force and menace of a wholly different order. Typically visitors had no problem reaching the lip of the crater, but this day the rumblings seemed particularly ominous, even to the guides, who would travel no further. The baseballists were not to be deterred, however, and continued their climb toward the smoking mouth of the behemoth. Eventually they reached the summit, and were rewarded with a view across a percolating bed of ash and lava. They had made it, and they glanced sidelong at each other with that certain sense of shared accomplishment they had known so often on the diamond.

That satisfied feeling was short-lived, wiped away as the dull rumble beneath their feet was transformed into a violent shake and a spectral shower of rock and cinder. Without a word, Carroll took off at a full gallop down the mountain. But Fogarty—irrepressible jokester, team funny man—was somehow transfixed by an awesome power he could hardly comprehend. "I could not have stirred from that spot to save me," he told his mates that night over a stiff drink in the Vesuvio's bar. "I stood there not knowing whether I wanted to remain or to follow Carroll's example, when I was suddenly startled into immediate activity. The ground seemed to actually rise under my feet. A wave of hot air almost overpowered me and then an explosion, which sounded as though the whole top of the mountain must be leaving its moorings, made me imagine my last hour had come. I did not know which way to run. But when the lava began to fall in pieces as big as my fist, and larger, all about me, I made up my mind that any place was safer than the one I was in."

Was he having them on again? After four months together, the tourists knew better than to take Fogarty's word at anything close to face value. But there was something on this night that made them all believers, and Carroll was not there to dispute Fogarty's account. Whatever the case, conversation soon shifted to other matters. A sign posted in the hotel lobby told them that there would be baseball in Naples the next day, at two o'clock sharp, on the Campo di Marte.

Any great expectations for the tourists' first exhibition of the national pastime on European soil might well have been tempered by the fact that the teams had not mounted a game since their visit to the pyramids, now ten days in the past, and that contest had come after a month-long period during which they had played but one game, at Colombo. A pleasingly large crowd estimated at between three and four thousand had nevertheless assembled for the competition; by the time the players arrived at the field, there were nearly a hundred carriages waiting, most belonging to the diplomats, royalty, military officers, and other dignitaries invited by the U.S. consul, Edward Camphausen. It certainly made for a picturesque tableau: the ballplayers in their uniforms, the handsome crowd, the snow-capped Apennines in the distance, a smoking Vesuvius in deep center—who could have guessed that such a pretty picture would, in short order, devolve into a scene of angry chaos?

The Campo di Marte, a military parade ground, turned out to be a poor venue for baseball, as it provided no physical barrier between diamond and spectators. The eager crowd, unfamiliar with the American game, seemed unaware of the dangers posed by flying bats and balls, and pushed forward until they were sitting right along the foul lines. Spalding could sense trouble, and when Camphausen told him that "*In di a tros!*" meant "Get back!" he anxiously walked up and down the lines belting out the phrase, but to no avail.

The difficulties came to a head in the top of the fifth inning, after Fred Carroll put the All-Americas ahead with a two-run homer that soared off toward the smoking volcano in the distance. Anson, his club now down four runs to two, immediately began to complain to Tener, who was umpiring. The encroaching fans were disrupting the Chicago fielders, bellowed the captain. Meanwhile, the All-Americas kept pounding out hits against Mark Baldwin. By the time Carroll came up again, All-America had batted around and taken an 8–2 lead, and Anson was kicking with ferocity. Baldwin, however, was spent, and it showed in his next pitch. Carroll pulled that toss foul into the crowd, whereupon it struck a middle-aged gentleman over the eye, knocking him out cold. In the frenzy that followed, the spectators rushed the field, and Anson, sensing opportunity, absconded with home plate. Without it, the game would have to be called, and with his Chicagos having failed to hit in the bottom of the inning, All-America's rally would be negated. Ward was apoplectic. Spalding's concern was even greater: A near riot and a game-ending controversy were not exactly what he had in mind for his first European contest. Certainly these events would do nothing to quell suspicions about the "vulgar" nature of his sport or its traveling exponents—to say nothing of the nation from which they came.

Fortunately for everyone, cooler heads prevailed. After the crowd was tamed and the injured man was revived, Anson offered to bring his team back onto the field. Spalding knew better than to let that happen. Instead, the All-America runs were allowed to stand, and they were given the game, which put them ahead by two in the series (now at 17 to 13, not counting the tie in Colombo). The next afternoon, the tourists departed for Rome, no hard feelings.

"What is there for me to see in Rome that others have not seen before me? What is there for me to touch that others have not touched? What is there for me to learn, to feel, to know, that shall thrill me before it pass to others? What can I discover? Nothing. Nothing whatsoever." Such was Mark Twain's lament upon arriving in the Eternal City with his compatriots from the *Quaker City*. Twenty-odd years later that ground was even more heavily trodden. But Spalding and his men were happy to arrive; if there was little new for them to discover, they were content in their lot as tourists and more than happy to keep to the beaten track. In any case, they were not there so much to see new things as to present them. Rome, for all its antiquity, had yet to witness the great American pastime, at least on a professional level.

The city was so jammed with visitors that accommodations for the party had to be split between two hotels, both first class: the Allemagne, across from the Spanish Steps on the Via Condotti, and the Capitol, just a few blocks away, on the Corso. It was late by the time they checked in—their train had not pulled into the iron-and-glass shed of Termini Station until nine o'clock—and most of the men turned in early, conserving their energies for what promised to be a full day of exploration.

First thing the next morning an eager Spalding, armed with his letter from Secretary of State Bayard and accompanied by Leigh Lynch, walked briskly across the Piazza di Spagna to the residence of Judge John B. Stallo, America's envoy extraordinary and minister plenipotentiary in Rome. The greeting was anything but cordial. Word of Spalding's attempt to hire out the Coliseum had reached Stallo, and the German-born judge from Cincinnati was appalled. The minister was a serious man devoted to serious matters; in his youth he had rallied other German immigrants to the abolitionist cause and the Union war effort. More recently, he had devoted himself to intellectual pursuits. A skilled linguist and a polymath, he had authored a pair of scholarly monographs, *General Principles of the Philosophy of Nature* (1848) and *The Concepts and Theories of Modern Physics* (1882). Baseball, a children's game played by a lot of rowdy gamblers, was clearly beneath his dignity. "I have never been interested in athletics," he told the magnate. "And I do not propose to have my good name used for mercenary purposes."

Having one's name used for mercenary purposes was, however, par for the course for an American diplomat; indeed, the American diplomatic program was more than anything a support system for the nation's commercial interests abroad. America's exceptionalist worldview and lack of concern for the formal niceties of diplomatic discourse was signaled by Stallo's very title: *minister*. In 1888, the United States had neither ambassadors nor embassies, which were considered needless aristocratic trappings. This policy served American politicians well at home, but the perception of America as a relentlessly commercial and ill-mannered nation did not serve it so well in the Old World, as Spalding and his men were finding out.

Spalding, however shocked he may have been by Stallo's rude reception, could do little except smile politely and return to the Allemagne, frustrated but determined. Of this he was sure: It would take more than a self-important bureaucrat to derail Albert Spalding. Fortunately, he could count on several other allies of some standing in the expatriate community: Charles Dougherty, secretary of the American legation, was a serious baseball fan, as was Reverend Dennis J. O'Connell, the rector of the American College in Rome, a seminary for American Catholic clergy. Through O'Connell Spalding applied for an audience with Pope Leo XIII. That request was regretfully denied on account of the pontiff's full schedule and fragile health, but at least Spalding and his men had a chance to spend a bit of time with O'Connell's students. "We are fond of baseball, even if we are studying for the priesthood," one seminarian told Harry Palmer. "We get out every Saturday during the summer and have some slashing good games."

In lieu of the pope, the ballplayers spent their first day in the city, guidebooks in hand, touring the Vatican, an attraction nearly as daunting as Pompeii. "It is an immense pile of buildings, irregular in plan, and composed of parts constructed at different times, without regard to general harmony," noted John Murray's popular *Handbook of Rome*, published in 1888. The ballplayers divided into small parties and roamed through its immense colonnaded piazza, designed by Bernini. (It would have made a far more commodious playing field than the Coliseum, but this was a request too cheeky even for Spalding.) They visited the Sistine

Chapel, the Stanzes of Raphael, and the Etruscan Museum. Inside St. Peter's, they inspected Bernini's gilded bronze baldachino with its towering Solomonic columns (*Baedeker* labeled it "tasteless" and Twain called it a "considerably magnified bedstead—nothing more") before ascending 142 steps to the roof of the basilica. This was just a staging ground for their climb to the lantern of Michelangelo's dome, some three hundred feet above ground, where they found a panoramic view of the city. A few more steps brought them into the copper ball that surmounted the lantern. Sixteen people could fit in the orb. From the ground, wrote Palmer, it looked no larger than a pumpkin.

The following day the focus of the tourists' perambulations shifted from ecclesiastical to ancient Rome. For many of the American ballplayers, these sites were quite interesting, if a tad overwhelming. Ryan, in his diary, recorded trips to the "Trojan" Forum and along the "Akien" Way. Palmer, however, seemed fully open to the historical magnitude of the Eternal City, writing:

> As one stands upon the steps of the Capitol and looks over the waste of columns and arches and magnificently carved pillars of stone of the Forum; or stands within the Coliseum and looks upon its great tottering walls; or passes under the Arch of Titus and out over the stones of the Appian Way, the same over which rolled the chariots of the imperial rulers of Rome in the days of its splendor, he is confronted on every hand with evidences of the fact that centuries ago there dwelt on this spot a people which, in point of wealth, power, and science, was not inferior to any of the nineteenth century.

At the end of another long day of sightseeing, the men were understandably tired, and after a promenade along the fashionable Corso, returned to their respective hotels for sleep; tomorrow they would play ball.

Spalding had not won the right to bring America's game to the Coliseum, but as a consolation he could take home a commemorative team photograph from the old stadium. Palmer made arrangements to have the picture taken with the men in uniform, on the way to their exhibition

The tourists at the Roman Coliseum. Spalding's offer of five thousand dollars for the right to play in the ruin was rejected, much to his dismay. Here he stands in the top row, between the All-Americas (on the left) and his Chicago White Stockings (on the right).

game. When the teams arrived in their parade of carriages, the photographer was patiently waiting for them. Once inside the arena, he placed the men on the podium, where senators and vestal virgins had watched as, Anson wrote, "the mighty athletes of an olden day battled for mastery." Spalding, dressed in formal attire, placed himself at the center of the photo, with the Chicagos and All-Americas lined up on either side of him. The rest of the party gathered on the dusty floor below. The big group of American gladiators and their retinue turned out to be as much of an attraction as the Coliseum itself, drawing the attention of the many other tourists present, and in particular that of a few Italian boys who seemed terribly excited by the players' snappy flannel uniforms, which they eyed with unvarnished desire.

The venue chosen for the actual contest was distinguished in its own right: the Villa Borghese, a sprawling garden estate of villas, lagoons, fountains, and pavilions just beyond the Piazza del Popolo. Established as a formal retreat by Cardinal Scipione Borghese in 1608, by the time Spalding and his men arrived it had been transformed into an elaborate English-style romantic garden, complete with faux-antique ruins. The game was played on the grass hippodrome of the Piazza di Siena—"a picturesque glade, its surface as smooth as any ball park at home," according to Palmer. When the ballplayers arrived, the seminary students of the American College were already there, and greeted them with three cheers. Also on hand were Prince Borghese, Princess Torlonia, and Signora Crispi, third wife of the controversial Italian premier, Francesco Crispi. King Umberto, who had been expected to attend, sent apologies and excused himself on account of illness. But the queen, accompanied by the prince of Naples, drove by and watched a few innings from the sheltered confines of her carriage. The rest of the crowd, which would grow to some four thousand, gathered on the tree-shaded terraces that bordered the field; this time there would be no encroaching on the diamond.

Proceedings began with a crisp warm-up session; once the men were good and limber, the All-Americas took the field behind Cannonball Crane, who cut down the Chicagos one, two, three. In the bottom of the inning, Fred Carroll, enjoying a macaroni-fueled power binge, drove a home run deep onto the piazza terrace, plating two runs and earning himself a standing ovation. It was his second home run in two games, but his dominion over Italy, much like Napoleon's, would be short-lived. Chicago tied the game in the second, and sent home the winning run on a passed ball in the seventh for a 3–2 victory.

———

After Sunday morning services at St. Peter's, the party departed for Florence. There, in less than twenty-four hours, they managed to pack in a frantic morning of sightseeing and one of the more artistically satisfying games of the tour. The day began with a trip from their hotel to the Duomo, Santa Maria del Fiore—the famous cathedral capped by Brunelleschi's ribbed dome. But it was the recently completed façade of the cathedral, not the marvel of Renaissance engineering that capped

it, that drew most admiration from the ballplayers; Palmer reported
that it was "unanimously voted by those of us who saw it to possess the
grandest exterior of any structure we had yet seen." (This was no advertisement of the tourists' taste; Florentines were already in the habit
of deriding its ostentatious ornamentation as too "American.") The
morning's whirlwind tour continued with the Uffizi Gallery, the Piazza
della Signoria, the Ponte Vecchio, the Pitti Palace, the Casa Buonarroti,
Santa Croce, Santa Maria Novella, and points in between—all this *be-*
fore their afternoon game. Moving about Pompeii with such alacrity
might have been recommended, but this "been there, seen that" tour
was an absurd parody of thoughtful travel, although this seemed to
trouble the tourists only slightly. "One would fain spend weeks where
we spent hours," lamented Palmer halfheartedly. Alas, hours were all
they had.

Given the morning's schedule, it is all the more impressive that the afternoon's game was played, in MacMillan's words, with "dash and spirit,
from start to finish," a considerable endorsement given that writer's general reluctance to sugar-coat matters. The setting was the Cascine, a
large park that, like the Villa Borghese, had once been a private estate but
was transformed in the nineteenth century into a vast English-style public park with a host of amenities for sports and general leisure. (*Cascine,*
literally "barns," refers to the structures that once occupied the site.) The
announcement of the game had put Florentine society "in a flurry," and
two thousand spectators—including enough contes and contessas to fill
half the palaces of Florence—made the trip beyond the city limits to
view the match. What they saw was a treat: an aggressive exhibition of
the American pastime, with slick displays of fielding by both squads—
Ward was notably impressive. In the end, the All-Americas won the day,
stealing eleven bases en route to a 7–4 victory.

Spalding had originally hoped to take his baseball stars north, making
stops first in Vienna and then Berlin, before heading for Paris. Upon his
arrival in Naples, however, Spalding learned that this plan would have to
be scrapped. Stamford Parry, his advance agent, reported that there was

The ballplayers lined up at the Villa Borghese in Rome. It wasn't the Coliseum, but the field was deemed a "picturesque glade" worthy of the American game. Spalding, as usual, is in the center.

snow a foot deep in both cities. In Vienna, an indoor venue was available—the main building from the 1873 international exhibition—but this was hardly adequate, and in any case Spalding wanted as much time as possible for the exhibitions in England, which he considered the most important of the trip, not least because they offered the greatest potential for profit. There was also the matter of getting the ballplayers back to the States in time for the beginning of the 1889 season. Opening day, April 24, was still a good ways off, but transatlantic travel was unpredictable, and he wanted to get back home with enough time to parade his two teams across the country to Chicago so that he might fully cash in on their newfound popularity. And so Spalding cabled instructions to Parry to head directly for Paris and begin preparations for their arrival; the tour would meet him there, stopping along the way in Nice and Lyon.

The ride from Florence to Nice took the better part of a day, but any sense of boredom was leavened by the scenery. The route skirted the

Mediterranean coastline, passing through Pisa (where the tourists had time for a quick peek at the famed Leaning Tower) and Genoa (where they had lunch) before moving on to the Italian Riviera. *Baedeker* described this route as "a delightful succession of varied landscapes, bold and lofty promontories alternating with wooden hills, and richly cultivated plains." The train continued on along the Ligurian coast, passing through Diano Marina, a fishing village that had been leveled by an earthquake in 1887—"there did not seem to be a building in the city," noted Palmer—and San Remo before finally coming to a halt at Ventimiglia, on the French border. Here, the tourists had their final confrontation with Italian authorities.

The combatants in the previous contretemps had been Anson and Sullivan. This time the perpetrator was Cannonball Crane, and again the circumstances suggest that the tourist had only himself to blame. Crane, it seemed, had been having a little fun at the expense of some of the Italian passengers on the train. The extent of his crime is unclear, but as a bit of retribution one of those passengers pointed out to the Italian customs agents that Crane was not traveling unaccompanied, as his ticket required. He was, as it happened, "sharing" his seat with the miniature monkey that had been given to him back in Colombo and was at present stowed happily in his coat pocket. The same pet that had been so entertaining on the ride from Suez to Cairo here proved to be a costly encumbrance. When the pitcher was informed that he would have to pay full fare—26 francs—for the diminutive animal's passage, he naturally balked. "So be it," was the conductor's reply, and with that, the tourists' train departed for Nice. Without the tourists. There would be no fighting the system.

An hour later, the men were on board the next train. Crane had paid his fine.

In Nice a large contingent of expatriate Americans was anxiously awaiting the arrival of the tour, and with it a reminder of the joys of their homeland. Unfortunately, Leigh Lynch, who had come to the city several days ahead of Spalding and the rest of the group, was having an impossible time finding not only a venue for a ballgame, but a hotel at which the tourists might sleep. Winter was high season in Nice, a time when vacationers and invalids from England, Germany, Russia, and other northern climes gathered along its rocky beaches to soak in the healthful Mediterranean sun. Exacerbating the problem was the fact that the tourists had arrived on the eve of Carnival, Nice's great civic party.

Lynch eventually secured accommodations at the second-class Interlachen, not far from the rail station, but he had made no progress on the field when the men pulled into the city. "Here are twenty of the best ballplayers in America, and we cannot see a game. It is too bad," complained Howard Conkling, an expatriate American resident of Nice, to the local correspondent for the *Paris Herald*.

Rain the next morning washed out any hopes for an exhibition of the American game, not to mention the flower parade that was the cornerstone of the Carnival celebrations. For the tourists, gamblers to a man, this represented nothing so much as an opportunity, for it left them free to spend the day ten miles down the coast in the tiny principality of Monaco, where they could try their luck at Europe's most storied gaming tables.

Coming after Rome and Florence, bastions of so much that was sacred in Western culture, religion, and history, Monte Carlo offered Spalding and his men grandeur of a wholly different kind. Sitting high up on a bluff above the sea was the famed Casino, a magnificent neo-rococo pleasure palace set in a carefully tended formal garden. Designed by Charles Garnier, architect of the Paris Opéra, the building was a study in opulence entered through a stunning marble atrium flanked by onyx columns. Inside, the gaming rooms were decorated with stained-glass windows and florid academic paintings. "Duchess and courtesan, prince and adventurer, gentleman and confidence man, may be found jostling each other as they place their bets," Palmer wrote. "Richly dressed women, some wrinkled and gray headed and others lovely and fair to look upon, pass from table to table in search of the luck that comes to but few of them, all seemingly slaves to the one consuming passion of gambling."

The sport of choice was roulette, for which there was a five-franc minimum, though the men could also experiment with *trente et quarante* (literally, "thirty and forty," a card game similar to blackjack) and several other European games, but unfortunately not their favorites, poker and craps. At the end of the day, Fogarty claimed four hundred francs in winnings; Spalding, too, had the good sense to quit while ahead. Anson was not as lucky; one day at the tables proved "quite enough" for him. The tour's greatest victim, however, was John Ward, who dropped the equivalent of thirteen dollars on a simple lunch of chicken, asparagus, and coffee—this at a time when dinner at a fine restaurant could be had for a dollar. "Those who have gold seem to regard it as so much dross," wrote Palmer. "Those who have not gold and who cannot obtain it, too frequently end their lives as not worth the living."

Improved weather the next afternoon allowed for the resumption of the Carnival festivities, and in particular the *bataille des fleurs*, the battle of blooms. Spalding and his fellow tourists joined the people of Nice, who gathered along the main boulevard, the Promenade des Anglais, to throw flower bouquets at the many carriages traveling up and down the avenue, whose occupants were busy throwing them right back. The goal: to fire your floral salute at a comely member of the opposite sex, of which, by all accounts, there was no shortage.

Notable among the revelers was a squat, red-bearded gentleman who rode on the back of a handsome drag pulled by four black horses. That man was Albert Edward, the Prince of Wales, future monarch of the United Kingdom and a man the tourists anticipated playing for in London in just over a week's time. The prospect of that meeting, however, did not deter the ballplayers from a little fun at "Bertie's" expense. Boys will be boys. Chosen to carry out the attack were Mark Baldwin and John Healy, pitchers whose accuracy would offer the best chance to land a blow on the royal proboscis. Armed with a pair of bouquets chosen "more for weight and efficacy as projectiles than for beauty," the two hurlers stepped forward and launched their missiles. Baldwin's struck first, his toss traversing the avenue in a slow arc that terminated on the prince's cheek. The accurate throw drew the attention of the future king, but he would have done better not to have looked, for Healy followed up Baldwin's pitch with a fastball that scored a direct hit on the royal nose. For Healy, who took pride in his Irish blood, the blow was a particularly satisfying score against a colonial oppressor. But the prince did not seem to mind. Bertie, who was well known for his fondness for the ladies, was busy lining up targets of his own among the throng. He soon demonstrated what Palmer called an "excellent eye for womanly loveliness."

The next morning, at six, the ballplayers departed Nice for the French capital. They made a stop for lunch in Marseilles, then tacked north for Lyon, where they spent a chill night at the Hôtel d'Universe. By eleven o'clock the next evening they had achieved their destination: Paris's Hôtel St. Pétersbourg, a comfortable five-story block on the rue Caumartin. There were snow flurries in the brisk Parisian air as their drags took them from the Gare de Lyon across the city to the hotel.

They had arrived in Paris at a propitious moment. France was celebrating the centennial of its 1789 revolution, and in just two months would open the spectacular Exposition Universelle of 1889 to mark the anniversary. Paris, in a fit of beautification, was on a mission of its own: to demonstrate to the world that it was indeed the City of Light, a beacon of modernity in all its forms.

On this front it had little to prove. By the fall of the Second Empire in 1870, Baron Georges Haussmann, Napoleon III's all-powerful prefect of the Seine Département, had already transformed the city into a showpiece of grand avenues lined with grander apartment houses punctuated by works of monumental architecture that were grander even still. His new parks and gardens, designed by the engineer Adolphe Alphand, were unparalleled in extent and elegance (though *Baedeker*, rather ungenerously, described the Bois de Boulogne as "somewhat formal and monotonous"). Such quibbles aside, Paris was unquestionably the envy of the world, the city that all others aspired to equal or at least emulate. Even its sewers, efficient and clean, were attractions for the visitor; once a month they were opened for tours by specially designed boat and tramway. Chicago, Melbourne, Cairo, Naples—wherever the players traveled, and no matter the continent, planners seemed to be at work in imitation of the great French metropolis. "Certainly the most beautiful of all the great cities," wrote Palmer. "Its magnificent thoroughfares, its great institutions and beautiful boulevards, its broad public parks, its picturesque environs, with their historical palaces, its public squares, its monuments, its life, its gayety combine to make Paris wonderfully attractive both to the Parisian and the visitor within her gates, particularly if he be American."

There was much to explore, and the tourists set out to take it all in: Notre Dame, the Bastille, the Louvre, the Place de la Concorde, the Madeleine, the Invalides, the Arc de Triomphe. They shopped everywhere: at Bon Marché, the spectacular *grand magasin*, designed by Gustave Eiffel, that was the cathedral of French commerce; in shops on the stylish boulevards of the Right Bank; at the booksellers and art hawkers on the rue de Rivoli. "Although we remained in Paris but a week," Palmer wrote, "it is safe to say that we saw much more of the city than many Americans who have tarried there for a much longer period." Their daily excursions, as often as not, concluded with a walk past the Paris Opéra, just a few blocks from the St. Pétersbourg. Charles Garnier's Beaux-Arts masterpiece was the crown jewel of Haussmann's Paris and set the tone of opulent spectacle that would come to define Paris in the Belle Époque.

By the time Spalding and his men arrived in March of 1889, however, the focus of Parisian spectacle had shifted to another structure, one more populist in nature and certainly more visible: the Eiffel Tower, still under construction but already having climbed to 790 of its eventual 986 feet. The colossal iron pylon, centerpiece of the 1889 exposition, seemed at once the ultimate realization of nineteenth-century technological ingenuity and a symbol of French prosperity and republicanism.

The tower did have its detractors, however, and none were more fierce than the great Beaux-Arts architect Garnier, who spearheaded resistance to the "useless and monstrous" invention he saw fouling his city. A host of intellectual luminaries, including composer Charles Gounod and author Guy de Maupassant, signed an open letter of protest against its construction, and their attack had a distinctly anti-American ring: "You may not doubt that the Eiffel Tower, unwanted even by commercial America, is the deflowering of Paris," they wrote. Stereotypes, of course, cut in two directions. Anson, an enthusiastic if inconstant capitalist, offered this bit of analysis when he later reflected on his sojourn in the French capital: "As a businessman the Parisian is not a decided success when viewed from the American standpoint, but as a butterfly in pursuit of pleasure he cannot be beaten."

The stereotypes disguised a truth that insecure nationalists on both sides of the Atlantic would not care to admit. The United States and France, the two great republics, were in fact very much alike: a pair of societies increasingly transfixed by the commercialized spectacle created by their own industry. The Spalding tour and the Tour Eiffel, beyond a bit of linguistic coincidence, were products of this shared spirit, works of monumental hubris made possible by nineteenth-century technological advances whose primary function was to call attention to themselves, and in the process accrue prestige and financial advantage to both their namesakes and their national sponsors.

It is a shame that the esteemed progenitors of tour and tower never met, for Albert Spalding and Gustave Eiffel were kindred spirits. Both men managed to parlay extraordinary natural ability into personal and then business success, and both were showmen unafraid to shape the historical record to augment their own position in it. Spalding achieved this through his persistent exaggeration of his role in the development of the National League. Eiffel, for his part, had no problem attaching his own name to a design that was in fact not his own, and for which he had initially evinced little enthusiasm. The great tower on the Champs de Mars was in fact designed by two young engineers who worked in Eiffel's firm, Émile Nougier and Maurice Koechlin; they had conceived it in 1884, and the architect Stephen Sauvestre designed the arches that framed the views from its base. Today, their names are all but forgotten.

———— ••◦•• ————

In the evenings, Spalding and his men explored the more risqué aspect of Parisian spectacle, the dance halls and cabarets for which the city was either famous or infamous, depending on one's perspective. The Folies Bergère, the Ambassadeurs, the Alcazar—more than a century later, these clubs' names remain familiar. Two francs would have gained the men admission to the Chat Noir, where they could listen to the bohemian composer-pianist Erik Satie. (The Moulin Rouge opened in October, six months after the ballplayers' departure.)

For the tourist, the Parisian nightclub presented an evolving challenge to propriety. "The company is not the most select and the performance tends to the immoral," reported John Murray's 1872 *Guide to Paris*. "Respectable people keep aloof." By 1893, according to Thomas Cook's *Guide to Paris*, the conventional wisdom had changed: "The majority of these establishments, though presenting some attraction to the visitor on account of the 'fast' reputation which they formerly had, are now of the most dreary description. Nine-tenths of the company consists of men, attracted by simple curiosity."

Neither guide got it quite right. Bathed in electric light and clouded with pipe smoke, unpretentious in clientele if not decoration, the Parisian night club known as a *café-concert* or *café-chantant*—was a social blender, a place where dandy and shop girl, soldier and prostitute, bohemian and tourist might share a beer, a song, or something more. It was in their mirrored halls that *la vie moderne* was truly lived, its action captured for posterity in a new style, beautiful yet raw, by the likes of Edouard Manet, Edgar Degas, and Henri de Toulouse-Lautrec.

For Spalding's tourists, men of working-class background who enjoyed nothing so much as a good time, these clubs were a revelation, a stunningly cosmopolitan alternative to the seedy tenderloins they were used to back in Victorian, teetotaling America, where such high living was far less acceptable. Away from home and thus removed from public scrutiny, Spalding saw no reason to curtail the activities of his charges—apparently he extended his "when-in-Rome" policy for Sunday ballgames to all extracurricular activities. Even Anson, a notorious martinet traveling with his wife, reported "a week of late hours and wild dissipation."

The debauchery reached its peak on the tour's fourth day in the city, Shrove (Fat) Tuesday, which marked the end of Mardi Gras and was capped by citywide "*bal masque*" celebrations. This was the most raucous night of the Parisian year; by midafternoon the boulevards were already crammed with celebrants deep into their cups. Meanwhile, back at the St. Pétersbourg, Palmer and Ward sat with Crane, Hanlon, and MacMillan, plotting a systematic "programme of wickedness" over dinner. By universal consent, they decided to begin their evening with a bit of light entertainment at the Comédie Française. From there, things became a lot more interesting. Crossing over to the Left Bank, they made their way to the Latin Quarter and the Jardin Bullier, where two francs gained the men admission to the "Students' Ball," a raucous party with a "rough and tumble" crowd fully dedicated to a night of prurient pleasure. "What a crush, what wild hilarity, what exaggerated costumes, and what shockingly short skirts!" wrote Palmer. There were girls everywhere, and they all seemed to be doing the high kick of the cancan; one lithesome specimen in red stockings knocked Hanlon's silk hat clear up onto a chandelier. He retrieved it, but had seen enough. "Come on," he said to his mates, "let's get out of here." Hanlon was by no means the first American to be taken aback by the sexy dance. Twain, upon seeing it for the first time, could barely watch. "I placed my hands before my face for very shame," he wrote in *The Innocents Abroad*. "But I looked through my fingers." The missionaries of Hawaii, men who had proscribed the relatively tame hula, would surely have been appalled.

The tourists left the students behind, but their evening was still just a baby. From the Bullier the party moved back across town to the Eden, an Egyptian-themed theater-cum-nightclub that was home to the city's most famous ball. The midnight show was just set to begin when the men arrived and took seats in the dress circle. From there, they had a clear view of the action below. Soon enough a full orchestra began to play, and the stage doors were pulled open to reveal a hundred dancing girls dressed, but just barely dressed, in frilly costumes. Out they poured into the orchestra, performing the cancan in pairs and quadrilles, drawing the audience into their dance in the process. Before long, the entire theater was on the floor, and nearly all of the tour's bachelors—Hanlon, Crane, MacMillan, Fogarty, Wood, even Professor Bartholomew—were kicking up their heels. The women of Paris were hard to resist. They even spoke English—perhaps not fluently, but, as Palmer wrote, "just enough to make them all the more interesting."

Festivities at the Eden concluded at three, but the boys were hardly done for the evening. They spilled out onto the rue Boudreau together with the rest of the crowd, and headed out for the bohemian cafés of Montmartre. By the time they returned to the St. Pétersbourg, it was well past dawn.

All the revelry was fine, but Spalding had brought his tour to Paris to do business. He had failed on his first attempt to bring baseball to Paris, back in 1874, and now he was determined to succeed. Certainly, the timing felt right to him. On the tour's stopover in Colombo he had come across a news story that reported a thousand-dollar reward on offer from the French banker Henri Louis Bischoffsheim to the individual who could introduce a new sport that would be suitable for French schools and colleges. Sensing opportunity, Spalding immediately dispatched a letter to the financier:

> Sir—A newspaper paragraph, recently published in the United States, calls attention to the fact that French educationalists are seeking a game suited to the needs of physical education in French schools, and that M. Bischoffsheim has greatly interested himself in the subject.
>
> In this connection permit me to state that the Spalding baseball party, containing the best exponents of the American national game, will visit Paris early in March, en route around the world.
>
> Will M. Bischoffsheim kindly consider himself the guest of the management and the exhibitions given in Paris, and do them the kindness also to consult them freely for any information concerning the game which has done so much for American schoolboys. . . .
>
> I have the honor to be, monsieur,
>
> > *Yours very truly,*
> > *A. G. Spalding*

The impetus for Bischoffsheim's offer was a lingering scar on the French national psyche, a sense of physical inadequacy that grew out of

France's humiliating defeat in the Franco-Prussian War of 1870–71. As one segment of French society veered toward the hedonistic life of the *cafés-concerts*, another movement was gaining force, a movement to rehabilitate the French character, beginning with the body. The effort was itself politically loaded, for sport in France had heretofore been the fairly exclusive province of the elite, and even then the chosen forms were hardly the most demanding, at least from a physical standpoint. As Alphonse Dumont, a Parisian visiting the United States in 1888, told the *Washington Post*, "The Frenchman cares little to contest anything where muscular ability is at an advantage. He prefers sport as he does art— striving to develop its fine points, aiming to become expert, and admiring only the skill that may be attained in the exercise." If pressed, a Frenchman would have named fencing as the national sport.

But by the time Spalding and his men arrived, things were beginning to change. For one thing, the development of a fit population capable of military service was a matter of national security. Gymnastics had become compulsory for French schoolboys in 1880, and in 1888 Paschal Grousset, in his youth a leader of the Paris Commune, founded La Ligue Nationale de l'Éducation Physique, whose mission was to democratize sport across all segments of the French population.

Spalding naturally saw baseball, which by his own account had taught the youth of America traits ranging from "courage, confidence, and combativeness" to "vim, vigor, and virility," as the perfect solution to the French problem. He could attest personally to the game's formative influence on his own life: It was baseball that had rescued him from his orphaned loneliness so many years ago in Rockford, transforming a shy and twiggy boy into a figure of national—and now international— prominence. He might also have pointed out how baseball had seemed a balm on American society, soothing wounds sustained in the nation's own devastating war experience.

A meeting between Spalding and Grousset was arranged by Robert MacLane, the American minister in Paris, and Grousset and his Ligue enthusiastically received the magnate, generously offering their playing fields in the Bois de Boulogne when it appeared Spalding would be unable to secure a venue for a ballgame in central Paris. The challenge of finding a site for the historic exhibition had troubled Spalding for much of his week in the city. Paris was endowed with countless formal parks and squares, but a large, enclosed space that would allow Spalding to charge admission was proving harder to come by. He even considered the idea of playing indoors, but the only appropriate structure, the cavernous Palais de l'Industrie, built near the foot of the Champs Elysées for the international exhibition of 1855, was unavailable.

In the end, Spalding managed to obtain the right to use the Parc Aérostatique, a sandlot adjacent to the Trocadéro on the Quai de Billy (now the Avenue de New York), in the shadow of Eiffel's rising tower. Earlier in the week, Spalding's party had gathered there to witness a balloon race. The professor, apparently still ailing from his fall in Australia, did not participate.

The game finally took place on the afternoon of Friday, March 8, the tourists' last day in the city. A makeshift grandstand was suitably decorated with French and American flags, and "plush" chairs were provided for the many dignitaries expected to attend. That list included the French president, Sadi Carnot, whom Leigh Lynch had met with and personally invited while the rest of the tour was still making its way to Paris from Rome. Carnot had in fact been enthusiastic, but at the last moment he sent a letter of regret through his military attaché, General Brugère. It read: "The President of the Republic is warmly appreciative of the invitation to attend the baseball match tomorrow at the Parc Aérostatique. It is with regret, due to his numerous obligations, that he will be unable to be present, as he attaches much interest to the development of physical exercise in the education of our youth. He will, however, be represented by officers from his military staff." Carnot was indeed a busy man in March of 1889; the threat of a coup d'état hovered over his administration for much of the year. As the tourists arrived, Paris was still fraught with the possibility that Georges Boulanger, a populist ex–military commander, might overthrow Carnot's administration and establish himself as dictator. Carnot would manage to hold onto his post (Boulanger was forced into exile later in the year), but his military staff failed him in 1894, when he was assassinated in Lyon by an Italian anarchist.

Though the president could not make it, there were many dignitaries who could, and none stands out more in history than Pierre de Coubertin, father of the modern Olympic movement. Much like Grousset, Coubertin was a passionate advocate for the promotion of sport within the French educational system. But unlike Grousset, who had an almost militaristic attitude toward physical education, Coubertin was a thinker with an international outlook. In 1894 he would organize the international congress that created the modern Olympic Games. Spalding was an ardent supporter of the movement—it was yet another opportunity for the convergence of patriotism and self-interest. In 1900 Spalding returned to Paris as the head of the American delegation to the second Olympic Games, a position he would hold again in 1904, in St. Louis. Spalding knew a good idea when he saw one, a fact that Coubertin would later come to regret. Spalding all but co-opted the American Amateur Athletic Union, which became a promotional tool for his sporting-goods empire, and in 1901 James Sullivan, Spalding's chief deputy, surreptitiously floated the idea of a new international athletic union to run the Olympics, one that would have taken them away from their founder. (The plot faded.)

Those events were for the future however. For the moment, there was a baseball game to be played. Unfortunately, the conditions for the exhibition were poor: Rain the previous day had turned the field into a quagmire of mud and gravel, a situation that would have severe consequences. Play began at half past two, with Crane pitching for the All-Americas and Tener for Chicago. For the first few innings the game proceeded with expert precision, each side failing to score. Then, in the fourth, Chicago Shortstop Ned Williams, who had reached first on a walk, took off for second in an effort to put himself into position to score the tour's first run in France. He didn't make it. Sliding into the bag, he caught his spikes in the gravelly mud and opened a large cut across his kneecap. At first no one thought it too serious; Mark Baldwin replaced him in the lineup, and Williamson's wife, Nellie, helped him from the field and back to the St. Pétersbourg. But things were much worse than initially suspected. Williamson's knee soon became infected, and he never fully recovered. The reigning home-run king played ball for two more seasons, but never again was the player he had been before departing on the tour. In a most unlikely turn of events, Chicago's great Stone Wall infield succumbed to a Parisian pebble.

The game turned out to be a complete loss for the Chicagos. A sixth-inning home run by Jimmy Ryan was one of only three hits they could muster off Crane, and All-America won by a final score of 6–3. Still, with the severity of Williamson's injury still unclear, the general feeling was that the exhibition had been a great success. "An almost faultless game," MacMillan reported back to the *Sun*. The verdict in the French press was also positive: "It's enough to say that batting, throwing, and fielding develops a superb musculature, and that the two teams demonstrated qualities of speed, precision, and coordination that won the admiration of all," wrote the *Revue des Sports*, though it did note that "few could understand the game or follow all of its phases and subtleties."

That was not entirely true; certain members of the French sporting press found the game quite familiar. "Base ball or '*balle aux bases*' is nothing more than a version of the French game *grand thèque* advocated by the Ligue, and which the English call *rounders*," claimed an article in *Le Temps*. "It's a form of exercise that consists, essentially, of players divided into two teams, of which one is placed 'home' within a figure traced on a ground marked by posts, while the other takes up position outside of this figure. The idea is to hit the ball as far as one can with a swing of the bat, and while the ball is traveling to make a tour of the 'bases,' or angles of the figure. The opponent, however, tries hard to catch the ball as quickly as possible to 'retire' the hitter while he is in the process of moving. It's a very exciting and very amusing game that our school children practice in its French form with ardor in many schools in Paris and the Départments."

News that such a similar game was already in practice must have come as an interesting surprise to Spalding and his compatriots; the subject undoubtedly came up during their week in the city, as much of their time was spent out on the town in the company of members of the Parisian sporting press, in particular the editor of the *Revue des Sports*, M. G. St. Claire. In fact, the tradition of bat-and-ball games in France could be traced all the way back to the Middle Ages. An illustration in "The Romance of Alexander," a French manuscript of 1344, depicts a group of monks and nuns engaged in such a pastime, and references to *thèque* occur as early as the fifteenth century. But St. Claire and Spalding could not have known of this broad history, and even if they had, what relation *thèque* might have had to American baseball would have been far from clear.

Clear or not, it would certainly have reopened the already heated debate over the game's origins, as it cast in doubt the two most popular theories about the game's genesis—Chadwick's assertion that it was derived from the British game of rounders, and Ward's argument that it had developed sui generis on native shores. Could there have been a French antecedent to the American game? The idea must have seemed preposterous, though Ward, in *Base-Ball: How to Be a Player*, had been willing to concede the possibility of some minor outside influences. He compared the game to the American system of government, writing that although "it has doubtless been affected by foreign associations, it is none the less distinctively our own."

In the past, Spalding had tried to remain aloof from this whole controversy, but the time was coming when he would have to take a stand. For him, the question seemed as much as anything a matter of branding, though that term hardly existed at the time. "While authorities differ as to [baseball's] origin, no one, so far as I know, claims that it is other than American," he would write upon his return to the States. Spalding had conceived his tour as a way to clearly establish baseball as *the* American game, both at home and abroad, regardless of its genetic origin. He would soon find that hedge to be inadequate, and eventually would settle on an explanation that better suited his patriotic needs, if not the facts. But in the meantime, the tour was headed for England, where the game's origin would become an even more intense subject of debate, and a politically loaded one at that.

CHAPTER 9

IN THE PRESENCE
OF ROYALTY

W HEN THE SPALDING PARTY ARRIVED AT THE PORT OF
Dieppe after a five-hour ride from Paris, a foreboding wind
was blowing off the Channel. Their fate, however, was already sealed: they were booked to make the crossing on the *Normandie*,
one of the flimsy paddle-wheel steamers that were notorious for leaving
passengers seasick. They took their seats uneasily, and their confidence
didn't improve when a steward passed out tin basins. "Are these for washing?" asked Palmer. "No," he was told, "they have a different purpose."
Enough said. The day after the journey, James Ryan sat down with his di-
,ary to make a record of that unhappy overnight passage, its terrors still
fresh in his mind.

> The night was pitch dark and a severe storm was brewing; inside
> the harbor the sea was very rough and the ship tugged away at her
> anchor chains, as if eager to get under way. We soon started, how-
> ever, and in a short space of time our miseries began. The ship
> plunged and pitched, tossed and shivered while the wind whistled
> through the rigging, threatening to carry the ropes and spars with
> it. The storm now burst upon us with all its fury, and the little ves-
> sel laboured heavily under the tons upon tons of water which she

was continually shipping. The scene below deck was indescribable, and as all the hatches were battened down tight, the smell was horrible. Men, women, and children were huddled together in the first cabin, some singing, others joking, but the greater majority praying. Then aside from there was another party who were so awfully seasick that they couldn't do either if they wanted to. Of course I was one of that class, and it lasted for seven hours. I suffered as I have never done before; it seemed, at times, that I would turn inside out, and if I had I think I should have been perfectly satisfied. Nor was I alone either, for, on glancing around I saw many of the boys in the same deplorable condition; they were lying about on the cabin floor, wholly unmindful of everything around them, even to the grip sacks and valises, and from the manner in which [they] were tossed about one would think they were holding high carnival or dancing the Lancers♦ to the vibrations of the ship, as she creaked and groaned under the heavy pressure of water. Soon after day break we came close to shore and at seven thirty a.m. landed at Newhaven, safe and sound, after passing through the worst storm that had visited the Channel in years. The only damage sustained by the ship was the losing of the bridge, which was washed overboard during the night. We boarded the train [there] and in two hours arrived in Victoria Station, London, and were driven to the First Avenue Hotel, and remained there the rest of the day. Weak and hungry but too miserable to eat, I sought refuge in sleep and dreamt of old Neptune and Davy Jones's locker until a late hour the next day.

———

For Spalding, the unpleasant trip might have been considered a poor omen for what was already a difficult mission. After fifteen years, memory of professional baseball's 1874 introduction to England had been largely (and fortunately) forgotten—at least by the English. Albert

♦ Lancers: an energetic dance popular at the time.

Spalding, however, could remember well that first, ill-conceived tour of the National Association's Boston and Philadelphia teams; after all, he had organized it. And this time, he would not repeat the mistakes of his youth. The small-town naïf of twenty-four traveling abroad for the first time had in the intervening years transformed himself, through skill and bluster, into an honest-to-goodness titan of American business. To the London press, this new man was not even recognizable. "In Mr. A. G. Spalding, our present visitors have got a first-rate showman, which the other lot had not," one paper wrote. "He has worked up the excitement beautifully. Our appetites have been whetted by judiciously timed paragraphs announcing the enthusiastic receptions which have been accorded to these peripatetic apostles of American sport in all parts of the globe."

To be sure, Spalding had learned how to conduct an international publicity campaign, but in that decade-and-a-half hiatus he had also become a far more savvy political operator, as evidenced by one well-considered decision: Though he was bringing the American sport to the most hallowed ground of England's national game—the playing fields at Kennington Oval, Lord's, and Old Trafford—his men absolutely would not play cricket. There was nothing to gain and everything to lose in their doing so. If they did play, the best that could be hoped for was a showing that was free of embarrassment—hardly a stirring advertisement of American athletic prowess. But Spalding also understood that he must at all costs avoid setting up America's national game in opposition to that of England. If baseball was seen as mounting a challenge to cricket, it would never get a fair shake from patriotic Britishers. And so from the outset Spalding advertised baseball as a supplement to and not a replacement for the English sport, albeit one better suited to a busy modern lifestyle.

Spalding faced one additional problem, the "rounders" problem. Although John Ward could expound with professorial erudition on the American origins of baseball, the British press, not surprisingly, took a different view. Story after story described baseball as a thinly veiled version of what was in essence an English children's game. A cartoon in the London humor magazine *Punch* made that point clear, and with a David vs. Goliath spin: A smiling English schoolboy in a check scarf brazenly poked a gargantuan American ballplayer in his massive gut, telling him, "Look 'ere, Mister, we represent the 'Ackney an' 'Omerton United Boys Rounders Club, an' we're game to play you on 'Ampstead 'Eath any Sat'day you likes." Thus, Spalding had a double (and potentially contradictory) challenge: to convince the British that the American game was not a threat to their own revered national pastime, while also demonstrating that it was something more than a childish sport played by a childish nation.

The odds seemed to be stacked against him, but Spalding was never short of optimism, and he could argue that the time was right to give baseball another shot on English soil. After a winter of worry over the identity and possible return to bloody form of Jack the Ripper—he had last struck in November—London was in need of a little diversion. Spalding might also have been encouraged by the wildly enthusiastic reception, in 1887, of another touring production that advertised itself as a demonstration of the American experience: William "Buffalo Bill" Cody's Wild West Show. That extravaganza, which counted the Indian chief Red Shirt and the sharpshooter Annie Oakley among its varied attractions, was such a popular success that Queen Victoria herself ordered a command performance—and the Queen was not much for public appearances. "It is often said on the other side of the water that none of the exhibitions which we send to England are purely and distinctively American," Mark Twain told Cody before his departure, words of advice that could equally have benefitted Spalding.

Of course, the first great American showman to visit England, and the man to whom both Cody and Spalding were clearly indebted, was P. T. Barnum. In 1844 he had created a sensation in London with the midget entertainer Charles Stratton, better known as General Tom Thumb. While there was nothing intrinsically American about Barnum's show— indeed, he falsely billed Thumb as a Briton and his appearance as a "homecoming"—his promotional strategy was uniquely American, at least in its audaciousness. That plan was to exploit the English fascination with its own royalty: If he could just capture the attention of the English aristocracy, he knew the general public would naturally follow along. The strategy worked for Barnum, it worked for Buffalo Bill, and it would work for Albert Spalding, too.

———<small>◆</small>———

Unlike Barnum, who was forced to rent out a mansion in London's exclusive West End in his effort to cultivate the English nobility, Spalding had a direct line to that distinguished set in the person of Charles W. Alcock, an ally who had been Spalding's primary contact during that first trip to England, in 1874. In the intervening years, he too had risen in prominence, having achieved a comparable level of esteem in the English sporting world as Henry Chadwick in the United States. But where Chadwick was principally identified with one game, baseball, Alcock was perhaps the foremost authority on England's *two* favorite pastimes, football and cricket. Alcock was the secretary of both the Surrey County Cricket Club and the national Football Association, and it was in the former capacity that he could provide Spalding with entrée to the upper crust of English society. That is exactly what he did on the afternoon of Tuesday, March 12, when the tourists arrived at Kennington Oval, home ground of the Surrey club, for a luncheon in their honor. Following that meal they would play their first game in England.

Two princes, two dukes, four earls, two viscounts, and five lords were waiting in the clubhouse saloon when Spalding and his men walked through its doors; the Prince of Wales—the same man the boys had pelted with flowers in Nice—was expected to arrive a bit later, when the game was already in progress. Alcock had the honor of introducing the ballplayers, and after a series of toasts—to the Queen, the American president, the still-absent prince and his family, and the tourists themselves—the party was ready to eat. The fare, which included Gloucester salmon, aspic of lobster, pigeon pie, ox tongue, champagne jelly, and a variety of other delicacies, was perhaps a bit heavy for a pre-game meal, but the men were nevertheless happy to indulge, and a pleasant time was had by peers and players alike. "Royal good fellows," said Anson of the distinguished company. "We forgot entirely that we were lunching with lords and dukes. I never felt more thoroughly at ease in my life, and the

Surrey County Cricket Club
TAVERN,
KENNINGTON OVAL.

Reception Luncheon
OF THE
American Base Ball Players.

TOAST LIST.
THE QUEEN.

PRESIDENT OF THE UNITED STATES.

PRINCE AND PRINCESS OF WALES
AND REST OF THE ROYAL FAMILY.

THE AMERICAN BASE BALL CLUBS.

March 12th, 1889.

The toast card for the reception given by the Surrey County Cricket Club for the tourists at Kennington Oval in London. Game was, quite literally, on the menu.

rest of the boys seemed as much at home as I did." Spalding, perhaps, had become a bit too comfortable.

A great crowd had turned out for the game at Kennington Oval, but unfortunately the weather was not cooperative. A thick fog covered the field from the outset, and rain intermittently poured down on the players and spectators who had gathered in what the London *Times* called a "living hedge" some twenty-five feet deep around the field. (A mesh barricade

Spalding and Charles W. Alcock surrounded by the world tourists and their
fans at Kennington Oval. Spalding hoped an impressive showing would set off
baseball fever in England.

kept fans from the diamond, and foul balls from unsuspecting fans.) From
the far side of the field it was nearly impossible to see the action.

The game commenced shortly after three o'clock, when George
Wright, serving as umpire, called for the teams to play ball. Chicago,
the home team for the day, had already taken the field; Ned
Williamson, still incapacitated and back at the hotel, was replaced at
short by Jimmy Ryan. (His outfield slot was filled in turn by John
Tener.) Mark Baldwin pitched a scoreless first half for the Chicagos,
who went ahead in the bottom of the inning on a sacrifice fly by Anson
and a run-scoring single by Pfeffer. The All-Americas responded in the
top of the second with four runs to take the lead, but the crowd, now
quite damp and confused by the unfamiliar game, seemed fairly disin-
terested. The truth was that many of the spectators had come simply

for a look at the prince, who arrived, as advertised, at a quarter to four. Play, then in the bottom of the second, was stopped, and the teams lined up beneath the clubhouse to give the prince a salute, a gesture for which the ballplayers received perhaps their biggest hand of the day. In the middle of the fifth there was another break in the action, at which time the ballplayers were each allowed the opportunity to shake the future monarch's hand.

Meanwhile, Spalding had joined Prince Albert and the prince's brother-in-law, Prince Christian, in the royal box, where he might explain the proceedings to Bertie, who considered himself something of a sportsman. Indeed, he proved to be far more interested than many of his future subjects. "Why's he doing that?" he repeatedly asked Spalding, who had taken up a position behind him. Unfortunately, the prince had a stiff neck, and this precluded his turning around. Showing typical brazenness, Spalding grabbed an empty chair from the back of the room and stationed himself squarely between the two royals. This was something of a faux pas, but it seems no one mentioned it, least of all Albert Edward, who slapped Spalding on the thigh after a triple by Anson. "That was a hard clip!" said the prince. Feeling a sense of camaraderie, Spalding slapped His Royal Highness right back on the shoulder after a Pfeffer hit scored Anson from third. This left the prince's courtiers aghast, but Spalding was hardly contrite when advised of his breach of decorum. Recalling the incident in *America's National Game*, he wrote:

I see nothing in it to make me blush. If I violated the code of court etiquette, I must plead that I was not at court, but at an American ball game. If I sat in the presence of Royalty, it is certain that the Royalty sat in mine. If I tapped the future King of Great Britain on the shoulder, it was nothing more offensive than a game of tag, for he had first slapped me on the leg. If British Royalty honored us by its presence, which I am willing to concede, we repaid it by a splendid exhibition of our National Game. No, I am not able to see wherein honors were not quite even.

Spalding could indeed look back at the day as a success; even his Chicago team had been victorious, 7–3. If there was any note of dissatisfaction, it was likely the product of a survey card handed out to each of the spectators by the London and New York *Herald*. Among its questions: "Do you think baseball more scientific than cricket?" and "Do you think it will ever be adopted in England?" Even Albert Edward was polled, and was quick-witted enough to come up with a tactful response: "The Prince of Wales has witnessed the game of Base Ball with great interest, and though he considers it an excellent game he considers cricket a better one." What else could he say? Some of his countrymen were less flattering. "Appears childish," "A silly game," and "It is rot," were a few of the responses printed in the next day's paper. No reviewer, however, seemed as genuinely cranky as the author of the *Daily Spectator*'s anonymous "Penny for Your Thoughts" column, who offered his readers a stream-of-consciousness critique of the action that would have made even the most foul-tempered bleacherite cringe:

HUMPH!. . . Wonder how All-America and Chicago like playing their national game in a fog on a mud-swamp. . . . Fine-built fellows though, and natty dress. Look at that broad-shouldered chap in spotless—*Bang!* By Jove what a downer! He's not spotless now either; plastered with Surrey slime from neck to ankle. . . . What are they up to? Look to me like a lot of tipsy fellows in a fog. Somebody sprawling every half minute. Find it difficult to follow the game, and as to the scoring—well, do they score at all? Br-r-r! it is cold. *All out?* Why I hardly knew they were in. Score? *Nothing?* And after all that scampering and stumbling! Rum game this!

Ah! *that's* a good spank. First fare hit I've seen. . . . What are they doing now? Ah! there's a swipe! Run, Sir, run!!! Why, he never stirs? Foul hit? Oh! Hang it all!. . . Yes, they do catch well, certainly, and throw straight, only nothing seems to come of it.

Pitcher throws as if he were pelting frogs in a pool. . . . Game resembles a glorified—and more dangerous—Rounders. . . . Without the prolonged charm of cricket or the swift, short excitement of football, but with the tedium of the one, and all the mud-tumbling of the other. . . .

Eh? Game's at an end? Well, well—and who's won? Don't know? Neither do I—nor care. . . ." *More scientific than cricket?*" Bosh! "*Likely to be popular in this country?*" Walker! Fancy a grown-up Rounders, with few hits and scarcely any score superseding Willow and Stumps! *Don't understand the game?* Well, no, I daresay not, and up to now, somehow, I don't want to. . . .

I will not fill up the [*Herald*'s] card, thankye! Never "down upon" a fellow's wife, children, wine, cigars, country, or *favourite game*. I love America, but if I gave my true opinion about Baseball it might not be flattering enough to make public for a penny. And now for a 'nip'!

Fortunately for all, this fellow was nowhere near the royal box. And it must also be said that a good portion of the crowd seemed downright enthusiastic with what it saw. "Our American cousins are here, and they are heartily welcome," wrote one such scribe. "We may safely conclude that the time is not far distant when they will find that the sincerest form of flattery—which is imitation—has followed upon their trip to 'Yurrup.'"

———✠———

With a schedule that would have them play ten games in eleven days, the ballplayers had little time for the conventional tourist trappings during their time in England. They did, however, have two free days before they began their string of exhibitions, and in this time they set out about London in an acquisitive mood, for the city was known as a nineteenth-century shopper's paradise. Their results were mixed. As far as Harry Palmer was concerned, the famed haberdashery and bespoke tailoring of Saville Row was overrated. "The London tailor is a miserable failure, so far as his ability to fit an American with a suit of clothes is concerned," he wrote. Indeed, Palmer was less than impressed with the sartorial aptitude of the nation as a whole. "It is a noticeable fact, or was to me, that in London, Englishmen seem to be utterly indifferent to the matter of fit.

They seem perfectly willing to wear their clothes as though they had been thrown at them."

Josie Spalding was having shopping troubles as well, though in her case the problem wasn't the wares on offer. Her difficulty was of the more traditional sort: the mother-in-law. Those trying early years in Byron and Rockford, when Harriet Spalding had been a widow twice over and a single mother of three, had left her reflexively frugal in her full maturity, though she could certainly appreciate the finer things of life. It was, no doubt, hard on Josie, who returned to the First Avenue Hotel after a day out on the town and complained to her husband, "Mother says, 'Don't buy,' but when we go out together, the first pretty store window we come to, Mother says, 'Let us come in here.' We go in, I buy something, but Mother doesn't." Albert just smiled.

The tourists had another chance for a bit of sight-seeing on the morning after their exhibition at Kennington Oval. Henry White, the American chargé d'affaires in London, had arranged for a private tour of the Houses of Parliament. When the men arrived, there was a lively debate in progress in the House of Commons concerning Irish home rule, and in particular the treatment of Irish political prisoners—a subject of some interest for the ballplayers who claimed Irish heritage. They did not stay long, however. Westminster Abbey was still on the morning's itinerary, and in the afternoon they were scheduled to play their second game in London, at Lord's Cricket Ground, home of the fabled Marylebone Cricket Club.

Seven thousand fashionably attired spectators came out to see the festivities at Lord's, considered the "swellest of the swell cricket grounds of London." Certainly, the Marylebone Cricket Club directors were not to be outdone by their competitors in Surrey. The duke of Buccleuch, president of the club, welcomed the men to the grounds, and he was joined by nearly a dozen lords and knights of the realm. Cooperative weather contributed to one of the prettier exhibitions of the tour, the highlight being a spectacular diving catch in the outfield by Ned Hanlon. This came off a ball hit by Marty Sullivan, making it a veritable replay of the catch Hanlon had made off the Chicago left-fielder back in Denver. Behind

Hanlon's defense and seven strikeouts by Cannonball Crane, the All-Americas went on to win the game 7–6. This was the last time they played as an intact unit, at least in Europe. The next morning, as the rest of the tourists headed off by train for an exhibition at the Crystal Palace in Sydenham, their captain, John Ward, sailed for New York. If he felt any sense of guilt about his early departure, he could take solace from the fact that he had left his All-America charges in a good position: They had a comfortable five-game lead (20–15 with one tie) in the series with the Chicagos—perhaps not an insurmountable margin, but one that would be difficult to lose.

———

Speculation that Ward might abandon the trip had been rampant since the tourists received news of the Brush classification scheme in Cairo. That talk had been fueled by additional reports that Ward himself might be sold or traded to either the Boston or Washington clubs. This double-whammy left him with serious concerns over both his own situation and the broader state of relations between the players and the National League, for which he naturally felt responsible. "Ward knows that the Brotherhood wants him at home and he is going there. That is all there is to the matter," one of the traveling players told Palmer, who included the statement in his dispatch to the *Herald*, though he did not name its source. The anonymous player continued: "If it had not been for the action of the National League clubs in undertaking to put a yoke upon the necks of ball players Ward would not be going home at present." But the truth was somewhat more complicated.

The first formal word of Ward's intention to return to the States ahead of the tour came in one of his own syndicated dispatches from Paris, on March 12. "From advices which I have received here I am convinced that it is imperative for me to leave for New York, which I shall do the last of this week, abandoning the trip through Great Britain, much to my disappointment," he explained, before adding, "I have arrived at no decision concerning my future movements; nor shall I until I reach home."

Later that week, in a story that ran in the *Sun*, Simon Goodfriend reported that Ward was returning to take care of "personal affairs," in particular, a "note due" on the property he had purchased in Denver in October. He also wrote, more cryptically, of "other affairs requiring his attention."

The "other affair" in question was Helen Dauvray, Ward's estranged wife. Back in October, she had claimed "urgent business" of her own as an excuse to abandon the tour in Denver as it was driving west toward San Francisco. What particular argument had set things off between the couple is unclear; certainly, there were plenty of options. Perhaps it was Ward's affair with it-girl Jessie McDermott, or perhaps it was Helen's desire to return to the stage, an idea to which Ward very much opposed. (In marriage, Ward seemed to be a traditionalist; a working wife wouldn't do, and certainly not one who would compete with her husband in the realm of public adulation.) Whatever the case, Ward had expected Dauvray to at least rejoin the tour in London. When it became pointedly clear to him, in Paris, that she would not do even this, and that she was in fact planning to resume her acting career, he knew it would be necessary to return home at once. Spalding was displeased with this development, but looked upon the matter with resignation, ostensibly figuring that British audiences wouldn't much know the difference anyway. "I deeply regret it," he said. "Ward tells me that nothing can alter his determination; that matters of a private nature demand his presence in New York, and with this explanation he leaves me."

For Anson's Chicago squad, at least, the absence of the All-Americas' top player was good news. With Ward gone, Hanlon was elevated to team captain, and Fogarty shifted in from the outfield to cover shortstop. Henceforth, the reserve pitcher (alternately Healy and Crane), would have to play in the outfield. Their first game with this new alignment came in Sydenham, southwest of London, the home of the Crystal Palace Cricket Club.

On the way to that game, the tourists stopped in for a peek at the structure for which the cricket club was named: the Crystal Palace. The titanic iron-and-glass hall, designed by Joseph Paxton, was constructed for the International Exhibition of 1851, the first of the great world's fairs. Over sixteen-hundred feet long and bisected by a series of naves, the structure remained, nearly four decades after its construction, one of the signature architectural works of the period. (The building, a master-piece of prefabricated parts, had originally been erected in Hyde Park; it was taken down and rebuilt in Sydenham in 1854.) The exhibitions on of-fer inside were, as *Baedeker* noted, "of such vast extent" that the guide could only give a brief outline, though it was careful to recommend the themed "courts" with reproductions of architectural monuments (the tomb of Abu Simbel) and arts (the *Venus de Milo*) from great civiliza-tions past.

Moving on to the local cricket grounds, the tourists found a field that was "velvety soft," and they rewarded the enthusiastic crowd that had come out to see them play with a fine showing. The All-Americas won by a score of 5–3, though it took a dramatic two-run home run by Tom Brown in the eighth inning to give them the lead. That ball sailed clear over the outfield and into a stand of trees bordering the field, prompting a prolonged cheer as Brown circled the bases. Anson wasn't too happy about it—Chicago was now six games back—but he did note with ap-proval the response of the crowd: "They're catching on," he told Palmer after the game.

The next morning, the tourists departed from London's Paddington Station for Bristol, a sea-faring city of more than two hundred thousand residents located a three-hour train ride to the west. No citizen of that city was more famous than W. G. Grace, England's preeminent cricketer and the president of the Gloucester County Cricket Club. A burly man with close-cropped hair and a thick beard that fell to his chest, he was an impressive physical specimen. At the age of forty, he was still very much in his prime, and could already boast nearly every record the sport had on its books.

Grace was waiting at the station when the tourists' train rolled in, and he proceeded to escort them to the Grand Hotel, where they were treated to lunch with the duke of Beaufort—"one of the finest examples of an old English gentleman I ever met," according to Palmer. Then it was off to do business at the cricket grounds. Unfortunately, the typical English weather, cold and damp, was again uncooperative. Both

Chicago pitchers, Baldwin and Tener, claimed to be ill, forcing Anson to start Ryan. Figuring he might as well take advantage of the opportunity, Hanlon chose to rest the two All-America pitchers as well, sending Brown to the box for his side. That decision backfired: Chicago cranked out hit after hit for a 10–3 victory. (Anson, however, was 0–5, his worst game of the tour.)

The day's proceedings were not yet complete. Grace, along with several other members of his club, wanted to give baseball a try. And so the Chicagos stayed on the field, and Ryan and Crane whizzed pitch after pitch past the Englishman. "I tossed him some easy ones," Crane later recalled, "and Grace missed 'em by about two feet. I gave him snakes, and in-curves, out-curves and twisters, all very slow, but he couldn't get his bat within a yard of 'em." After fifteen minutes, only one ball had been hit into fair territory. Even the crowd was impressed. Grace, for his part, was nonplused. "I should like to have been a 'pitcher' when I was a young man," he said. "I don't think anyone would have hit the ball." If this was rounders, it sure had come a long way.

The following afternoon the Americans played their final game in the London area, a 12–6 victory for Chicago at Leighton. In the evening, as a farewell, they were treated to a banquet at a venue that brought them, at least visually, a little closer to home. At an exhibition space on York Street, the tourists found themselves in the midst of a massive cyclorama, *Niagara Falls*, painted by Paul Philippoteaux, a graduate of the French Académie des Beaux Arts and a specialist in the genre. (His other panoramic works included *The Siege of Paris* and *The Battle of Gettysburg*.) Dramatic lighting effects brought the falls, seen from an elevated platform, to life. Admission, normally one shilling, was waived for the ballplayers.

The next day, a Sunday, they packed, for the following morning they would begin a new adventure: a breathless, six-day, six-city, six-game tour that would bring them to Scotland in the north before depositing them on the eastern coast of the island, whence they would take leave of England across the Irish Sea to Dublin. It would be a busy week, no doubt, but at least they would be traveling in grand style. Stamford Parry (who, in addition to his role as tour advance man was European agent of the Burlington Route Rail Road) and Alcock had combined their clout to convince the London & Northwestern Rail Company to prepare a private train for the travelers "the like of which had not before been seen in England." It certainly put to shame the two-car caravan the Burlington Route had provided for the tour back in the States. This train was *nine* cars long: two for dining, two for smoking and receiving guests, and five sleepers equipped for six to eight persons. Inside, wrote Palmer, there was "every comfort one could ask." The exterior was white enamel with brown trim, and on the side of each car was an inscription lettered in handsome type: "The American Baseball Clubs." Spalding could not have asked for more.

Sadly, the party that would be making the journey aboard this luxury liner had been reduced by two. Chicago Shortstop Ned Williamson, still ailing from his fall in Paris, missed the train tour through northern Britain in its entirety. Doctor's orders were for him to remain in bed at the First Avenue Hotel, where his wife could minister to his needs. Indeed, Williamson's health seemed to be worsening. On March 26, while the rest of the tour was traveling across the Irish Sea to Belfast, the *Herald* reported that his condition had become desperate. "He experienced a relapse yesterday which assumed something like the form of paralysis of his lower extremities. The intensest agony followed, and for the greater part of a day his physician was in constant attendance upon him." Recovery was anticipated, but the slugger was confined to bed for another week. Adding insult to his injury was Spalding's refusal to pick up the tab for his hotel bill—by contract, he was not obliged to do so. This was standard for the time. Nineteenth-century teams did not have training staffs, and players were responsible for their own medical care. If they missed time, they were not paid. Nevertheless, Williamson, understandably, would never forgive Spalding for that stinginess.

———

The luxurious rolling hotel made its first stop in Birmingham, the great industrial city some 113 miles to the northwest of London. The train arrived at New Street Station shortly after noon, and the tourists were there met by members of the Warwickshire Cricket Club, who had arranged a lunch in the players' honor at Queen's Hotel. The game, at Edgbaston, was scheduled for half past three, and despite less than ideal conditions—it was rather cold and cloudy—it turned out to be a memorable one, an exciting ten-inning affair called for darkness with the score knotted at four. "The most interesting and brilliant yet played on the trip," Palmer commented after it was over. "A prettier or more desperately contested game is rarely seen anywhere."

That contest began well for Chicago; Anson's men touched up a shaky Healy for four runs—all they would get—in the first inning. Healy settled down, however, and All-America tied up the game with a run in the third and three more in the fourth. The score remained locked at four until the top of the seventh, when the Chicagos were again poised to take the lead. Tom Daly led off the frame with a double, and advanced to third base on a grounder by Ryan. The next batter, Robert Pettit, then sent a Healy pitch high in the air to center. Daly returned to third base to tag, and when Hanlon caught the ball, Daly sprinted for home. But the savvy captain had anticipated Daly's play and had lined himself up accordingly; when the ball fell into his hands, he immediately wheeled and sent it whizzing back toward the plate. Daly was out by a good five feet. "One of the grandest throws to the plate ever seen on a ball field," wrote Palmer.

The All-Americas would have their own chance to put the game away. Hanlon led off the bottom of the tenth with a single into the outfield gap, which he hustled into a sliding double. Two batters later Hanlon found himself on third, ninety feet from victory, with just one out. If Mark Baldwin, the Chicago pitcher, was nervous, he did not show it; indeed, he seemed to toy with the All-America captain, faking pick-off throws and taunting him to try, just try, to make it home. He never would. Perhaps the creeping darkness gave Baldwin a bit of extra confidence. Whatever it was, the next two batters, Carroll and Wood, struck out. And that's where the game ended, for there was no longer enough light to begin another inning.

From Birmingham, the tourists continued north into Yorkshire for Sheffield, a city in England's industrial heartland then known primarily for its cutlery manufacture. *Baedeker's* 1887 guide described it as "smoke-begrimed," and this is just how the tourists found the Bramball Lane Grounds, a walled-in field of green surrounded by belching chimneys. The rain was so heavy and the fog was so thick that the game had to be called in the fourth, before it became official (a good thing for the Chicagos, who were already down 10–0). It was an ugly day, weatherwise, but the crowd of three thousand seemed happy nonetheless. Throughout, wrote Palmer, they showed "more enthusiasm than any audience the boys have had yet on the way through England." Conditions were only marginally better the next day in the Leeds suburb of Bradford; on the morning of their arrival snow blanketed the ground. In the afternoon, on a field so muddy that it had to be covered with straw, Chicago plodded its way to a 6–3 win.

It is indicative of Spalding's conviction that baseball's future as an English sport lay with the kind of blue-collar workingmen who filled up the Chicago and All-America rosters that he chose Glasgow and not Edinburgh as the tour's one stop in Scotland. Most tourists would have picked the latter; it was, after all, the capital, and famous for its beauty. "Perhaps no fairer or more harmonious combination of art and nature is to be found among the cities of the world," wrote *Baedeker*. Glasgow, by contrast, was a city of commerce and industry with a population roughly triple that of its elegant rival to the east.

In any case, Spalding and his men had little time to explore the city. Glaswegians, however, found themselves drawn to the American athletes who had ceremoniously rolled into their midst. "Had our train borne the Shah of Persia himself, it could scarcely have been an object of greater curiosity," wrote Palmer. Some five hundred rubber neckers were gathered at Northwestern Station when, at two o'clock, a pair of double-decker, four-horse drags picked the uniformed men up and carried them off to the West of Scotland Cricket Club. Three thousand more fans were waiting at the field to see the tourists play, and for seven innings they got their wish. The game was cut off (with All-America in the lead, 7–4), so that the party would not be late to a performance of *King Lear* at the Grand Theatre, where they were the honored guests. After the final curtain, the boys returned to their train, and chugged south through the night toward Manchester.

Another day, another city, another ballgame. The next afternoon the tourists played in "Cottonopolis" (Manchester was the capital of the English textile industry) at the historic Old Trafford Cricket Ground, since 1856 the home of the Lancashire County Cricket Club. "Undoubtedly the most beautiful athletic grounds the teams have yet seen in Great Britain," wrote Palmer. (Ground was broken for Old Trafford Football Stadium, home of the celebrated Manchester United football club, in 1909.) The teams did the storied field justice, the All-Americas winning in the bottom of the ninth on a dramatic double by Fogarty that brought Hanlon in with the clincher.

The whirlwind trip continued the next morning at seven, when the tourists departed Manchester; an hour later they pulled into Liverpool's Lime Street Station. This was to be the last stop on their English tour, which probably was all for the best. With the relentless itinerary of the previous week, Britain's industrial cities were inevitably coalescing into a murky physical soup. After a few hours walking about Liverpool's streets, even Palmer found it impossible to put his finger on a distinguishing characteristic: "Just where or what the existing difference is between it and other English cities, I cannot say."

Confusion was the order of the day. The men arrived at the Police Athletic Club Grounds to find a large crowd already clamoring at its gates; when one of those gates gave way, fans poured into the stadium. Players were conscripted into service as ticket takers in an attempt to stem the flood of humanity, but the effort was of little use.

The reason for all the excitement was that national pride was very much on the line. Spalding knew better than to let his men compete at cricket, but he had consented to a game of rounders between his tourists and a picked team from England's National Rounders Association. Following that contest, the rounders men would try their luck at baseball. Spalding's hope was that these two contests would finally dispel any suggestion that baseball was a mere children's game and at the same time showcase the prowess of the American athlete. Of course, there was the ever-present danger that his men might embarrass themselves at the British game, and if that were to happen, the entire tour through Britain would be cast in a thoroughly unflattering light.

The two games against the rounders men were set to take place after a first contest between the Chicagos and the All-Americas, an arrangement that did little to encourage interest on the part of the English in the finer points of the American sport. That game was called, mercifully, after five innings with the score tied at two. Having dispensed with this obligation, the rounders contest could begin, and in its opening moments it looked as though the English might just hand the Americans the embarrassing defeat they so feared. Though familiar, the ground rules of rounders required some getting used to for the visitors. The arrangement of players on the field was similar to that of baseball, but with an extra fielder behind the "catcher" position, and an added hand in the outfield. Batters hit one-handed with a short paddle, and attempted to make a circuit of five stakes in the ground before being hit—as opposed to tagged—with the ball. (This method of retiring the runner, called "soaking" or "plugging," had been a feature of baseball in its early years.) The Americans' lack of experience allowed the English to build a sizable lead, but by their second at bat the visitors had caught on and had stormed back, closing to within 16–14 before the game was called so the rounders men could try baseball. Though technically a loss, the Americans had acquitted themselves impressively, and would likely have won the day had the game continued—a moral victory.

In the baseball game that followed, the tourists gave their hosts a thorough beating. Mark Baldwin, pitching for a mixed team of Chicago and All-America players, struck out the first three men who came to the plate. With that, the visitors took their turn at bat, and put up eighteen runs before the game was called in their favor. Throughout, a crowd running twenty deep stood in a slashing rain watching the tourists at work. Spalding had made his point. Though he might have made it too well. Embarrassing the British was no way to win them over to the American sport.

Whatever the case, there was little time for the Americans to savor their victory or worry about hurt feelings. At nine o'clock, the tourists boarded their specially outfitted train for the last time. A 50-mile trip north took them to the coastal city of Fleetwood, where a small steamer, the *Princess of Wales*, was waiting to ferry them to the Emerald Isle.

The tourists welcomed the slackening of the tour's heretofore frenetic pace on its final foreign leg, which for many of the men was a homecoming to an ancestral land. After the week spent charging through England's industrial centers, Ireland's verdant landscape was a revelation. As if to underscore the change, they arrived on a quiet Sunday morning shortly after breakfast, steaming up through the Belfast Lough and onto the River Langan, with the green banks of the Counties Antrim and Down framed to the north and south, respectively. By early afternoon they were checked into Belfast's first-class Imperial Hotel, and soon thereafter were out window shopping along Royal Avenue, the city's primary commercial thoroughfare. As a relatively new city—Queen Victoria had only given it official designation as such in 1888—and an industrial one at that, there were few landmarks of note for the tourists to attack. Instead, they spent their free day meandering about and taking rides in the city's famed "jaunting cars," two-wheeled carriages with back-to-back bench seats that faced out instead of forward.

The business of the tour recommenced the following afternoon on the grounds of the North of Ireland Cricket Club, a lush greensward on the Ormeau Road that was fenced in on three sides and bounded by the Langan on its fourth. The crowd drawn was "unmistakably fashionable," the men in dun-colored coats and the women—a large portion of the twenty-five hundred spectators—in pretty pastel-hued dresses. The All-Americas began and finished the contest with power, opening the top of the first with four runs against Chicago pitcher John Tener, who was making his debut on "home" soil. (Forty-two-year-old George Wright, Spalding's old Boston teammate, filled in for Ward at short.) Chicago fought back, however, and carried an 8–7 lead into the ninth inning. Then, with one out and two men on base, All-America catcher Billy Earle lashed a triple into the left-field gap, scoring two. John Healy closed the game out in the bottom of the ninth for a 9–8 All-America victory. The team had only lost three times since Ward's departure.

Early the next morning there was loud banging on the doors of the tourists' rooms at the Imperial Hotel. "Arf pawst foive. Wudge ye be gettin' oop, surrs? It's arf pawst foive!" In Belfast, wake-up calls were delivered in person, and apparently with a thick Irish brogue. A scheduled six-thirty departure for Dublin necessitated the early rising hour. When they arrived in that city after a five-hour journey, U.S. Consul James Mc-Caskill escorted them to their hotel, Morrison's (its primary claim to fame was as the place where the Irish patriot and home-rule advocate Charles Stuart Parnell was arrested in 1881).

None of the party seemed very interested in hanging around the hotel, whatever its history. With no game scheduled, most of the tourists spent the day shopping for shillelaghs and derby hats along Sackville and Grafton streets. But it was not so much the goods for sale that interested the men: "Our party was unanimous in awarding the palm for clear complexions, beautiful faces, and attractive figures to Ireland," reported Palmer.

For the Americans with Irish roots, prodigal sons returned home, the day off represented an opportunity to connect with family left behind. Tener visited relatives in Londonderry; Daly found his family in County Kildare. Manning returned to his ancestral home of Callan, a town of barely fifteen hundred in County Kilkenny. When he arrived at the station there he was swarmed. Everyone had come out to meet the hero from abroad, and everyone had to shake his hand. A parade of jaunting cars delivered him to the house of a long-lost uncle, its walls covered with newspaper clippings and photos of the town's famous American son. How was life in America? Was baseball like "hurley," the local sport of choice? Could you really earn a living playing a child's game? Manning answered their questions, and with pleasure. "Everything in Callan, even the scores of pretty girls, was mine," he recalled. "I wouldn't have missed it for a farm."

For the most part the reunions were heartwarming, but there was also something bittersweet in the fact that the tourists' lives had diverged so drastically from their origins. While their relatives appeared to be rooted firmly in a rural existence that evolved at a generational pace—if even that quickly—the travelers seemed to be hurtling toward the twentieth century, with all of its wonders, technological and otherwise.

———☞———

The tour's final game on foreign soil took place on March 27 at the Landsdown Road Grounds. A large society crowd that included Prince Albert of Saxe-Weimar, the commander of English forces in Ireland, Lord Mayor Thomas Sexton of Dublin, Lord Londonderry, U.S. Consul McCaskill, and a host of other luminaries came out for the event. With pride and bragging rights for the duration of the week-long transatlantic voyage in the balance, both teams were out to win—or at least anxious not to lose. Baldwin and Crane pitched for their respective teams, both men throwing heat that left batters all but helpless. Chicago could hardly keep the ball away from All-America first baseman Fred Carroll, who had fifteen putouts. Baldwin struck out five. Over the first six innings, neither team managed to put up a run, and the Dublin crowd was growing impatient. Finally, in the bottom of the seventh, Chicago broke through with a sacrifice fly to right that scored Pettit from third. The All-Americas would again win in their last at bat, however, erasing a 3–1 deficit with a four-run rally capped by a Carroll double. It was quite a day for the Bostonian, and it gave the All-Americas a commanding lead in the series between the teams, which would continue when the tour returned to the United States. The tally stood at twenty-six games for the All-Americas and just eighteen for Anson's Chicagos. Hanlon, demonstrating the strategic acumen that would serve him so well in the future, had been an effective leader.

Back at Morrison's the men barely had time to change out of their uniforms before they were whisked off to the depot, where a private three-car train had been outfitted in their honor by the Southern Railway Company. At eight o'clock, as its American flags fluttered in the evening light, the train pulled out of the station and began its six-hour trip southwest, to Cork. It arrived on time, at 2 A.M., whereupon the travelers immediately transferred to waiting carriages that had been sent by the Victoria Hotel. After a few hours of sleep, the men dragged themselves out of bed, downed a few cups of coffee, and headed out for one last touristic fling. Their destination: Blarney Castle, some five miles distant. After such a long trip, and with another ocean to cross, how could they fail to give its famous Stone of Eloquence a peck for good luck?

———◆◆◆———

It was but a half hour's ride from the station in Cork to the docks at Queenstown, where the tourists would board the White Star Line's *Adriatic* for the passage back home. A considerable crowd of well-wishers was already gathered at the pier when the group arrived; in addition to the ship's seventy-six first-class passengers (among whom were Spalding and company), nearly eight hundred were traveling to America in steerage. Servicing this mass of travelers were vendors selling supplies and goodies and trinkets of all types. One, a stooped older woman, had a patter that Harry Palmer found irresistible.

"Are yez goin' back to Ameriky?" she asked.

"Yes," he said. "Can I do anything for you there?"

"Do yez know me boy?"

"What's your boy's name?"

"Larry Donovan. As foine a bit of a boy as ever left old Ireland, and Oi hav'n't 'erd from him foor a year pawst."

"Where is Larry?"

"Sure Oi don't know. But if ye wud come across him, will ye take him this bit of shamrock from his old mither, and tell him that ye got it from her at the dock at Queenstown?"

How could he refuse?

CHAPTER 10

RETURN OF THE HEROES

T HE *ADRIATIC* ARRIVED IN NEW YORK HARBOR IN THE WEE hours of April 6, after a plodding nine-day trip across the Atlantic that had been slowed throughout by strong headwinds and generally foul weather. For the tourists, asleep in their berths, the first inkling that they had made it home came via the firing of the dawn gun at Governor's Island, a thundering boom that echoed across lower New York Bay just before 6 A.M. The rapport drew the men from their bunks, and when they looked out their staterooms' portholes they could finally see land.

On shore, preparations for their arrival had long since been under way. A reception committee had two boats ready to reel the tourists in from quarantine; inspection was a requirement for all international arrivals. With the cannon's blast, the *George W. Wood* zipped across the harbor, a brass brand on board tooting out "Auld Lang Syne" beneath a giant "Welcome Home" banner. Just behind was the *Laura M. Starin*, carrying more than one hundred and fifty friends and family members, including John Ward, Henry Anson, Walter Spalding, and James Hart. Also on board, chatting with Ward as the vessel made its way across the water to the *Adriatic*, was a man whose presence would loom large in the coming months: Al Johnson, a Cleveland streetcar kingpin eager to get into the baseball business.

With the Statue of Liberty as a backdrop in the foggy distance, the *Adriatic*'s 750 steerage passengers, confined to the after deck of the great ship, watched with mouths agape as the jubilant party of baseballists clambered down a gangplank and onto the *Starin*, where they fell into welcoming arms ready with champagne. James Manning, the All-Americas' second baseman, was the first to disembark, followed in short order by Tom Burns, Tom Daly, John Tener, and Fred Carroll. Harriet Spalding, grateful finally to be home, was carefully guided down the catwalk and onto the deck of the smaller vessel. "This is the best part of the whole trip," she said. Her son came soon after, and then Anson, who was greeted with three cheers and a hug from his father. "I'm crying boys, and I can't help it. I'm not ashamed," said the famously irascible Chicago captain. Having regained his composure, he later put into words just how much he appreciated the inspiring welcome. "I had been led to expect a reception of some kind, but did not expect anything like that which awaited us at daybreak," he told the *Evening Sun*. "If we had arrived here at noon and found a party of friends on a steamboat we would have been very much touched, but when we saw the steamboat and its crowd of merry-makers and well-wishers who had doubtless remained up all night so as to be on hand, then—then—well, I can't say anymore. I am overwhelmed."

Last off the ship was Cannonball Crane, though he was in fact not unaccompanied. In one arm the big pitcher carried a large grip sack; in the other, he held the long-tailed companion that had caused so much trouble over the last few months.

The *Laura M. Starin* deposited the travelers at the Twenty-second Street Pier, and from there they were taken by waiting carriages across town to the Fifth Avenue Hotel, which would be their base of operations over the next three days. After six months abroad, everyone seemed glad to be back on native soil, and the first order of business was a big American breakfast in the hotel's handsome dining room. "I've had some good old-fashioned buckwheat cakes and I hope to have a piece of pie before the day is over," Spalding said after the meal. "I hadn't the nerve to ask for it at breakfast."

The press of reporters milling about the Fifth Avenue's lobby were more interested in a recap of Spalding's tour than in the details of his morning repast—quotes were required for their afternoon editions. Spalding, his belly now full, was only too happy to oblige them. "Well, I'm glad it's over," he told the writers. "The trip was a success financially and every other way. I didn't make much money, but I have the proud consciousness of having established our game throughout the world, and feel certain that many countries will adopt baseball as a game." The truthfulness of any of these claims, aside from the first, was questionable to say the least.

It is telling that Spalding, who was prone to sugar-coat his dealings for the benefit of the press, later told the *Clipper* that the financial outcome of the trip was just "fair" and that he "about cleared all expenses." True or not, in the festive spirit of the morning few were willing to rain on the parade—anyway, Spalding's financial losses weren't the press's main concern. "We've had a splendid time, a great time indeed, right from the start," Spalding let them know. "The fact is we've had too much fun, and we are now ready to settle down to business. You never saw a lot of fellows so glad to get home as these boys are, and I'm with them. I am glad to get back, for we have the greatest country in the globe. Australia is a nice place, so is England and the other countries we visited, but there is only room for one United States on this globe."

With that, he set the tone for the reports that Americans would read of the world tour. A general sense of patriotic satisfaction was to be the order of the day. "It was when we stood in our rooms at the famous old hostelry and looked out over Madison Square that we felt once more at home, and were able to look back upon our great tour of the world as an accomplished fact," Palmer wrote. Anson, still touched by the grand reception, waxed philosophical: "A new feeling surges through me to-day," he said. "I am proud to be called an American, and you would, too, if you had passed six months in such sight-seeing and such travelling as we have. When you go over the same ground you will return to your native land with your heart overflowing with gratitude. And why? Because you are American." He closed his impromptu lecture with a declaration: "If you think you'll get me out of this country again you are greatly mistaken." Clarence Duval, the tour's mascot, shared that sentiment, though it was reported by the *Evening Sun* in dialect. "Had a fine time, sah. Never seasick once, even when we crossed the English Channel," said Duval. "But I'se mighty glad to git back to 'Merica again. Ain't no place like 'Merica." Only Cannonball Crane seemed willing to return to the seas. "The travel one has creates a desire for more," he said, "I wanted to go to Japan and China and the rest, but now I'm here I'm satisfied."

The travelers had little time to recuperate. In order to earn back some of Spalding's massive investment, now estimated at fifty thousand dollars— minus the contributions from Anson and Lynch—and to fully take advantage of the publicity capital accrued on the trip, the tourists would barnstorm their way back to Chicago, in the process playing exhibitions in every city on the National League circuit plus Brooklyn and Baltimore. As they traveled, they would be promoted as genuine American heroes, men who had conquered the world with bat and ball. (This campaign had been orchestrated in the tour's absence by Albert's brother, Walter, and a longtime Spalding ally, A. G. Mills, the former National League president.)

The ballplayers' first obligatory appearance came on the afternoon of their arrival home. After a few hours of relaxation at the Fifth Avenue Hotel, they crossed over the Brooklyn Bridge, still a newcomer to the city's skyline in 1889, for an exhibition game at Washington Park between the National League's New York Giants and the American Association's Brooklyn Bridegrooms. To the crowd's delight, Crane pitched for New York, and they won, 11–3. In the evening, the tourists were the guests of honor at the Palmer Theater for a performance of *The May Queen*, starring the notorious baseball buffs Digby Bell and DeWolf Hopper. Six boxes were reserved for the men, and the stage was decorated with flags and bunting; suspended from the proscenium arch was a gilt eagle bearing a shield with crossed bats, a catcher's mask, and a glove. The house was packed to its rafters for the event. "Positively no more money taken tonight," read a sign tacked up above the ticket office on the afternoon of the show. Throughout the performance, Hopper and Bell broke script to acknowledge the players, drawing applause each time they did. Then, in the final act, Hopper added a new kicker to one of their show-stopping numbers:

> *Our twenty American athletes who roamed*
> *In climes that are foreign have now returned home.*
> *They've played the world over before crowds and courts,*
> *They've shown effete Europe the noblest of sports,*
> *They've shown the old foreigners how to have fun*
> *With the mystical curve and the lively home run,*
> *And now let's greet them with all our main and might.*
> *Do you catch on? If you do it's all right!*

The last couplet wasn't quite a winner, but it didn't matter. As Hopper was finishing the stanza, he reached into the wing and drew a giant banner reading "Welcome Home, Boys" clear across the stage. The audience went wild. A stagehand then gave Hopper a mug of beer, and after blowing off the foam he raised it to the players' box in a salute: "Here you are fellows!" That brought down the house again.

Two days later, on Monday, the Chicagos and All-Americas were back at Washington Park, but this time they were in uniform. A healthy crowd braved a crisp spring afternoon for the contest, and most of them were on hand before the Chicago catcher, Tom Daly; he didn't bother to show up until the game was well under way, obliging Anson's men to play short-handed until his arrival. It was not to be their day. All-America pitcher John Healy tossed a no-hitter through six innings before the Chicagos caught up with him, and the picked stars held on for a 7–6 victory. Afterward, the entire party was driven back to the Fifth Avenue Hotel, where they dressed for the celebratory banquet being held in their honor at Delmonico's. "One of the greatest affairs ever held in New York," Ryan wrote in his diary of the soirée attended by Mark Twain, Theodore Roosevelt, and the other lords of the city. The *Clipper* was only slightly less adulatory: "The whole affair was a

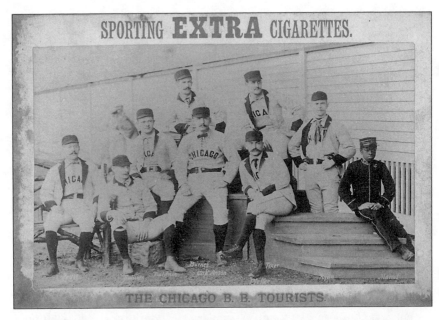

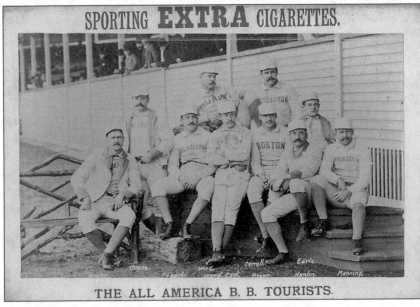

The first baseball cards were used to sell tobacco, not gum. The photographs of the Chicagos and All-Americas on these cabinet cards were taken at Brooklyn's Washington Park upon the tour's triumphant return home.

brilliant success, and will long be remembered by every participant." That was a fact no one would dispute.

Heroes for a night, the next afternoon the Chicagos and All-Americas were once again back at work at Washington Park—their third appearance in three days at the Brooklyn ballyard. In a bid to increase attendance, Spalding dropped the admission from fifty cents to a quarter, but even that was a bit steep for some of the local fans. Though a good-sized crowd packed the stadium, the stand of trees overlooking the park was filled with freeloading young men taking in the action from their perches. What they saw, according to Palmer, was a "rather uninteresting exhibition" won by Chicago 9–6. You get what you pay for.

Following that game, the tourists began their barnstorming trip through the cities of the East, beginning the next afternoon with a contest at Oriole Park in Baltimore (Chicago won 5–2). The very next day they were in Philadelphia, where Francis Richter, the editor of *Sporting Life*, tendered them a banquet that vied in extravagance with that thrown at Delmonico's, though this time the guests were drawn more from the sports world than the society pages. For the event, the grand ballroom of the city's famed Bellevue Hotel was decorated floor to ceiling with floral displays ensconced with baseball equipment—Spalding brands, to be sure. The speeches ran well into the night. "I should like to pay Mr. Spalding the tribute he deserves," Charles Byrne, the president of the Brooklyn Bridegrooms, told the audience. "The man who conceived and organized and carried out this marvelous enterprise is worthy of all consideration." Byrnes's encomium was extended to the rest of the athletes—"these magnificent specimens of American manhood"—who "carried themselves like gentleman, like American citizens, animated by a purpose and a spirit which has been a surprise to everybody." Spalding, Ward, and Anson all responded to toasts in their honor with brief speeches. Fogarty amused the crowd with a ten-minute soliloquy on his many escapades, and Harry Wright and Henry Chadwick, baseball's two most revered elder statesmen, both addressed the audience. The evening was brought to a close with the reading, by Chadwick, of a proclamation that dispensed a bit of retribution for the only real slight of the tour.

RESOLVED: That the sincere and hearty thanks of all lovers of baseball in America be, and they are hereby, extended to Mr. Charles Daugherty, the present Secretary of the American Legation at Rome, for his kindness and attention to the American representatives of the national game on their recent tour around the globe; that this thoughtful and unselfish friendship, rendered the more conspicuous by the ill-mannered conduct of his superior officer, United States Minister Stallo, shall be treasured as one of the most enjoyable and delightful memories of our tour around the globe.

Again there was little time for recovery. After a reception the next morning at Philadelphia's City Hall—"You have been a credit to your country," Mayor Edwin Fitler told the men—they were driven to the local ballpark, where Chicago dispatched the All-Americas 6–4, their third consecutive victory. Had they been paying attention to such things—and by this point, after so many miles and so many games, they seemed to have lost track and interest—they might have noticed that with the victory Chicago had climbed within five games of the All-Americas, with just six left to play in the tour. As it was, the count stood at twenty-six wins for the All-Americas to twenty-one for the Chicagos, with three ties.

The clinching game came the next day, in Boston, but one member of the All-Americas would not be on hand for the team's celebration. While standing on the platform at Philadelphia's Broad Street Station, catcher Billy Earle had his attention distracted by several attractive young women, and the overnight train departed without him. Fortunately his teammates did not need his help. The *Boston Globe*, after lauding the tour as "the biggest venture our national game has ever known," described the proceedings on the field as "well worth the price of admission." A crowd of twenty-five hundred was on hand for the contest, and their loudest cheers were reserved for Anson and Tom Brown, a Hub native. In the eighth, Chicago even managed a triple play. Alas, they could not win the game. Behind strong if somewhat wild pitching from Ed Crane, the All-Americas were victorious by a score of 10–3. The first and only true "World Series" was theirs. The next morning, after spending the night at Brattle Square's Quincy Hotel, they departed for Washington, where they would again be received at the White House, but this time by Benjamin Harrison.

The visit came on the morning of their arrival from Boston, after the men had cleaned up and breakfasted at their usual place of accommodation, the Arlington Hotel, which was just a few blocks from the executive mansion. It was, apparently, a challenging morning at the White House. The tourists had originally been scheduled to appear at eleven o'clock sharp, but word came to the hotel just after nine that they would be expected an hour early, at ten. When they arrived, there was hardly a wait before they were escorted in to meet the president, with Spalding leading the way. This time, Anson was not given the opportunity to put his foot in his mouth. Walter Hewett, a director of the National League's Washington club and a longtime friend of the president's, introduced the players, and Spalding invited Harrison to attend the afternoon's exhibition between the Chicagos and the All-Americas at Capitol Park. Unfortunately, Harrison was not able to make it out to the ballpark.

"I used to go to the games once in a while in Indianapolis, and also at Chicago," said the president. "I enjoy seeing a good game, but I cannot see how I can spare the time to go today." That was the end of the meeting, and if it was abrupt, as some of the players grumbled after the fact, that was just too bad. Anson, a Democrat, seemed most insulted—he later claimed that Harrison's reception was "about as warm as an icicle," prompting inaccurate rumors that the players had been snubbed and that Harrison, like Judge Stallo in Rome, had declared baseball beneath his dignity. Spalding, good Republican that he was, happily cleared up that misperception. "I have no reason whatever to feel offended at the President on account of the short audience he gave us," he said. More to the point, he could take a certain pride in the fact that the president, whatever his true feelings, felt behooved to at least pay lip service to the national pastime. In the future, such obeisance would become a happy requisite of the job.

Harrison didn't miss much by skipping the afternoon game. "A Baseball Burlesque" was the *Washington Post*'s headline the next morning, "Two Thousand Disgusted Spectators at Capitol Park: A Game Wholly

Devoid of Interest." Ward was charged with three errors in the 18–6 Chicago rout.

With that game complete, the tourists embarked on the final leg of the tour, a three-game, four-night swing through Pittsburgh, Cleveland, and Indianapolis that would, at last, return them home to Chicago. Those last three games were unremarkable—the first ended in a tie; they split the next two—and the attendance was mediocre, with Indianapolis drawing just a thousand spectators. The country's interest, along with the tourists' stamina, had been exhausted. Everyone was ready for the great tour to end.

Everyone, that is, except the people of Chicago. The city of broad shoulders would not be outdone by the likes of New York and Philadelphia in the celebration of its globe-girdling hometown heroes. All of Chicago had mobilized for their arrival. As word came down the line the that they were on the way, a reception committee was dispatched to Hammond, Indiana, roughly twenty-five miles from Chicago, to greet the tour's train and escort the party home. "Dress to the nines," the players were told. A parade and a banquet were in the offing, and there would be no down time in between.

At five o'clock, when the train carrying Spalding and his men finally pulled into Polk Street Station, there was bedlam. "Every kid on the South Side was alive and 'onto' the entrée of the Chicagos," wrote the *Inter Ocean*. A platoon of police officers was overcome by the surging crowd, which swarmed past the station's iron gates, surrounded the tourists as they descended to the platform, and carried them on their shoulders to the line of carriages waiting out on Madison Street. From there, the party made its way across town to the corner of Peck and Wabash, where a massive parade had already begun to form.

At the front was the National Guard Band, under the direction of Grand Marshal C. I. Wickersham. The fifteen-man unit included a showman who would go on to make a name for himself as America's greatest theatrical producer: Florenz Ziegfeld, Jr. Following that ensemble were ten Scotch pipers from the Highland Association of Illinois and a pair of twenty-five piece marching bands. Fifty-eight amateur baseball teams, all in uniform and arranged by league, marched to welcome the players. The city's athletic clubs—the Union, Universal, and Pullman, to name just a few—were represented, as were its cricket, cycling, and lacrosse clubs. The tourists themselves were placed in six horse-drawn carriages with a "special bodyguard" composed of Spalding Company employees. In all there were some sixty carriages, four of them equipped with calcium lights and pyrotechnics that would transform the city into one "great blaze of light." Finally, bringing up the rear in one fantastic sea of motion, were a thousand bicycle riders—members of the Chicago, Lincoln, Douglas, Pastime, Eaglewood, Oakland, and Aeolus cycling clubs.

Of this tumultuous welcome Palmer wrote: "The great crowd that filled the depot, that crushed our carriages, that lined the streets along which lay our line of march, and howled and cheered at the sight of each familiar face in line, as well as the music, the calcium lights, the colored torches, the rockets and the Roman candles that burst above our heads, all combined to make the reception tendered us the most enthusiastic ever given any body of athletes upon American soil." An estimated 150,000 Chicagoans lined the parade route to cheer the tourists. "Every one seemed to be out," wrote the *Chicago Tribune*, and the crowd "represented all classes. Business-men were in it, toughs and sports were in it, and also a great many ladies. And they went fairly crazy." The city would not know such revelry again until the opening of the World's Colombian Exposition, in 1893.

Engulfed by the jubilant crowd, the immense parade made its way up Michigan Avenue, at Congress Street passing in front of the still unfinished Auditorium Building, the latest and greatest of Chicago's skyscrapers. (Sullivan & Adler were the architects; much of the design work was performed by an ambitious young apprentice named Frank Lloyd Wright.) Crossing over to Wabash, the parade continued north, finally arriving at its destination, Palmer House, the city's great hotel and social hub, a building so luxurious that silver dollars were set into the tile floor of its barber shop. Potter Palmer, the dean of Chicago society, was there to greet the men, and by his side were most of the city's leading citizens. Inside, in the hotel's resplendent dining hall, twenty-four tables with

twelve places each had been set. The souvenir menus were no less elaborate than those for the banquet at Delmonico's: Each had a fringed-silk
dustcover and a frontispiece with a montage of landmarks from the tour.
The speeches, which commenced at eleven thirty, began with a welcome
from Mayor DeWitt C. Crieger. Carter Harrison, who had already served
four terms in that post (and would hold it once more before being assassinated by a deranged office-seeker), followed soon after with a toast of
his own to the touring ballplayers. Even Hiram Waldo, Spalding's old
mentor from Rockford, was there to say a few kind words about his erstwhile protégé.

For Spalding—a man who would always be, somewhere deep inside,
an orphaned boy in need of paternal attention—the adulation of the
city's fathers must have been especially gratifying, and he knew just how
to extend it. "I never realized what a dear thing it was to be home again,"
he told the crowd. "I want to tell you that though there may be some
great and good places in the corners of the earth I think that Chicago is
the sweetest, dearest place on this globe. I love the bustle and the life of
this city—our home." The audience roared its approval, but Spalding
was not done. This was a night for magnanimity—though perhaps not
truth—and he was, as ever, up to the task. "I want to say a word to our
players who have accompanied me on this trip," he said. "I want to thank
the players individually for their temperate habits and their faithful observance of their contracts with me. They have been as exemplary a body
of men as ever went out of this city."

The tour was now completed but for one last obligation: a farewell game
for the city of Chicago at Spalding's West Side Park. And so the next afternoon Clarence Duval led the two teams onto that diamond with a
good crowd of five thousand diehard cranks ready to cheer on the hometown heroes. Up in his private box, Albert Spalding must have allowed a
proud smile to cross his lips. But it could not have lasted for long. After
the previous night's festivities the men were physically and emotionally
exhausted, and Spalding's Chicagos seemed in even worse shape than the
visiting All-Americas. There was, anyway, little but pride at stake; the

*Souvenir menu from the celebratory banquet at the Palmer House in Chicago—
the last of the tourists' many grand meals together.*

All-Americas had already clinched the series between the two teams. Mark Baldwin, the normally hard-throwing Chicago pitcher, all but lobbed the ball over the plate. All-America first baseman Fred Carroll tripled twice before the end of the second inning. Tom Brown also tripled, and hit a home run for good measure in the fifth inning. The hits kept coming, and with them run after run, until the game mercifully came to an end with the All-Americas ahead, 22–9. It was the most lopsided game of the tour, the coup de grâce in a series that finished with twenty-nine victories for the All-Americas and twenty-three for the Chicagos, plus four ties.

In the aftermath, the men gathered on the field for one last good-bye, knowing that they would face one another on the diamond again but with the All-Americas scattered back to their respective teams. A few moments later, as the All-Americas boarded the carriages in which they would set off on their journeys home, Anson led his men onto the veranda of the Chicago clubhouse, and the White Stockings offered three final cheers to their departing mates. From their drags Ward and his men responded in kind.

That night, Jimmy Ryan made one last entry in his diary:

To day we have completed the circumference of the globe, for six months ago to day we bid good bye to Chicago and entered upon our tour Around the World. We have given exhibitions of our National Game in every continent on the face of the globe and also in thirteen foreign countries and travelled upward of a distance of thirty thousand miles. This afternoon as Tourists we played our last game and a great crowd greeted us as we appeared on our native diamond. The game concluded and so did the greatest trip in the annals of sport, namely a Baseball Tour "Around the World."

STUPIDITY,
AVARICE, TREACHERY

J
UST A FEW MONTHS AFTER THE TOUR'S RETURN, SPALDING SAT
down to pen an essay on baseball's history and future for the popular magazine *Cosmopolitan*. Cribbing from the many toasts he had
delivered as the tour made its way back across the United States to
Chicago, Spalding pronounced his mission to disseminate the national
pastime around the globe a substantial, if not absolute, success. In
Hawaii, an American colony in all but name, baseball was solidly established. In New Zealand, the future looked bright. "There is no doubt the
game will become a fixture there," he wrote. In Australia, where Harry
Simpson had remained to promote the game, there were already as many
as sixty amateur clubs. India and Ceylon he was willing to write off owing to their tropical climate, and Egypt seemed too backward to take seriously: "In a country where they use a stick for a plow, and hitch a
donkey and camel together to draw it, and do many other things as they
did twenty centuries ago, it is hardly reasonable to expect that the modern game of base-ball will become one of its sports."

The Continentals were another matter. "We found very little interest
in athletic sports in France and Italy," he wrote, though he did think it
might be good for them. "In looking at the small stature of the Italian
and the Frenchman, and comparing it with the Englishman, Australian,

and American, I was impressed with the idea that athletic sport has had its influence in developing the physical nature of the English-speaking countries." Spalding was more optimistic about baseball's chances in England and Ireland, though he freely admitted that challenging cricket and football for space both on the athletic fields and in the collective imaginations of these two nations would require "some little time and patience." In any case, it seemed important to him that the nations of the world, and in particular the English-speaking ones, come together on the field of sport. "I believe international contests would do more to cement a friendly feeling between these nations than anything else that can be suggested," he wrote. As to which sport they should play, he had no question: "Without wishing to disparage any other game, I unhesitatingly pronounce base-ball the peer of them all, and expect to see it become the universal athletic sport of the world."

John Ward shared Spalding's inclination to publicly speak of the tour in dulcet tones, as he did in his toast at Francis Richter's *Sporting Life* banquet in Philadelphia. "There is no period in my professional life that I will look back to with more genuine pleasure than upon the six months past," he told the luminaries who gathered for that event. "I am glad to have been a member of this pioneer combination and proud to have been a member of the All-America team. In my entire experience as a player I have never been associated with a more companionable lot of boys, and I am sure when the memory of our struggles on the field have faded from us we will recall with affection the many happy hours we have spent together. . . . It has been a delightful tour."

Ward may well have enjoyed certain aspects of the tour, but his happy-soldier act was just that—an act designed to mask his true feelings. The reality was that his union, the Brotherhood of American Base Ball Players, was on the verge of an all-out war with Spalding's National League. Whether or not Spalding had intended for his tour to result in an escalation of tension between the two sides had been a moot question since February, when the players, then in Cairo, first got word of the league's new labor policy. From that day on, Ward and his Brotherhood cohorts had spent their "happy hours" on the tour secretly plotting the overthrow of the league they saw as their oppressor. That was most assuredly not what Spalding had in mind when he invited Ward on his world tour.

Despite Ward's deep concern about the Brotherhood, in the days immediately following his early return from England his focus was on personal issues. Chief among these was his unhappy domestic situation. Helen Dauvray had likely found out about his affair with Jessie McDermott, and she was demanding to return to the stage. With so much else on his plate, Ward relented; he was too busy managing his own career to worry about hers. Exactly where Ward would play out the coming season was, aside from the tour, one of the primary topics of conversation over the winter's hot stoves. As Ward was circling the globe, New York owner John Day was threatening to sell him either to Washington or to Boston, where Mike "King" Kelly would take over as team captain. The situation was not resolved until Opening Day, when Ward re-signed with New York for $4,250. (Kelly's ill-fated tenure in Boston would end in May.)

With his private affairs in some semblance of order, at least temporarily, Ward could retrain his attentions on larger issues. On May 19, Brotherhood representatives from each of the league's teams, led by Ward, gathered at the Fifth Avenue Hotel to discuss strategy for the coming season. One option was a general strike, but Ward was opposed to this on the grounds that it would alienate the public and make it all the easier for the league magnates to smear the ballplayers as un-American, left-wing radicals—their usual tactic. Instead, Ward cleverly positioned the Brotherhood as an organization of capitalists blocked from selling their wares in a fair market by a tyrannical monopoly. This lawyerly hedge allowed the Brotherhood, which was a union in everything but name, to play on the sympathies of both blue- and white-collar audiences.

A belief in the righteousness of their cause prompted Ward and the Brotherhood to pursue their battle in the press with the hope that Spalding and the other league magnates would see the error of their ways. If that did not work, the players could shift to a far more aggressive course of action. That plan, a wholesale baseball revolution, called for the players to quit the National League en masse and start their own circuit, the Players' League.

That bold idea was a fruit—for Spalding, a most bitter fruit—of the world tour. Just when it first popped into Ward's imagination is unclear, but so many days of ocean travel with nothing to do but ruminate and stare at the waves had certainly provided ample opportunity. Ned Hanlon, Fred Pfeffer, and James Fogarty were all in on the early discussions. When they learned of the league's draconian new labor policy, what may have been an idle fantasy was suddenly transformed into a real alternative, as Ward hinted in his angry dispatch from Cairo: "Will it be necessary to sweep away the entire tangled network of stupid legislation and begin all over on a new basis?" he asked. The answer, it would seem, was a resounding yes.

The Brotherhood scheme bore all the hallmarks of Ward's legal education; its tactical genius was that it used the league's odious contract as the means of its undoing. Because the standard player agreement was only one year in duration, the players could simply refuse to re-sign. With a circuit of their own in the offing, the "reserve" provision was made moot, as was any threat that they would be blackballed from picking up with another team within "organized baseball"—the National and American leagues, and the various independent and minor circuits with which they were associated. Freeing themselves from the National League yoke was by far the most difficult obstacle for the players in the establishment of their new league. Grounds on which to play would be fairly easy to acquire. Ballparks, at the time, were rough-and-ready grandstands that could be thrown up in a matter of weeks. All that was needed was a bit of capital, and Ward already had someone in mind on that front: Al Johnson, the Cleveland trolley kingpin and baseball fan who had taken the trip out to greet the returning world tourists with him on the *Laura M. Starin*.

For all of their plotting, compromise with the league remained the players' preferred solution to their plight, and over the coming weeks they publicly aired their grievances with the hope that doing so would draw the league to the negotiating table. Instead, the league defended its position, arguing that salaries were restricting the ability of small-market teams (at the time, Washington and Indianapolis) to compete. Ward responded that those clubs should either quit the league or be subsidized by the profitable big-city teams. It was a stalemate—and more than a hundred years later, the terms of the debate are eerily familiar. With this open feud as a backdrop, on June 17 Ward proposed a meeting between representatives of the Brotherhood and the league to "take definite action in regard to the classification system." Three days later, Ward sidelined himself with a "sore arm," an injury that would keep him off the field until July 8. That conveniently came just as his New York Giants were making a swing through the league's western cities. Ward, it seems, was playing a double game: on the one hand suing for peace with the league, on the other taking time away from the diamond to recruit additional investors for his would-be league.

When the Giants reached Chicago, Ward took up his case for a labor summit between Brotherhood and National League leaders with the one man who could make it happen: Albert Spalding. On June 24, the pair met for two hours behind closed doors at Spalding's Madison Street office. Afterward, the magnate announced that he had taken the Brotherhood's request for a meeting with league leaders "under advisement," but that he nevertheless felt matters were not "of a sufficiently urgent nature to warrant such an action." Spalding, uncharacteristically, had gravely misjudged the situation. Ward, not wishing to show his hand, claimed to be "well satisfied" with the meeting, though his disappointment was clear. A more honest (and ominous) appraisal came from Ward's New York teammate Tim Keefe, who called the league's refusal to meet with the Brotherhood "the crowning point to the arrogant despotism of these dictators."

Henceforth, the sides became increasingly acrimonious and a showdown looked inevitable. On July 3, Ward squelched a Brotherhood motion to strike the following day, Independence Day, traditionally the most profitable date on the league schedule—an indication that the die had finally been cast. Two days later, Keefe told the *Clipper*, "The League will not classify as many men this Fall as they think," and rumors began to circulate about just what the players had up their collective sleeve. On July 14— Bastille Day, it was noted—the plan for insurrection was officially set in motion at the Fifth Avenue Hotel. There would be a new league after all, though it would remain a secret, at least for the moment.

If Spalding had not quite figured out exactly what the Brotherhood was up to, he could see that some action was necessary to recapture the moral high ground for his side. Despite his previous admonition that the league would not "fight its battles" in the press, on the same day that the Brotherhood was meeting to formally decide on its plan of patricide, Spalding publicly announced his own plan to refashion baseball on more player-friendly terms. According to Spalding's scheme, current players with three years or more of major league experience would be "grandfathered" out of the classification system, and any player who was sold would receive a quarter of his sale price. But Spalding's attempt at conciliation was too late. As one anonymous player told the *Times*, "This man Spalding is for himself all the time, and he cares little or nothing for players."

The Brotherhood's plan for a new league hit the papers for the first time in the September 8 edition of the *Chicago Tribune*. "To Start an Opposition League" read the headline. "A rumor has gained circulation in other cities that Albert Johnson of Cleveland is engaged in forming a circuit of baseball clubs in league cities in opposition to the present National league. The rumor further has it that Johnson is working with John M. Ward and the ballplayers' Brotherhood, and that the members of the latter organization will join Johnson's forces and leave the league magnates to hustle for players." The story was accurate, and two weeks later, on September 22, the players revealed their hand. "A Great Ball Trust," announced the *Tribune*. "The Ball Players' Revolt: To Cast Off the Yoke of the League Bosses," was the headline in the *New York Times*.

The Players' League was to be an eight-team circuit overseen by a sixteen-man senate; each team would have two representatives, one to be chosen by the players and one by the capitalists who backed them. Each team would be run by an eight-man board, also equally divided between labor and capital. Gate receipts would be shared evenly between home and visiting clubs. Income would go first to meet expenses, then to player salaries, and then into a purse for end-of-year prize money. Following that, the backers and players would be entitled to draw on revenues, the first ten thousand dollars to go to the backers and the next to the players. Those players would be allowed to invest in their own clubs, and all would be given three-year contracts at their 1889 salaries, except for those players who had been reduced in the National League classification scheme—they would be returned to their 1888 rates. Moreover, there would be no reserve clause, and no salary limit. Better still, players could only be released at the end of the year, and then by majority vote among the club's directors.

The insurrection must have been a tough blow for Spalding. It was in many ways a personal failure that things had been allowed to reach their current state, a failure compounded by the fact that several of Spalding's allies and friends had taken up the players' cause, including his old team-mates George Wright (whom he had brought on his tour, no less) and Ross Barnes. Indeed, nearly all of the tourists decamped for the Players' League. Only Anson remained, and even he might have departed had he not been a minority stockholder in the Chicago club. When push came to shove, he always seemed to be under Spalding's thumb.

With the gravity of the situation now clear and momentum on the Brotherhood's side, Spalding made a last-ditch attempt at conciliation. "I will be pleased to have you name a date when it will be convenient for your committee to meet the league committee," he wrote Ward on September 28. But it was now too late for that. Ward's reply was curt. The league had missed its chance, and now he was turning the tables: The players would consider Spalding's offer of a sitdown at *their* winter meetings. In case anyone was unsure of the meaning of that message, the *Tribune* spelled it out: "The time for conference and compromise has passed. The Brotherhood plans for 1890 have been formed. The league will be given no chance to redress any real or imaginary grievances."

Public opinion was divided. The *Sporting News* and the *Sporting Life* took the side of the Brotherhood. Much of the mainstream press, and in particular the *New York Times*, fell in behind the league. To ensure a steady stream of positive coverage, Spalding went so far as to purchase the New York–based *Sporting Times*, and there installed as editors his own partisans, O. P. Caylor and Harry Palmer. (Palmer had just completed his book, *Sights Around the World with the Base Ball Boys*, available for $3.50 in cloth, $5 bound in morocco leather.)

A formal declaration of hostilities came on November 4, just six days after the conclusion of a World Series in which Ward's National League Giants defeated the Brooklyn Bridegrooms of the American Association, six games to three. (Ward hit .417 in the series; fellow tourist Cannonball Crane had four victories for the champions.) This came in the form of an open letter, ostensibly written by Ward and addressed "To The Public":

There was a time when the League stood for integrity and fair dealing. To-day it stands for dollars and cents. . . . Players have been bought, sold and exchanged as though they were sheep instead of American citizens. "Reservation" became for them another name for property right in the player. By a combination among themselves, stronger than the strongest trust, they were able to enforce the most arbitrary measures, and the player had either to submit or get out of the profession he had spent years in attaining a proficiency. . . . We believe that it is possible to conduct our national game upon lines which will not infringe upon individual and natural rights. We ask to be judged solely by our work, and believing that the game can be played more fairly and its business conducted more intelligently under a plan which excludes everything arbitrary and un-American, we look forward with confidence to the support of the public and the future of the national game.

The response, harsh and digressive, came three weeks later in a statement, signed by Spalding and two other owners, that framed the issues in the context of the league's history of fighting player misconduct:

The National League of Base Ball Clubs has no apology to make for its existence, or for its untarnished record of fourteen years. It stands to-day, as it stood during that period, sponsor for the honesty and integrity of Base Ball. It is to this organization that the player of to-day owes the dignity of his profession and the munificent salary he is guaranteed while playing in its ranks. . . .

How false [the players'] promises and pledges, how evasive, contradictory and malicious have been their every act and deed, from first to last, we leave to the readers of the daily and weekly press for verification.

An edifice built on falsehood has no moral foundation, and must perish of its own weight. Its official claims to public support are glittering generalities, that lack detail, color, and truth, and the National League, while notifying its recalcitrant players that it will aid its clubs in the enforcement of their contractual rights to the services of those players for the season of 1890, hereby proclaims to the public that the National Game, which in 1876 it rescued from destruction threatened by the dishonesty and dissipation of players, and which, by stringent rules and ironclad contracts, it developed, elevated and perpetuated into the most glorious and honorable on the green earth, will still, under its auspices, progress onward and upward, despite the efforts of certain overpaid players to again control it for their own aggrandizement, but to its ultimate dishonor and disintegration.

From the outset, the two sides fought an ugly war, and, as in all such conflicts, even the winners would come out badly damaged. "It was announced at the beginning that it was to be a fight to the death, and it was carried to a finish along these lines," Spalding wrote in the aftermath. The tactics on both sides were vicious. Spalding offered King Kelly, who had signed with the Players' League, a $10,000 bribe to return to the National. (He refused it.) The Players' League sought to rent out National League grounds, which drove up the rents for their regular tenants. (Not all teams owned their ballparks, as did Spalding's.) National League owners sought aid in the courts, pressing to enjoin players from entering the Players' League on the grounds that doing so would violate the reserve clause of their contracts. These cases, with one minor exception, were tossed out. The National Leaguers also set out on a path of mutual destruction, scheduling their games to conflict with those of the Players' League. Meanwhile, the Players' League followed several National League policies that did little to help it at the box office or to engender popular support: Alcohol was prohibited and Sunday ball was proscribed, policies that foolishly alienated the blue-collar audience that might have been inclined toward a "worker"-owned league. The unspoken ban on black players remained in effect. Throughout the bitter 1890 season, the American Association, which had its own financial problems, maintained neutral; the last thing it needed was a revolt among its own labor force.

By end of the year all three circuits were running heavily in the red. The Players' League had a reported operating loss of $125,000. The National League, stripped of its top players, was in even worse shape. Its Pittsburgh franchise, depleted of all talent, had put up an appalling 23–114 record; its New York team required a financial bailout. Across the board, interest was down. The public, fed up with the infighting among players and owners, was staying away in droves, a point made clear on a late-summer afternoon in Chicago, when a reporter asked one of Spalding's assistants about the day's attendance at West Side Park. "Twenty-four eighteen," he replied. Even Spalding was taken aback by that work of inflation. "How do you reconcile your conscience to such a statement?" he asked when the coast was clear.

"Don't you see?" his man replied. "There were twenty-four on one side of the grounds and eighteen on the other. If he reports twenty-four *hundred* and eighteen, that's a matter for *his* conscience, not mine."

In retrospect, the failure of the Players' League appears inevitable, a foregone conclusion. Against the entrenched power of Spalding's National League, the upstarts were unquestionably fighting an uphill battle. But there was a moment, however brief, when it appeared that its unique collaboration of labor and capital just might succeed, and in doing so overthrow a structure that had become too powerful for its own good. What the Players' League's survival would have meant for the subsequent history of professional baseball, or even the history of American labor politics is impossible to know, though it is worth noting that the model of profit sharing pioneered by the Players' League more than one hundred years ago is not wildly dissimilar to the current system for dividing revenue between players and owners in the major leagues.

There was, indeed, every reason for the Players' League to win its war with the National League. Though both reached the end of the 1890 season in dire financial straits, the Players' League had the only asset in the game of any real value: the players themselves. What it did not have was a patient and fully committed leadership, and that would be its downfall.

The decisive moment came in October 1890, when Al Johnson and two other Players' League backers approached Spalding on a peace mission. Like so many before it, the meeting took place at the Fifth Avenue Hotel. With everyone losing money, the Players' League contingent proposed a truce. For Spalding, it was the perfect opportunity to drive a wedge between the Brotherhood members and their financial backers— the divide that was the league's essential weakness. The money men were naturally more interested in saving their shirts than in retaining their progressive labor structure. As on so many previous occasions, Spalding's gambit was to consolidate business—to co-opt the Players' League backers by bringing them into the National League. The final blow against the upstarts came on October 22, at a tripartite meeting of National League, American Association, and Players' League magnates. Ward was not invited, and when he and two other Brotherhood members tried to crash the party, claiming it was their legitimate right, they were turned away. When that meeting was over, the Players' League had effectively been dismantled.

"Stupidity, avarice, and treachery" were the reasons Ward gave for the collapse of the Players' League. Its official demise came on January 16, 1891, when it was ratified out of existence at a joint National League–American Association meeting in New York. Afterward, the men who had been responsible for the circuit's life and death gathered at

Nick Engel's Home Plate Saloon, on Twenty-seventh Street, a regular haunt for ballplayers and other athletes. Johnson and Ward were already there when Spalding and Anson arrived. If there were any hard feelings— and there most assuredly were—on this day they would be washed away by alcohol. "Pass the wine around." said Ward. "The League is dead. Long live the League."

⌒ EPILOGUE ⌒
THE GLOBE TROTTERS CLUB

FOUR YEARS AFTER THEIR HEROIC RETURN TO AMERICA, THE
Spalding tourists, or at least a good number of them, appeared in
New York as a group once again. This reunion, however, was free
of acrimony and bitter subtext. The date was March 8, 1893, and the occasion was their cameo, en masse, in the hit show *Ninety Days*, which had
been inspired by their trip. Ward had organized the appearance and timed it
to coincide with the annual National League meeting in New York, when
much of the party would already be in town. Spalding made it, as did Tom
Burns, Tom Daly, and Bob Pettit of the touring Chicagos. Ward's All-
America teammates Ned Hanlon, Ed Cannonball Crane, and George Wood
also came, as did the journalists Harry Palmer and Simon Goodfriend, and
the sporting-goods dealers George Wright and Irving Snyder. Cap Anson,
Fred Pfeffer, Jimmy Ryan, and Ned Williamson sent their regrets.

Written by Broadway stalwart William Gillette, *Ninety Days* tells the
story of one Matilda Epps Watkins, a comely young maiden who has been
willed eighteen million dollars by a beloved uncle, the condition of this be-
quest being that she marry the son of her uncle's best friend, and do so
within the titular time period—the rub being that this handsome young
gentleman is presently in Burma, and incommunicado. It is on her globe-
circling mission in search of remunerative love that Watkins comes across
the touring baseballists, who extricate her from a variety of travails along
the way.

If the concept was somewhat less than Shakespearean in ambition—
"sufficiently interesting" was about the best thing anyone had to say of
the plot—it did offer considerable possibilities for the scenic artist. "The
collision between a steamer and an iceberg is especially noteworthy for
the ingenuity and originality of the mechanical effects," noted one reviewer. Prescient, too.

On their special night, the real-life baseballists made their entrance
during scene three, to the wild cheers of the Broadway Theater audience
and the great relief of Miss Watson, who was then being held against her
will in a Cairo "mad house." (So much for Khedive Ismail's "Paris on the
Nile.") The American athletes, in full uniform, proceeded to liberate the
heroine from her captors by vanquishing a horde of Oriental scoundrels
with their bats. After the performance, they celebrated their victory at a
banquet for the "Globe Trotters Club" hosted by Ward. It was a night of
beer and revelry, and at its close it was agreed by all that the dinner
should be an annual affair, and that only those who were on the original
tour would be welcome. It was a grand idea, but there is no record that
the club ever reconvened.

———

While the shipwreck of *Ninety Days* seems prophetic of the *Titanic* disaster, it also suggested the future of the liners Spalding and his tourists
had taken themselves. The *Salier*, which carried the ballplayers from Australia to Egypt, wrecked in a storm off the Spanish coast in 1896; all 796
of its passengers and crew were lost. The *Alameda*, which took them
across the Pacific, crashed into a Seattle dock in 1912, destroying itself
and the dock in the process (there were no fatalities). The *Adriatic*, the
flagship of the White Star Line when it was launched in 1874, was sold
off and cut up for scrap in 1899.

Crashes were also an unshakable problem for Professor Bartholomew.
Though his ill-fated leap in Ballarat apparently put a temporary halt to
his own parachute jumping, once back in the United States he continued
to produce his balloon act, usually leaving the aerial duties to his assistants. But those assistants did not appear to be particularly well trained.
In September 1891, one of Bartholomew's "aeronauts," Edward Cole,

was severely injured after a sixty-foot fall at a Detroit-area county fair. The balloon ascension and ensuing jump had been advertised as taking place every day of the event, however, so the next afternoon, with Cole disabled, another of the professor's charges, John Hogan, made the ascent. But Hogan was even less comfortable on the trapeze than Cole, a fact that became increasingly apparent as the balloon rose through the air with the rookie aeronaut dangling awkwardly below.

"Get on the bar, man, get on the bar," Bartholomew shouted from the ground, but the apprentice either could not hear him or could not execute the command. The inevitable followed shortly thereafter. With the balloon at approximately 2,500 feet in the air, Hogan's right hand slipped from the trapeze. "My God, he has lost his hold," shouted Bartholomew. When Hogan's body hit the ground, witnesses said it rebounded four feet into the air.

Clarence Duval, the tour's other sideshow attraction, seemed to fare better in the wake of the trip. In September 1898 he was treated as an honored guest by Spalding's Chicago team at a game in Philadelphia. (The only original tour member on that squad was the diarist Jimmy Ryan, who was coming to the close of an eighteen-year career in which he hit .306.) By that time, Duval had attached himself to the pioneering African-American vaudeville-minstrel act of Bert Williams and George Walker, in which he likely performed in such numbers as "I Don't Care If Yo' Neber Comes Back" and "Quityerkiddin'." For all of the "coon" play, however, Williams and Walker were instrumental in presenting Americans with more rounded portrayals of black life. At the turn of the century they became popular recording artists and then made a smash on Broadway with *In Dahomey*, billed as a "Negro Musical Comedy." Of Williams, Booker T. Washington wrote, "He has done more for our race than I have."

Not all of the post-tour stories ended so hopefully. The *Ninety Days* reunion night came two years too late for Jim Fogarty, the tour's funny man. In February 1891 he returned to Philadelphia from his native California, apparently the picture of health and hoping to secure a spot on the roster of the local National League squad in the wake of the Players' League collapse. When he found himself in the hospital with a sudden case of pneumonia just a few days after his arrival, he blamed the change in climate. The truth was that he had contracted tuberculosis, and he never recovered. Fogarty, a bachelor, died on May 20 at the age of twenty-seven. Just two years earlier he had led the National League with ninety-nine stolen bases.

Ned Williamson, the cornerstone of Chicago's legendary Stone Wall infield, died three years later. His career never recovered from the leg injury he suffered at the Parc Aérostatique, in Paris, and he still held a grudge against Spalding for not supporting him financially through that ordeal. (Spalding's stinginess may have been prompted by the fact that Williamson had been sending reports on the tour, not all of them flattering, to the *Sporting News*.) In the spring of 1894, Williamson traveled to Hot Springs, Arkansas, hoping the waters would cure a liver problem, and perhaps help him to cut down his soaring weight, which had reached 280 pounds (he played at about 200). The treatments didn't work. Williamson died on March 4 with his wife, Nellie, by his side. His ballpark-aided single-season home-run record of twenty-seven, established in 1884, survived until 1919, when it was broken by Babe Ruth, who hit twenty-nine.

The story of Cannonball Crane was perhaps more tragic, if only because his troubles were self-inflicted. Alcohol, if not the root of his pain, became his undoing. Signs of his problem were evident before the Spalding tour even departed the United States; the hung-over pitcher was too ill to take the field for the All-Americas in their first exhibition in San Francisco. The consequences of Crane's alcoholism became even more serious during the 1890 season, when he was expected to be the frontline pitcher for the Players' League's New York franchise. "Just when we wanted his services he was not in a fit condition to do any work, a state of affairs due to his desire to partake of intoxicating liquors," said Edward Talcott, the principal backer of the team. "Our failure to win the pennant can only be attributed to one reason: Crane's poor work." That failure was not without consequence: Talcott was among the first of the Players' League capitalists to sue for peace with Spalding and the National League.

Over the next few years, Crane bounced around the minor leagues of the Northeast on a permanent bender, taking work where he could find it, usually as an umpire. He was in a Rochester flophouse on a gloomy Saturday in September 1896 when his funds finally ran out. He had nowhere to go. The next morning a clerk found him dead on the floor, having overdosed on chloral hydrate, a sedative. The coroner generously ruled the death accidental. In its obituary, the *Sporting Life* blamed the tour for Crane's drinking and his subsequent demise, claiming: "Until then, he never drank, but when the aggregation reached Paris, Crane fell." Whatever the cause of his problems, that was certainly not true.

There were positive stories. John Tener, who served Spalding ably as a traveling secretary during the tour, quit baseball after a subpar season in the Players' League, but moved on to a successful political career during which he would often call back on his days of diamond glory, few though they were. "Honest John" was elected to the U.S. Congress from his home state of Pennsylvania in 1909. The next year he became its governor. Tener's progressive Republican administration passed legislation on women's rights, labor reform, education, and road building. When a colleague claimed that an important bill was the highlight of Tener's "inspiring career," he replied, "No, gentlemen, I once shut out Boston." He did briefly return to the game he loved; he served as president of the National League from 1913 to 1918.

Fred Pfeffer, Williamson's double-play partner in the great Stone Wall infield, also kept close to the game. In 1889 he published his own primer, *Scientific Ball*, and he occasionally managed. Always a firebrand, he was temporarily expelled from the league during the 1890s for railing at the owners about their treatment of players. Later, he was a candidate to manage the New York Giants, a job he seemed happy not to win. "The lot of the manager there is not so rosy as in other places," he said. "If the team happens to be a winner the manager is the biggest manager in baseball, but if the team is a loser than the manager is condemned from the Battery to Harlem." In the meantime he continued as a player, and opened a popular Chicago bar, Pfeffer's Theater Court Buffet. He died in 1932 at the age of seventy-two.

No member of the Globe Trotters Club has had a more enduring influence on the game of baseball, at least as it is played today, than Ned Hanlon. After the failure of the Players' League, he signed on as player-manager of the National League's Pittsburgh franchise, but a lousy record and a knee injury soon washed him out of the game. He returned in 1892, this time in Baltimore, and there "Foxy Ned" proceeded to build one of baseball's great dynasties. The team's brainy, hyperaggressive (and quite often dirty) play was exemplified by Wee Willie Keeler, who famously quipped, "Hit 'em where they ain't." They did that, and also made unprecedented use of tactics such as the squeeze play, the sacrifice bunt, and the double-steal. Hanlon's Orioles won pennants in the three years from 1894 to 1896, and he captured another pair while at the helm of the National League's Brooklyn team from 1899 to 1900. In the process, Hanlon—a shrewd judge of talent, a capable political operator, and a solid businessman—established himself as a master of the strategic game-within-a-game known as "inside baseball." Hanlon's legacy was assured by the men who learned their craft at his side: John McGraw, Wilbert Robinson, Hughie Jennings, Miller Huggins, and Connie Mack all played for Hanlon. As skippers of, respectively, the New York Giants, Brooklyn Dodgers, Detroit Tigers, New York Yankees, and Philadelphia Athletics for much of the early twentieth century, these men transformed his practices into conventional wisdom, and disseminated his techniques of game and personnel management to generations of baseball leaders. All six, Hanlon included, have been inducted into the Baseball Hall of Fame. The eminent baseball historian and analyst Bill James has written, "Ned Hanlon is the great-grandfather of most modern major league managers."

John Ward's Players' League outlasted his marriage to Helen Dauvray. In January 1890, while he was still feverishly organizing the new circuit's plans, the two moved into separate quarters, his in Brooklyn, hers in Manhattan. In March, news of their separation broke in the papers, the split being attributed to her desire to return to the stage. This she denied, saying, "I go back to the stage because I am separated from my husband. I am not separated from my husband because I want to go back to the stage; there is a vast difference between the two." The vast difference was the future Maxine Elliot, with whom Ward was still entangled. Eventually their affair ended, but the demise of the Ward-Dauvray marriage became something of a spectacle, and she sued for a formal divorce in 1893.

Upon the failure of the Players' League, a chastened Ward returned to Spalding's National League, playing two years each for its Brooklyn and New York franchises before calling it quits and entering law practice full-time. His interest in the game remained strong, however, and he counted several ballplayers as clients. By 1909 he was perceived, at least by some, to be one of the game's gray eminences, and was even considered as a possible president of the National League—an idea that would have been apocalyptically unthinkable twenty years earlier. (His candidacy was derailed by Ban Johnson, the American League president, with whom Ward had tussled as a lawyer.) Ward became involved with another upstart circuit, the short-lived Federal League, serving as business manager for its Brooklyn franchise in 1914. Meanwhile, golf was replacing baseball as his primary avocation. He remarried in 1903, and in subsequent years seemed to spend an increasing amount of time on the links, often playing tournaments, and often coming in first. He died in 1925, at the age of sixty-five, in Augusta, Georgia—the future home of the Masters Tournament.

—————————

The world tour stands as a fulcrum in Adrian Anson's career, the point of both his greatest fame and the pinnacle from which he would begin a long, inexorable fall. Spalding was generous about sharing the spotlight, at least when doing so was in his interest, and he was happy to have the great captain—*his* captain—share in the glory bestowed by a proud nation upon the tour's return home. But the good feelings engendered by the trip soon dissipated. The tour lost money, and $1,500 of it was Anson's; he would forever resent that Spalding held him to it, despite the fact that it was Spalding who had chosen to extend the trip around the world (and thus pile up more expenses), and it was Spalding's business that would profit from the contacts generated overseas.

But a worse rub came in 1891, when Spalding chose to formally remove himself from the day-to-day operation of the Chicago club. Anson
had always envisioned himself as Spalding's successor, and was indig-
nant when he learned that this post would go to a man for whom he had
a well-known distaste: James Hart. Their acrimony could be traced right
back to the tour, when Anson had refused, publicly, to contribute to the
purchase of a pair of diamond cufflinks for Hart, a token of appreciation for his work on all of the tourists' behalf. Now Hart was his boss,
and the two did not get along, a problem compounded by the decline of
the team.

Ever the firebrand, Anson seemed to become more and more demanding every year. In 1897 he finally snapped, berating his team as a bunch of
loafing drunkards in the *Chicago Inter Ocean*. That was it. His contract
was up for renewal at the end of the year, and it was clear that Hart
would not be asking him back. Instead, Anson begged the retired Spalding to help him put together the capital to purchase controlling stock in
the club. The public was squarely behind Anson (the team, by most
counts, was in fact a bunch of loafing drunkards), but Spalding must
have thought the prospect ridiculous, and parried. Later, he offered to
put together a fifty-thousand-dollar honorarium (an astronomical sum
at the time) for Anson as a kind of pension payment. But Anson was too
proud to accept the offer. Instead, he walked away from the game, taking
with him his 3,418 hits and .333 career average in the major leagues. No
one had ever done better.

In the following years, Anson drifted in and out of baseball, taking on
various managerial and administrative positions, but not staying anywhere for long. He served briefly as clerk of the city of Chicago. His businesses failed. He went bankrupt. Another attempt was made—by John
Tener, his old Chicago charge and fellow tourist—to provide him with
some kind of pension from baseball. Anson turned that down, too.

In the meantime, he had taken to the stage; for a man who had always
enjoyed the roar—if not the approval—of a crowd, it was a natural fit.
(The vaudeville circuit was a useful moneymaker for many an athlete, a
handy way to capitalize on their personal fame during off-seasons and in
retirement.) Anson had made his theatrical debut in the late 1880s with a

brief appearance in *A Parlor Match*, at the Theatre Comique in Harlem. That role consisted primarily of being kicked in the rear end—not the most dignified of parts, but one that got a big laugh. In any case, he had caught the acting bug, and in 1895 he landed on Broadway in a production designed to take advantage of his celebrity. The vehicle, *A Runaway Colt*, was a comic farce in which Anson, playing himself, led a young pitching phenom, Manley Manners, through various trials and tribulations. Reviews were mixed, though Anson's notices were fair enough for him to proclaim himself, on the letterhead of his stationery, "A better actor than any ballplayer. A better ballplayer than any actor." Over the years he would repeatedly return to the stage. George M. Cohan wrote a monologue for him in 1914. Two years later he hit the road with *Aid to Father*, a one-act comedy penned for him—at no charge—by Ring Lardner. (If his shows failed, he could hardly complain of subpar writers.) The highlight came when Anson's daughters lobbed papier-mâché baseballs to the self-professed "Grand Old Man of Baseball," and he knocked them into the audience with a silver bat. After running into the songsmith Jack Norworth in Baltimore, they added "Take Me Out to the Ballgame" to the show. In New York it had a nice run at Proctor's Fifth Avenue Theatre, and in Chicago at the Palace and then the Majestic.

However popular Anson's shows may have been, he was all but broke when he died, at age sixty-nine, in 1922. His only request was that his epitaph read "Here lies a man that batted .300"—a rare Anson understatement. Of the old gang, only Fred Pfeffer made it to the funeral. The nation, however, mourned the loss of one of baseball's foundational heroes. "The secret of Anson's greatness was not only due to his great skill and rugged integrity but also to the fact that he loved the game with an intensity that the long caravan of years could never weaken," wrote Grantland Rice, the legendary sports columnist, in his elegiac obituary. "He fought for the love of fighting and he played for the love of his profession, where a base hit meant more than a week's pay."

Having orchestrated the downfall of the Players' League, Spalding was left with one more competitor to vanquish: the American Association. As always, his first impulse was to consolidate, and in fact the National League had already begun that process, having taken (or stolen, depending on one's perspective) the association's profitable Brooklyn and Cincinnati franchises to gird itself for the fight with the players in 1890. Spalding had long been a proponent for the merger of the two circuits—just so long as it was the American Association that was to be merged into his National League and not the other way around. In the aftermath of the Players' League collapse, he saw that dream become a reality. As with the Players' League's downfall, the American Association's demise would be the product of weak leadership and the increasing willingness of a great many parties to place their own interests above that of their combination. The American Association held out for one last season, 1891, before it was collapsed into a reformed twelve-team National League.

With the dissolution came the satisfying fall of Spalding's old nemesis, St. Louis Browns owner Chris Von der Ahe. After so many years of playing the fool in the press, "Der Boss" had a serious credibility problem, and he did himself few favors by micromanaging his able team captain, Charlie Comiskey. In the free-for-all that followed the 1890 season, Von der Ahe saw a mass exodus of American Association players to Spalding's National League, and decided to take matters into his own hands. Showing typically poor judgment, he had the former world tourist Mark Baldwin, who had been recruiting for the National League's Pittsburgh franchise, yanked from a St. Louis pool room and tossed in jail on a conspiracy charge. Baldwin got revenge by winning a $2,500 settlement against Von der Ahe in court. Pittsburgh owner W. A. Nimick then retaliated by having detectives kidnap Von der Ahe back to Pennsylvania, where *he* was tossed in the clink. Meanwhile, the Browns were fast becoming a perennial National League laughingstock. Der Boss, broke and embarrassed by a public divorce, was forced into a series of stunts—a roller-coaster in the outfield being one—to attract crowds that his players alone could not. He died in 1913; by that time, the club had long since slipped from his possession and had even adopted a new name, the Cardinals.

With the National League now on solid footing, and with his own club turned over to James Hart, Spalding could finally retire from the game. But he would always be hovering in the distance, ready to step in to protect the league he had done so much to found—or at least to protect his own interests in it. That time came in the late 1890s, with the appearance of a new challenger to the National League's dominance. Ban Johnson, president of the Western League, had all of Spalding's ambition and every intention to transform his minor league circuit into a major league, the American League. What's more, he was fully possessed of the centralized authority that had been so lacking in Ward's Players' League and Von der Ahe's American Association.

Spalding's response to this upstart was to fall back on his tried-and-true business strategy—consolidation—but this time with an added twist: Not only should the National League absorb its opponent, Spalding suggested, but the reformed league's various clubs should be collapsed into a single corporation. If the plan seemed novel, it wasn't. This was an era of trusts and monopolies in many branches of industry, and Spalding had recently used the technique to bolster his bicycle business, this in response to intense competition that was eating away at the Spalding company's profits in this sector. Spalding in 1899 organized a massive trust, the American Bicycle Company, which combined more than forty manufacturers into a single $22 million conglomerate. (This trust broke up after two years largely because of a declining interest in bicycling, then something of a fad sport.)

Spalding failed to get his baseball trust off the ground, but the idea was adopted, much to his chagrin, by his old antagonist John Brush, now at the helm of the National League's Cincinnati franchise, and Andrew Freedman, the much-reviled owner of the New York Giants. They sprang their "syndicate" plan on the league at its winter meetings in 1901. Spalding responded by pronouncing himself appalled at the very idea of such a proposal, despite the fact that he had introduced it in the first place. "Think of a trust in baseball," he claimed in the press. "Is it all commercialism? Is there no more of the glorious sentiment attached to our sport?" What he no doubt found most appalling about the scheme was that it called for the New York franchise to be assigned 30 percent of the stock in the new business while his Chicago club would garner only 10 percent. That wouldn't do. Several days of bickering between the camps ensued, a situation that reached a level of absurdity when Spalding, after a bit of parliamentary gamesmanship, absconded with the league books. So ended "syndicalism."

When the National and American Leagues reached a mutually beneficial detente in the years following the turn of the century, Spalding was left with but one final challenge to round out his baseball career: to establish once and for all the American patrimony of the national game. His experience watching rounders in Liverpool left him certain that Chadwick's theory about the game's origin was wrong. "I am satisfied that baseball has no connection with rounders whatever," he had written in his *Cosmopolitan* article in 1889. "It is no more like that game than battledoor and shuttlecock are like rackets and lawn tennis." In the years following, Spalding became ever more militant on the subject, insisting that the sport had evolved from a series of bat-and-ball games developed on native soil and that it was American through and through. But Chadwick's authority was a problem, and so in 1904 Spalding felt compelled to establish a committee to determine, once and for all, the game's origins.

It was this committee to whom one Abner Graves, late of Denver, sent a pair of letters in which he claimed to have been in attendance back in 1839, when Abner Doubleday sketched baseball's first diamond in front of a Cooperstown, New York, tailor shop. Spalding pounced on the news: Here was a genuine American hero (Doubleday, a Union general during the Civil War, fired the first shots on Fort Sumter) with whom he could align his sport, never mind that the story seemed implausible. Indeed, Graves was an occasional lunatic (he was put in asylum on at least three occasions) and frequent fabulist (among his false claims was that he had ridden for the Pony Express). In 1924, then well into his eighties, he shot to death his forty-eight-year-old wife.

To contemporary historians, and Chadwick in particular, the immaculate conception scenario suggested by Graves and endorsed by Spalding's commission was patently absurd. "Spalding must realize that the rounder argument overwhelms the ridiculous fraud of Mr. Graves and the findings of the commission which are inherently flawed," Chadwick wrote to a friend. "It seems 'Young Albert' is overzealous in his patriotism to a fault. Indeed, baseball is a truly American Game—but it evolved." Ward, had he still been engaged in the debate, might have noted that Oliver Wendell Holmes had spoken of playing the game as a college student at Harvard in the 1820s. Spalding, however, was no longer interested in such complications. The Doubleday story suited his needs, and he had the stature and the power to make it law. And so the myth that baseball was created on a Cooperstown street in 1839 became received wisdom, and historians have been fighting an uphill battle to correct the record ever since.

The great irony in this situation is that all of the theories floating around at the turn of the century were wrong. Baseball was not invented by Abner Doubleday in Cooperstown, it is not the finished product of in-digenous American ball games, and it is not derived from rounders. Re-cent scholarship suggests that the American pastime evolved from an English children's game known as, of all things, *base ball*. The first ap-pearance of that term can be found in a book of children's pastimes, *A Little Pretty Pocket-Book*, published in England in 1744. In it, beneath an illustration of three boys at play, a verse describes an embryonic version of the pastime Americans consider their own:

> The Ball once struck off,
> Away flies the Boy
> To the next destin'd Post,
> And then Home with Joy.

That game arrived on American shores in the eighteenth century, and was here adapted into the sport we know today. (The first recorded use of the term *base ball* in the United States was in a 1791 ordinance that pro-hibited ballplaying within striking distance of the windows of the new town hall in Pittsfield, Massachusetts.) Curiously, it appears that rounders is simply a regional variant of this sport.

———

It is difficult not to read Spalding's obsession with the game's patrimony as a manifestation of his own orphanhood. Fatherless himself, he had always been drawn to figures of surrogate male authority. Harry Wright and William Hulbert served this role earlier in his career. Now it was Abner Doubleday, another revered American, who appeared as a most perfect vessel for Spalding's needs. That the evidence for Doubleday as baseball's "father" was so obviously flawed only reinforced the perception within the game that it was Spalding himself—the man so clearly behind the curtain—who was baseball's ultimate creative power.

An additional factor that may have disposed Spalding to the Graves story was his knowledge that Doubleday was an ardent believer in Theosophy, the quasi-occult religion established in 1875 by Madame Helen Blavatsky. Spalding had his own connection to that group. In 1900, barely two years after the death of his first wife, Josie, he married Elizabeth Churchill Mayer, a committed Theosophist in her own right. The two moved from Chicago to Point Loma, a San Diego suburb, where the group's chief American prophet, Katharine Tingley—known as the "Purple Mother"—had established a compound.

Spalding and Mayer had known each other in Rockford as young adults, and had been carrying on an affair for years, perhaps since as far back as 1888, when Spalding departed on his world tour. In 1892 they had a child together, Spalding Brown Spalding, who was sent off to live with Albert's sister, Mary. After Josie's death, Albert formally adopted his son, who was rechristened Albert Spalding, Jr. (Walter Spalding also named his first son after his famous older brother, the confusing result being a family with three Albert Spaldings).

The newly married couple constructed a massive and wildly idiosyncratic home for themselves at "Lomaland." If nothing else, it was unique: a whitewashed single-story octagon (the shape had Theosophical meaning) with a wraparound veranda, a fanciful external staircase, and an amethyst-colored dome surmounted by a spherical lantern. Inside, Albert's baseball treasures could hardly compete with the ornate symbolist carvings of the sculptor Reginald Machell. Every inch of the house, it seems, was a reflection of Theosophy's obscure teachings, which claimed the "essential oneness" of all things and a belief in reincarnation. These concepts were laid out by Blavatsky in a pair of immense and inscrutable treatises, *Isis Unveiled* (1877) and *The Secret Doctrine* (1888).

It is, perhaps, difficult to reconcile Albert Spalding, the Machiavellian sporting-goods magnate and champion of American values, with the man who allowed himself to become intimately involved with a barmy camp of spiritualist eccentrics. Love can do funny things. That Spalding went along with the whole thing more out of a desire to make his wife happy than out of any real commitment to Theosophical ideas seems clear from an interview he gave to the *Chicago Tribune* in 1903. "I'm sure that I am in sympathy with work done in this society," he told the paper, before adding, "I am not, however, so ardent a Theosophist as Mrs. Spalding," and that he was "perfectly willing to stand for it." In any case, he was "having a good time every week in the year" at Point Loma. Though the "good time" seemed more a product of hours spent on the private nine-hole golf course he had constructed for himself than any engagement with Helen Blavatsky's abstruse writings.

Despite its odd trappings, Theosophy was the perfect religion for Spalding, as it was the creation of a personality much like himself— a brazen and charismatic visionary known to bend the truth to suit her needs. For all of her adherents, Helen Blavatsky had no shortage of detractors, and none more diligent than Neville Maskelyne, an English crusader for the public good whose primary claim to fame was the invention of the pay toilet. Having provided that service, in 1913 he published *The Fraud of Modern 'Theosophy,' Exposed*, a withering attack in which he depicted Blavatsky as a phony of the worst sort. No doubt Spalding saw things differently. In an era bent on progress and progressiveness, Blavatsky's synthesis of religion, science, and philosophy, however convoluted, had the appeal of the new.

And when push came to shove, Spalding was willing to put his name on the line for the society. In 1902, eleven Cuban children en route from Santiago de Cuba to San Diego in order to attend Lomaland's Raja-Yoga Academy were detained in New York on the grounds that their welfare would be endangered if they fell into the hands of the Theosophists. The fate of the children became a cause célèbre—a situation with more than a few parallels to the Elian Gonzalez uproar of 2000. Spalding stepped in on behalf of the academy, using all of his personal and political clout to defend the school from a variety of slanderous accusations and to ensure that the children arrived safely at their destination.

By the turn of the century, Spalding's reputation was so strong that it could hardly be tainted by his association with Theosophy. In San Diego, he became a civic booster and advocate of road building. In 1910, he was recruited to run for the U.S. Senate as a Republican, but he was defeated in the primary, despite the fact that he had won the majority of California counties. He might well have won had he not run an equivocal and reluctant campaign. His heart just didn't seem to be in it. He was always more interested in baseball, his first love, and in 1911 he published his ode to it, *America's National Game*, a history that conflated his own personal saga with the rise of the sport. Actually, Spalding had originally commissioned Henry Chadwick to write the book, and gave him explicit directions as to just what it should and should not include. (He asked Chadwick to supply copies of the text as he wrote, for approval.) Eventually Spalding appropriated the project as his own vehicle, yet again upstaging one of the game's patriarchal figures. He had long imagined himself as one of history's great men. It was only natural that he would try to fix his own place in that pantheon.

When the book was finally complete he sent out copies to virtually everyone of any importance whom he had met. President Taft received a copy, as did New York Mayor William J. Gaynor. Pierre de Coubertin wrote from his office at the International Olympic Committee in Paris that he was "gratified indeed" to receive his copy. John Ward sent a note of thanks from his New York law office. "I received the book and am greatly indebted to you for the remembrance," he wrote. "I am sure it will be a valuable contribution to the history and literature of the game."

───⋅∘⋅───

When Albert Spalding died of a stroke on September 9, 1915, newspapers across the country eulogized the man the *New York Times* called the "father of baseball." In a final twist, he had posthumously assumed Chadwick's sobriquet. His lifelong campaign to promote himself as the benevolent patriarch of American sport had been won, his many battles and transgressions all but forgotten. Even the *Sporting News* was effusive in its praise. Indeed, no publication was more effusive. "Spalding Enters Games Valhalla" was the headline to its obituary; beneath the bold type it wrote:

> Mortals could ask no more of the gods than they granted Albert Spalding. . . . Strong physically and mentally, sensing and grasping opportunity when it came to him, he built for the world as much as for himself, took only his fair share of what his talents amassed and was satisfied and content to enjoy it, rather than strain and scramble in blind greed for more. . . . Baseball is proud to claim such a man as its own and points to him as an example of the real manhood that it enlists and develops.

If Spalding's passing called for a moment of national reflection and reverence, at least among baseball fans, the settlement of his estate proved an ugly fight. He left one hundred thousand dollars to each of his sons and the balance of his fortune to his wife. Keith Spalding contested the will, claiming his Theosophist stepmother had unduly influenced his father in his final years. Walter Spalding also sued, but on behalf of the estate of Albert Spalding, Jr., his brother's son with Elizabeth Mayer. The youngest Spalding would show some of his father's nerve. At the outbreak of World War I, he enlisted in the British army, and his gallantry in action led to his swift promotion from private to lieutenant. He was killed, on July 1, 1916, in the Battle of the Somme. (Spalding's other namesake, Walter's son, achieved considerable fame in his own right as America's preeminent concert violinist of the early twentieth century.) In the end, a settlement was reached that more equally divided the fortune. The Theosophists wound up with none of it. In fact, it turned out that Spalding had never been much of a financial supporter of the group. "I want you, wherever you can, to knock the statement into smithereens that Mr. Spalding was a great benefactor to this institution," Katharine Tingley wrote. "We have been looking over the books, and we find that in the fifteen years he lived here, he did not donate, on the average, over two hundred dollars a year." The situation was actually much worse than that. When Elizabeth Spalding died in 1926, her estate held a mortgage

on the Point Loma property. In a final reversal, the society owed her heirs
some four hundred thousand dollars.

———◦◦◦———

In his victorious 1888 presidential campaign, Benjamin Harrison called
America "an apart nation." That exceptionalism, which looked back to
the admonitions of the Founding Fathers, masked a certain ambivalence
as to the country's appropriate role in an ever-shrinking world. Though
Americans of the late nineteenth century were rightfully proud of their
burgeoning economic strength and mindful of their regional preroga-
tives, they were nonetheless concerned about the consequences of engagement, military or diplomatic, beyond native shores. Spalding's tour
allowed them to have things both ways, to proudly wave the flag abroad
without taking on any uncomfortable obligations.

Spalding's tour also allowed the world, or at least select parts of it, to
see the United States for what it was, for baseball was being sold without
apology as a reflection of American values. Ungenerous observers could
point to the unrepentant commercialism and cultural vulgarity of the
traveling ballplayers (to say nothing of their bigotry and labor problems)
as reasons for concern about America's growing international power. But
for Albert Spalding the values promoted by the American pastime—fair
play, teamwork, fortitude, ambition, opportunity, optimism—were nothing but positive. Indeed, the moment seemed to belong to America and
its modern game, as if the two were the logical products of a scientific
historical progression akin to natural selection. John Fiske, one of the
era's most prominent public intellectuals and an advocate of Darwin's
theory of evolution, asserted that from "pole to pole" nations would
soon be transforming themselves in America's image. In 1888, the same
year Spalding and his men departed on their trip, the British aristocrat
and historian James Bryce published a magisterial three-volume survey,
The American Commonwealth, in which he wrote, "The institutions of
the United States, are something more than an experiment, for they are
believed to disclose and display the type of institutions towards which, as
if by a law of fate, the rest of civilized mankind are forced to move, some
with swifter, others with slower, but all with unresting feet."

Bryce may not have considered baseball to be one of America's principal institutions—the Constitution, the presidency, the legislature, and the judiciary were more what he had in mind—but for many Americans baseball was the American institution par excellence, and Albert Spalding had every intention of ensuring that it remain one. His entire professional life was devoted to this cause, and his great world tour was a part of that enduring campaign. In the process, and not by accident, Spalding's personal history and private interests became inextricably conflated with the larger history of the sport he championed. It was a winning strategy, and one that made him an American institution in his own right.

The career Spalding built for himself was an undeniable success. As a ballplayer and team owner he was a champion many times over. The National League he did so much to build—though perhaps not as much as he would have liked the world to believe—is still thriving. The sporting-goods business he founded in 1876 lives on and still carries his name. (It has changed hands several times since his death, most recently in 2003, when it was sold to the Russell Corporation for $65 million.) His was a quintessentially American story, and not just because it was built on the American game. Even if he had a bit of help from family, Spalding's success was self-made, a product of innate ability, savvy, hubris, and an absolute determination for achievement.

Gauging the success of the world tour is an altogether more difficult project. From a financial standpoint it was not a triumph—it ran considerable losses—but profit was not its primary objective and was never really expected, despite Spalding's initial assurances. And whatever his ideas may have been about the correct course of action for addressing the National League's labor issues, there can be no doubt that absenting himself and Brotherhood leader John Ward from the United States during the 1888–89 off-season backfired. The tour did, however, have some positive impact on Spalding's business: Over the course of the trip Spalding established distributors for his sporting goods in Honolulu, Auckland, Sydney, Melbourne, and Adelaide. European markets soon followed.

More than anything, the tour was a promotional event, and its influence is best understood within the broader context of the subjects it advertised.

Spalding's own businesses were, as ever, the primary beneficiaries of his efforts, and they clearly did not suffer from the tour. If the trip did not quite get off on the right foot, at least according to the *Sporting News*, by the time of its return to the United States even that publication was writing of the adventure in positive terms. More important, it was writing about the adventure—and that was really the whole point: staying in the news. To be celebrated by the likes of Mark Twain and Theodore Roosevelt and Benjamin Harrison—well, that was just icing on a Delmonico's cake.

If Spalding and his men stand as a most unlikely combination of cultural diplomats, they nevertheless helped pave the way for a not-too-distant future when American forms of entertainment, movies in particular, would dominate world markets. Still, baseball did not turn out to be one of the more popular American exports—at least in Europe—and Spalding could look to his own actions for at least a partial explanation as to why. Spalding's success in so identifying the game with America and American values was something of a double-edged sword. Although the strategy most certainly solidified the game's stature in the United States, it had the effect of discouraging other nations, patriotic in their own right, from taking it on and adopting it as their own. That Spalding's athletes seemed so brilliantly skilled didn't help matters either, as they left the dispiriting impression that the game was so difficult that any attempt to challenge American superiority, honed over generations, would be forever hopeless. (In England, even W. G. Grace, the greatest of cricketers, could not compete.) Instead, it was soccer, like baseball a "modern" game attractive to a working-class demographic, a game that is relatively easy to play, that was able to shed its associations with the country in which it was born—England—and become the presumptive international sport of choice.

Today, as Americans once again find themselves struggling with their nation's role and image on the world stage, baseball's status as an international sport is at something of a crossroads. The game's popularity is growing rapidly in Eastern Europe, and it has a place at or near the top of the sports pyramid in much of East Asia. Latin America has practically surpassed the United States as the sport's hotbed, producing an ever-rising proportion of professional players, including recent Most Valuable Players in both the American and National leagues. In 2005, Hawaii's Ewa Beach team won the Little League World Series.

Despite its global popularity, a 2005 decision by the International Olympic Committee removed baseball (and its sister, women's softball) from the roll of sanctioned sports. That vote bears the ugly taint of anti-American politics, though it is also true that the Olympics have always presented something of a problem for baseball's American promoters. Mandatory amateurism and summer scheduling that conflicts with the professional baseball season have, in the past, prevented baseball's top players from participating. Bypassing the Olympics, in spring 2006 Major League Baseball sponsored a sixteen-team international tournament that featured many of its greatest stars playing for their home countries. Tour stops Australia and Italy entered teams.

It is worth remembering that Spalding had proposed just such a competition back in his 1889 *Cosmopolitan* article. More than a century later, that dream has finally come to fruition. Better still, today's athletes can still play the game with equipment—bats, balls, gloves, and more—produced by the firm he founded in 1876.

In October of 2005 a Chicago baseball club known as the White Stockings took home the Major League crown for the first time in eighty-eight years. Those White Sox were not Albert Spalding's White Stockings. His team saw its name change several times in the late nineteenth century, and today exists as the National League's long-suffering Cubs. But one suspects that if Spalding were alive today he would have been pleased with the victory for his hometown. And that he would have taken a bit of credit for himself, too.

☙ APPENDIX I ❧
THE SPALDING TOURISTS

ALBERT G. SPALDING, *president*
LEIGH S. LYNCH, *general manager*
CLARENCE DUVAL, *mascot*

The Teams

Lineups are presented in typical batting order.

CHICAGO

Jimmy Ryan, *center field*
Robert Pettit, *right field*
Marty Sullivan, *left field*
Adrian Anson, *first base*
  (team captain)
Fred Pfeffer, *second base*
Ned Williamson, *shortstop*
Tom Burns, *third base*
Tom Daly, *catcher*
Mark Baldwin, *pitcher*
John Tener, *reserve pitcher*

ALL-AMERICA
(home clubs in parentheses)

Ned Hanlon, *center field* (Detroit)
George Wood, *first base*
  (Philadelphia)
John M. Ward, *shortstop*
  (New York; team captain)
Fred Carroll, *left field* (Pittsburgh)
James Fogarty, *right field*
  (Philadelphia)
James Manning, *second base*
  (Kansas City)
Tom Brown, *third base* (Boston)
Billy Earle, *catcher* (St. Paul)
Ed Crane, *pitcher* (New York)
John Healy, *reserve pitcher*
  (Indianapolis)

FELLOW TRAVELERS

Ed Hengle, *catcher* (Chicago)♦
Frank "Silver" *Flint*, catcher
(Chicago)♦
Hermann Long, *shortstop*
(Kansas City)♦
George Van Haltren, *pitcher*
(Chicago)♦

George Wright, *coach*
Professor C. Bartholomew,
aerialist
Frank Lincoln, *comedian**

James Hart, *management*♦
Harry Simpson, *management**
Will Lynch, *management**

Simon Goodfriend, *journalist*
Newton MacMillan, *journalist*
Harry Palmer, *journalist*

Harriet Spalding, *mother of
Albert Spalding*

Josie Spalding, *wife of
Albert Spalding**
Keith Spalding, *son of
Albert Spalding**
William Pereiera, *servant of
Albert Spalding**
Maid of Josie Spalding*
Henry Anson, *father of
Adrian Anson*♦
Virginia Anson, *wife of
Adrian Anson*
Nellie Williamson, *wife of
Ned Williamson*
Anna Berger Lynch, *wife of
Leigh Lynch*
Helen Dauvray, *wife of
John Ward*♦
Irving Snyder, *tourist*
Leslie Robison, *tourist*

♦American leg only
*To Australia only
*Joined tour abroad

≈ APPENDIX II ≈
GAME RESULTS
OF THE TOUR

ALL-AMERICA VS. CHICAGO

Game 1
20 October 1888
City: Chicago
Venue: West Side Park
Score: 11–6 Chicago
Series: All-America 0, Chicago 1

Game 2
21 October 1888
City: St. Paul
Venue: Athletic Park
Score: 9–2 Chicago
Series: All-America 0, Chicago 2

Game 3
22 October 1888
City: Minneapolis
Score: 6–3 All-America
Series: All-America 1, Chicago 2

Game 4
23 October 1888
City: Cedar Rapids
Score: 6–5 Chicago
Series: All-America 1, Chicago 3

Game 5
24 October 1888
City: Des Moines
Score: 3–2 All-America
Series: All-America 2, Chicago 3

Game 6
25 October 1888
City: Omaha
Score: 12–2 All-America
Series: All-America 3, Chicago 3

Game 7
26 October 1888
City: Hastings
Score: 8–4 Chicago
Series: All-America 3, Chicago 4

Game 8
27 October 1888
City: Denver
Venue: River Front Park
Score: 16–12 Chicago
Series: All-America 3, Chicago 5

Game 9
28 October 1888
City: Denver
Venue: River Front Park
Score: 9–8 All-America
Series: All-America 4, Chicago 5

Game 10
29 October 1888
City: Colorado Springs
Venue: Colorado College
Score: 13–9 Chicago
Series: All-America 4, Chicago 6

Game 11
31 October 1888
City: Salt Lake City
Score: 9–3 All-America
Series: All-America 5, Chicago 6

Game 12
1 November 1888
City: Salt Lake City
Score: 10–3 All-America
Series: All-America 6, Chicago 6

Game 13
4 November 1888
City: San Francisco
Venue: Haight Street Grounds
Score: 14–4 All-America
Series: All-America 7, Chicago 6

Game 14
11 November 1888
City: San Francisco
Venue: Haight Street Grounds
Score: 9–6 All-America
Series: All-America 8, Chicago 6

Game 15.
14 November 1888
City: Los Angeles
Venue: Prospect Park
Score: 5–0 Chicago
Series: All-America 8, Chicago 7

Game 16
15 November 1888
City: Los Angeles
Venue: Prospect Park
Score: 7–4 All-America
Series: All-America 9, Chicago 7

Game 17
10 December 1888
City: Auckland, New Zealand
Venue: Potter's Paddock
Score: 22–13 Chicago
Series: All-America 9, Chicago 8

Game 18
15 December 1888
City: Sydney, Australia
Venue: Sydney Cricket Association
Score: 5–4 All-America
Series: All-America 10, Chicago 8

Game 19
17 December 1888
City: Sydney
Venue: Sydney Cricket Association
Score: 7–5 All-America
Series: All-America 11, Chicago 8

Game 20
18 December 1888
City: Sydney
Venue: Sydney Cricket Association
Score: 6–2 All-America
Series: All-America 12, Chicago 8

Game 21
22 December 1888
City: Melbourne
Venue: Melbourne Cricket Ground
Score: 5–3 Chicago
Series: All-America 12, Chicago 9

Game 22
24 December 1888
City: Melbourne
Venue: Melbourne Cricket Ground
Score: 15–13 All-America
Series: All-America 13, Chicago 9

Game 23
26 December 1888
City: Adelaide
Venue: Adelaide Oval
Score: 19–14 All-America
Series: All-America 14, Chicago 9

Game 24
27 December 1888
City: Adelaide
Venue: Adelaide Oval
Score: 12–9 Chicago
Series: All-America 14, Chicago 10

Game 25
28 December 1888
City: Adelaide
Venue: Adelaide Oval
Score: 11–4 Chicago
Series: All-America 14, Chicago 11

Game 26
29 December 1888
City: Ballarat
Venue: Eastern Oval
Score: 11–7 All-America
Series: All-America 15, Chicago 11

Game 27
1 January 1889
City: Melbourne
Venue: Melbourne Cricket Ground
Score: 14–7 Chicago
Series: All-America 15, Chicago 12

Game 28
5 January 1889
City: Melbourne
Venue: Melbourne Cricket Ground
Score: 5–0 Chicago
Series: All-America 15, Chicago 13

Game 29
26 January 1889
City: Colombo
Venue: Galle Face Green
Score: 3–3 (tie)
Series: All-America 15, Chicago 13, 1 tie

Game 30
9 February 1889
City: Cairo/Ghizeh
Score: 10–6 All-America
Series: All-America 16, Chicago 13, 1 tie

Game 31
19 February 1889
City: Naples
Venue: Campo di Marte
Score: 8–2 All-America
Series: All-America 17, Chicago 13, 1 tie

Game 32
23 February 1889
City: Rome
Venue: Villa Borghese (Piazza di Sienna)
Score: 3–2 Chicago
Series: All-America 17, Chicago 14, 1 tie

Game 33
25 February 1889
City: Florence
Venue: Cascine Park
Score: 7–4 All-America
Series: All-America 18, Chicago 14, 1 tie

Game 34
8 March 1889
City: Paris
Venue: Parc Aérostatique
Score: 6–2 All-America
Series: All-America 19, Chicago 14, 1 tie

Game 35
12 March 1889
City: London
Venue: Kennington Oval (Surrey Cricket Club)
Score: 7–4 Chicago
Series: All-America 19, Chicago 15, 1 tie

Game 36
12 March 1889
City: London
Venue: Lord's Cricket Ground
(Marylebone Cricket Club)
Score: 7–6 All-America
Series: All-America 20, Chicago 15, 1 tie

Game 37
14 March 1889
City: London (Sydenham)
Venue: Crystal Palace Cricket Grounds
Score: 5–2 All-America
Series: All-America 21, Chicago 15, 1 tie

Game 38
14 March 1889
City: Bristol
Venue: Gloucester County Cricket Club
Score: 10–3 Chicago
Series: All-America 21, Chicago 16, 1 tie

Game 39
15 March 1889
City: Leighton
Venue: Essex County Cricket Club
Score: 12–6 Chicago
Series: All-America 21, Chicago 17, 1 tie

Game 40
18 March 1889
City: Birmingham
Venue: Edgbaston Grounds (Warwick-
shire Cricket Club)
Score: 4–4 (tie)
Series: All-America 21, Chicago 17, 2 ties

Game 41
19 March 1889
City: Sheffield
Venue: Bramball Lane Grounds
Score: 10–0 All-America
(4 innings—unofficial game)
Series: All-America 21, Chicago 17, 2 ties

Game 42
20 March 1889
City: Bradford-Leeds
Venue: Bradford Cricket Club Grounds
Score: 6–3 Chicago
Series: All-America 21, Chicago 18, 2 ties

Game 43
21 March 1889
City: Glasgow
Venue: West of Scotland Cricket Club
Score: 8–4 All-America
Series: All-America 22, Chicago 18, 2 ties

Game 44
22 March 1889
City: Manchester
Venue: Old Trafford Cricket Grounds
Score: 7–6 All-America
Series: All-America 23, Chicago 18, 2 ties

Game 45
23 March 1889
City: Liverpool
Venue: Police Athletic Club Grounds
Score: 2–2 (tie)
Series: All-America 23, Chicago 18, 3 ties

Game 46
24 March 1889
City: Belfast
Venue: North of Ireland Cricket Club
Score: 9–8 All-America
Series: All-America 24, Chicago 18, 3 ties

Game 47
Date: 27 March 1889
City: Dublin
Venue: Landsdown Road Grounds
Score: 4–3 All-America
Series: All-America 25, Chicago 18, 3 ties

Game 48
8 April 1889
City: Brooklyn
Venue: Washington Park
Score: 7–6 All-America
Series: All-America 26, Chicago 18, 3 ties

Game 49
9 April 1889
City: Brooklyn
Venue: Washington Park
Score: 9–6 Chicago
Series: All-America 26, Chicago 19, 3 ties

Game 50
10 April 1889
City: Baltimore
Venue: Oriole Park
Score: 5–2 Chicago
Series: All-America 26, Chicago 20, 3 ties

Game 51
12 April 1889
City: Philadelphia
Venue: Philadelphia Baseball Grounds
Score: 6–4 Chicago
Series: All-America 26, Chicago 21, 3 ties

Game 52
13 April 1889
City: Boston
Venue: South End Grounds
Score: 10–3 All-America
Series: All-America 27, Chicago 21, 3 ties

Game 53
15 April 1889
City: Washington
Venue: Capitol Park
Score: 18–6 Chicago
Series: All-America 27, Chicago 22, 3 ties

Game 54
16 April 1889
City: Pittsburgh
Venue: Recreation Park
Score: 3–3 (tie)
Series: All-America 27, Chicago 22, 4 ties

Game 55
17 April 1889
City: Cleveland
Venue: National League Park
Score: 7–4 Chicago
Series: All-America 27, Chicago 23, 4 ties

Game 56
18 April 1889
City: Indianapolis
Venue: Seventh Street Park
Score: 9–5 All-America
Series: All-America 28, Chicago 23, 4 ties

Game 57
20 April 1889
City: Chicago
Venue: West Side Park
Score: 22–9 All-America
Series: All-America 29, Chicago 23, 4 ties

OTHER GAMES

Date: 21 October 1888
City: St. Paul
Venue: Athletic Park
Score: Chicago 5, St. Paul 8

Date: 22 October 1888
City: Minneapolis
Score: Chicago 1, St. Paul 0

Date: 6 November 1888
City: Oakland
Venue: Haight Street Grounds
Score: All-America 2, Greenhood &
Moran (Oakland) 8

Date: 8 November 1888
City: San Francisco
Score: All-America 4, Pioneers 9

Date: 8 November 1888
City: Stockton
Score: Chicago 2, Stockton 2
Date: 9 November 1888

City: San Francisco
Score: All-America 16, Stockton 1

Date: 10 November 1888
City: San Francisco
Score: Chicago 6, Haverly 1

Date: 17 December 1888
City: Sydney
Venue: Sydney Cricket Association
Score: All America 67, Chicago 33
(cricket)

Date: 17 December 1888
City: Sydney
Venue: Sydney Cricket Association
Score: Spalding Tourists 87, Australia
115 (cricket)

Date: 5 January 1889
City: Melbourne
Venue: Melbourne Cricket Ground
Score: All-America 20, Expats 3
(2 innings)

Date: 23 March 1889
City: Liverpool
Score: Spalding Tourists 14, Rounders
Association 16 (rounders, 2 innings)

Date: 23 March 1889
City: Liverpool
Score: Spalding Tourists 18, Rounders
Association 0 (baseball, 1 inning
incomplete)

☙ Notes ❧

Prologue

(page)

xiv   **Delmonico's:** Accounts from articles in the Spalding Scrapbooks, vols.
8–11, Spalding Collection, New York Public Library, and Harry Clay
Palmer et al., *Athletic Sports in America* (Boston: Hubbard Bros., 1889).
On Delmonico's, see Lately Thomas, *Delmonico's: A Century of Splendor*
(Boston: Houghton Mifflin, 1967), and Michael and Ariane Batterberry,
On the Town in New York (New York: Routledge, 1999).

xv   **"galaxy of stars":** A. G. Mills to Julian Curtis, 23 March 1889, Mills Papers, National Baseball Hall of Fame Library, Cooperstown, New York.

xv   **"It does my heart good. . . ":** Spalding's comments are a composite drawn
from several accounts in the Spalding Scrapbooks.

xvi   **"very symbol. . . ":** Paul Fatout, ed., *Mark Twain Speaking* (Iowa City:
Iowa, 1976), 244–47.

xvi   **the event's pompous air:** "Baseball at Delmonico's," *New York Times*, 9
April 1889.

xvii   **"Everything is possible. . . ":** Quoted in Peter Levine, *A. G. Spalding and
the Rise of Baseball* (New York: Oxford, 1985), xiv.

Chapter One

1   **History of nations:** Spalding, *America's National Game* (1911; reprint,
Lincoln: Nebraska, 1992), 199.

1   **no little plans:** The quote is generally attributed to Daniel Burnham, but it is unclear whether and when he actually stated it.

2   **"Who is Kenwood?":** Account of the meeting based on several reports in the Spalding Scrapbooks.

2   **The Chicago White Stockings:** Team names of the nineteenth century were informal and unstable. Most often, clubs were simply known by their city of origin: the Chicagos or the Bostons, for example. Those same teams might also sport nicknames derived from their uniform colors or some other defining characteristic. When the uniform changed, so might the name. Such was the case with Chicago's National League franchise, which was known as the White Stockings for much of the nineteenth century, but became the Black Stockings for the 1888 season. Most histories have simply referred to this team as the White Stockings, and for the sake of clarity and consistency this is how I refer to them here. This club survives today as the Chicago Cubs, a name the team acquired in the 1890s, when its roster was stocked with young and inexperienced players. Their cross-town rivals, the Chicago White Sox, adopted the name for its familiarity and storied history.

3   **"That inimitable boomer:"** Various newspaper clippings, Spalding Scrapbooks.

3   **a stickler:** "Spalding One of Baseball's Leaders," *New York Times*, 11 September 1915.

4   **the Spalding modus operandi:** On Spalding's personality and the events of his early life, I am greatly indebted to Peter Levine and his fine biography of Spalding.

5   **Spalding family:** Albert Goodwill Spalding, *America's National Game*; Albert Spalding, *Rise to Follow: An Autobiography* (New York: Henry Holt, 1943); Harriet Spalding, *Reminiscences* (East Orange: n.p., 1910); Levine, *Spalding*.

5   **homesickness:** Spalding, *America's National Game*, 510.

5   **"That ball came for me. . . ":** Ibid., 511.

7   **"I had a reputation. . . ":** Harriet Spalding, *Reminiscences*.

8   **"not favorably impressed":** Quoted in Albert Spalding, *Rise to Follow*, 15.

8   **life expectancy:** For statistics, see Society of American Historians, *Reader's Companion to American History* (Boston: Houghton Mifflin,

1991). Patent medicine ads appeared in nearly every issue of the *Sporting News* during the 1880s.

9   **"I suppose I looked. . . "**: Harriet Spalding, *Reminiscences*, 99.

9   **"Call it science. . . "**: Spalding, *America's National Game*, 118.

10   **a united cultural identity**: See Peter Morris, *Baseball Fever: Early Baseball in Michigan* (Ann Arbor: Michigan, 2003), 110–14. Morris also addresses the championship of the Northwest.

11   **Pioneers vs. the Mercantiles**: See Spalding, *America's National Game*, 117–18. I am indebted to John Molyneaux of the Rockford Public Library for alerting me to the discrepancies of Spalding's account.

11   **"Prince of Humbugs"**: Peter Levine made the connection between Spalding and Barnum. See *Spalding*, 9–10ff. On Barnum, see Neil Harris, *Humbug: The Art of P. T. Barnum* (Boston: Little Brown, 1973).

12   **"amusement and deceit. . . "**: Ibid, 62.

12   **ten-point plan**: Barnum, *The Life of P. T. Barnum, Written by Himself* (New York: Redfield, 1855).

13   **"Money getters. . . "**: Quoted in Harris, *Humbug*, 156.

14   **"I intend that. . . "**: Quoted in Spalding Scrapbooks.

15   **Nationals and Excelsiors**: See Stephen Fox, *Big Leagues: Professional Baseball, Football, and Basketball in National Memory* (New York: Morrow, 1994), 184–96; Morris, *Baseball Fever*, 171–74; Harold Seymour, *Baseball: The Early Years* (New York: Oxford, 1960), 54.

16   **Chicago-Rockford game**: Account from Spalding, *America's National Game*, 109–12. Chadwick quoted in Harry Palmer, *Stories of the Baseball Field* (New York: Rand McNally, 1890), 129–31.

17   **Knickerbocker Club**: Seymour, *Early Years*, 15.

17   **Article V**: *By-Laws and Rules of the Knickerbocker Base Ball Club* (New York: W. H. B. Smith: 1858), Swales Collection, New York Public Library.

17   **"dead letter"**: Spalding, *America's National Game*, 122.

17   **"I was not able. . . "**: Ibid., 123.

18   **With a budget**: Seymour, *Early Years*, 56–57.

18   **risqué uniforms**: See John Thorn, "Play's the Thing: The Color of Sport," *Woodstock Times*, 3 February 2005.

18   **Red Stocking's streak:** Game totals according to Greg Rhodes of the Cincinnati Reds Hall of Fame.

19   **"I was inclined to be obstinate. . . ":** Spalding, *America's National Game*, 141–43.

19   **National Association of Professional Base Ball Players:** See Seymour, *Early Years*, 75–85 and David Quentin Voigt, *American Baseball: From Gentleman's Sport to the Commisioner System* (Norman: Oklahoma, 1966), 35–59.

20   **Red Stockings stats:** Statistics via Retrosheet.org.

21   **"scenes of drunkenness and riot":** Spalding, *America's National Game*, 190.

21   **"I would rather be a lamp-post in Chicago. . . ":** Ibid., 207–8.

22   **"You're a Western Boy. . . ":** Ibid., 201–2. Details of Hulbert's recruitment of Spalding and of Spalding's secret contractual rider in Meeting Notes of the Chicago Baseball Association, 16 July 1875, Chicago Club file, Chicago Historical Society.

22   **Hulbert and the formation of the National League:** Seymour, *Early Years*, 75–85.

22   **Spalding's shifting claims:** Levine, *Spalding*, 24–26.

23   **A. G. Spalding & Bro. and Spalding's business career:** Levine, *Spalding*, 71–95.

24   **"No ballplayer, in my recollection. . . ":** Spalding, *America's National Game*, 143.

25   **Lakefront Park; West Side Park:** See Philip J. Lowry, *Green Cathedrals* (New York: Addison-Wesley, 1992), 127–29, and Steven A. Riess, *Touching Base: Professional Baseball and American Culture in the Progressive Era* (1983; revised, Chicago: Illinois, 1999), 100–104.

26   **"That ain't no shadow. . . ":** Quoted in Bill James, *The Baseball Book 990* (New York: Villard, 1990), 254. See also Adrian C. Anson, *A Ball Player's Career: Personal Experiences and Reminiscences* (Chicago: Era, 1900).

27   **"I never drank a lemonade. . . ":** Quoted in Spalding, *America's National Game*, 525.

27   **"For two years":** Quoted in story from the Spalding Scrapbooks.

28   **"It occurred to me. . . ":** Spalding, *America's National Game*, 175–76.

28   *Illustrated Sporting and Dramatic News*: For clips on the 1874 trip, see Spalding Scrapbooks, vol. 5.

29   "deep rooted prejudice of the English people. . . ": Anson, *Ball Player's Career*, 78.

29   The trip lost money: Voigt, *American Baseball*, 47–49, provides the best overview of the trip.

30   "I see great things. . . ": Quoted in John Thorn et al., *Total Baseball*, 6th ed. (New York: Total Sports, 1999), 499.

30   "Chicago was America's city": Donald L. Miller, *City of the Century: The Epic of Chicago and the Making of America* (New York: Simon & Schuster, 1996), 188.

31   prestigious new neighborhood: On Kenwood, see Jean F. Block, *Hyde Park Houses: An Informal History, 1856–1910* (Chicago: Chicago, 1978).

Chapter Two

33   "I prefer to assume. . . ": "Spalding's Surprise," *Chicago Herald* (n.d.), Spalding Scrapbooks.

33   "The prospects. . . ": Anson, *Ball Player's Career*, 141.

35   Anson's $3,750 stake: Ibid., illustration opposite p. 283. On Anson's failed business, see James, *Baseball Book 1990*, 247–56.

35   "In my judgement. . . ": Quoted in Harry Palmer, "To Australia," *Sporting Life*, 28 March 1888.

36   the Lynch family: See Betsy G. Miller, "Anna Teresa Berger, Cornet Virtuoso," *ITG Journal*, February 1998, 43–49.

36   "demoralizing to discipline": Spalding, *America's National Game*, 515.

37   "Is the Ball Player a Chattel?": Reprinted in Sullivan, *Documentary History of Baseball*, 162–73.

37   "It was understood between us. . . ": Spalding, *America's National Game*, 517.

38   Clarkson was a notorious grouch: On Clarkson, see Ivor-Campbell et al., *Baseball's First Stars*, 31–32.

38   "overdid the matter a trifle": Spalding, *America's National Game*, 518.

38   "I have not thought of it": Quoted in "Chicago Gossip," *Sporting Life*, 22
       August 1888.

38   "In the name of decency. . . ": Ibid., 29 August 1888.

40   "I know the lady. . . ": Quoted in "He Said Anson's Men Flirted," *Sporting
       Life*, 22 September 1888.

40   "The securing of teams for this voyage. . . ": Spalding, *America's National
       Game*, 252.

40   "No Australia trip for me": Quoted in the *Sporting Times*, n.d., Spalding
       Scrapbooks.

41   "Much to my surprise. . . ": O. P. Caylor, *Sporting Life*, 19 September
       1888.

42   "giving up drink": "Kelly to Give Up Drink," *Sporting News*, 21 July 1888;
       "Mike Kelly Leaves the Boston Club in a Hurry," *Sporting News*, 4 August
       1888.

42   "iron-clad" contract: "A Pitcher Full," *National Police Gazette*, 18 May
       1889.

42   "No one in Chicago. . . ": "Will Kelly Go to Australia with the Spalding
       Party?" *New York Clipper*, 13 October 1888.

43   "all reports to the contrary": "That Australian Trip," *Chicago Tribune*, 16
       October 1888; "Will Kelly Go," *New York Clipper*; "Kelly's False Move,"
       Sporting Life, 13 October 1888.

43   "Yes, and I am [also] told. . . ": "Will Kelly Go," *New York Clipper*.

43   "Am sorry, but it is impossible. . . ": "Getting Ready for Australia,"
       Chicago Tribune, 18 October 1888.

45   "the Chicago fakir": "The Windy City Fake," *Sporting News*, 22 Septem-
       ber 1888. The screed against Spalding's wares is in an untitled editorial in
       the same issue. On Comiskey, his tour, and his parsimony, see Elfers, *Tour
       to End All Tours*, and Asinof, *Eight Men Out: The Black Sox and the 1919
       World Series* (New York: Holt, Rinehart & Winston, 1963).

46   "would not have been cigar money": Later, Comiskey's comment took on a
       definite ironic twist, as Spalding always seemed to be something of a
       model for him. In 1914, Comiskey—by then the owner of the American
       League's Chicago White Stockings (Spalding's National League club had
       adopted a new nickname, the Cubs)—embarked on a round-the-world
       tour of his own for which the Spalding trip was the obvious inspiration.
       His parsimony with regard to player compensation eventually resulted in

the infamous selling of the 1919 World Series—the so-called "Black Sox" scandal.

46   "The Chicago Fake": *Sporting News*, 29 September 1888.

46   "Some months ago. . . ": Harry Palmer, "Baseball: The Great Trip," *Sporting Life*, 17 October 1888.

47   "Were the man possessed. . . ": Ibid.

48   "*Keep away from saloons*": John Ward, *Base-Ball*, 44.

50   "It is an exceedingly pretty design": Harry Palmer, "Mrs. Ward's Good Taste," *Sporting News*, n.d., Spalding Scrapbooks.

50   Dauvray was not the only woman: On the Dauvray-Ward-McDermott triangle, see the excellent biography by Bryan Di Salvatore, *A Clever Base-Ballist: The Life and Times of John Montgomery Ward* (New York: Pantheon, 1999).

51   "strongest base running and batting. . . ": "Chicago Neatly Whipped at the Crystal Palace," *Chicago Herald*, 15 March, in the Spalding Scrapbooks.

52   "Professor C. Bartholomew": The professor, who was most assuredly not accredited as such by any institution of higher learning, used the initial C in place of his first name. Michigan census records suggest it stood for Cornelius.

52   "Unquestionably the base ball event of 1888": "Chadwick Chats," *Sporting Life*, 17 October 1888.

53   The assertion that base-ball. . . ": Ward, *Base-Ball*, 21. On Chadwick and for a comprehensive look at the origins debate, see Block, *Baseball Before We Knew It*, 1–31.

53   the "American game *par excellence*": Spalding, *America's National Game*, 4–5.

54   meeting with President Cleveland: Dialogue reconstructed from multiple sources, including Anson, *A Ball Player's Career*, and clips from the Spalding Scrapbooks.

Chapter Three

59   "full of ginger": "Their Farewell Game," *Sporting Life*, 21 October 1888.

61   "No American can form. . . ": Palmer, *Athletic Sports*, 162.

62   "the Solace of the traveler": Anson, *Ball Player's Career*, 145.

62   "The Chicago players are probably. . . ": "The Chicago Players," *Sporting News*, 10 November 1888.

63   "radical departure from long-established rule": "Principle or Policy?" *Sporting Life*, 31 October 1888.

63   "Anson Annihilated": "Anson Annihilated: The Chicago Team Beaten by the Ruralists of St. Paul," Spalding Scrapbooks.

64   "a disappointment to all": "All-Americas, 6; Chicago 3," *Chicago Inter Ocean*, 24 October 1888.

64   "vim and snap": "Chicago, 1; St. Paul, 0," *Chicago Inter Ocean*, 24 October 1888.

65   The lurid glare of the red light: Palmer, *Athletic Sports*, 165–67.

66   "excited as much curiosity. . . ": James Ryan, "Tour of the Spalding B.B.C.," 23 October 1888 (unpublished diary), National Baseball Hall of Fame Library. Heretofore, Ryan Diary.

67   "a singer and dancer": Anson, *Ball Player's Career*, 148. On mascots in general, and on Duval and Boldt in particular, see Di Salvatore, *Clever Base-Ballist*, 219–21. On Hopper and Boldt, see "The New York Mascot," *Sporting News*, 28 July 1888. On Hahn, see Anson, *Ball Player's Career*, 125.

67   *Starlight*: "Amusements," *Washington Post*, 13 March 1888.

67   "Juno, herself": "By an Admirer" (no publication information), Vernona Jarbeau file, New York Public Library for the Performing Arts.

68   "a life on the diamond": Anson, *Ball Player's Career*, 148–49.

68   Anson and league racism: On this, see Di Salvatore, *Clever Base-Ballist*, 235–39, and James, *Baseball Book 1990*, 247–56.

69   "If you hear of any clubs. . . ": John M. Ward, "Ward's Experience," *Sporting Life*, 9 January 1892. For more on Ward and black players, see Di Salvatore, *Clever Base-Ballist*, 236–37.

69   "Where'd you come from . . . ?": Dialogue sequence taken (with some of the dialect altered) from Palmer, *Athletic Sports*, 169–70.

70   "This reminds me. . . ": Anson, *Ball Player's Career*, 149.

71   "They deceive nearly every one. . . ": Palmer, *Athletic Sports*, 172.

71. **Denver's identity as a frontier town:** "The End of a Bad Man," *Rocky Mountain News*, 27 October 1888; "Crows on the Warpath," *Denver Post*, 26 October 1888. For Denver in the nineteenth century, see Louisa Ward Arps, *Denver in Slices: A Historical Guide to the City* (Athens: Ohio, 1988).

71 **"Base Ball in Australia":** *Rocky Mountain News*, 28 October 1888.

72 **a sarcastic cartoon:** In "A Very Poor Exhibition," *Denver Republican*, 28 October 1888.

73 **"[Sullivan] got the ball. . .":** "Grand Base Ball Game," *Rocky Mountain News*, 29 October 1888.

74 **"one of the finest games":** "The Great National Game," *Denver Republican*, 29 October 1888; "Hanlon's Wonderful Catch," *Denver Times*, 29 October 1888.

75 **"It was positively the worst game. . . ":** "Roasted," *Colorado Springs Gazette*, 30 October 1888.

75 **"How fearful must have been. . . ":** Palmer, *Athletic Sports*, 182. On the history of the railroad, and for the Kipling quote, see website of the Black Canyon of the Gunnison, National Park Service, U.S. Department of the Interior.

76 **"We arrived there in time. . . ":** Ryan Diary, 31 October 1888.

77 **"very fine pipe organ":** Ibid.

77 **"The water. . . ":** Anson, *Ball Player's Career*, 158.

77 **"Conditions could not have been. . . ":** Palmer, *Athletic Sports*, 185.

77 **"A long dusty ride it is":** Ryan Diary, 2 November 1888; Palmer, *Athletic Sports*, 188.

78 **"We are the Howling Wolves. . . ":** John Ward, "Across the Continent," *Chicago Tribune*, 11 November 1888.

Chapter Four

79 **"a veritable Garden of Eden":** Palmer, *Athletic Sports*, 188.

80 **telegram:** Ibid., 189.

81 **Sackville-West:** Ironically, when Sackville-West, who was not a professional diplomat, was sent to America, in 1881, it was considered an assign-

ment in which he could do little harm. See Ernest May, *Imperial Democracy* (New York: Harcourt, Brace & World, 1961), 3–5.

82   **"I never saw men work harder. . . ":** Palmer, *Athletic Sports*, 191; Anson, *Ball Player's Career*, 162; unidentified clippings from the Spalding Scrapbooks; "The Chicago Fakirs," *Sporting News*, 17 November 1888.

83   **Hart on Spalding trip:** "World of Sports: Jim Hart Considering an Australian Trip," unidentified clip, Spalding Scrapbooks.

84   **"No one should leave. . . ":** Karl Baedeker, ed., *The United States: A Handbook for Travellers* (1893; reprint, New York: Da Capo, 1973), 431.

84   **Sergeant Burdsoll and Chinatown tour:** Account of this scene from Palmer, *Athletic Sports*, 195–96.

84   **"The memories of these after-dark trips. . . ":** Anson, *Ball Player's Career*, 168; Palmer, *Athletic Sports*, 197.

85   **the notorious San Francisco tenderloin:** Herbert Asbury, *The Barbary Coast* (New York: Garden City, 1933).

86   **"He will go to the outside limit. . . ":** Quoted in Di Salvatore, *Clever Base-Ballist*, 229.

86   **"Players cannot train on late hours. . . ":** *Daily Examiner*, 6 November 1888.

86   **"Roses in California. . . ":** Anson, *Ball Player's Career*, 162.

87   **"Can the tourists play ball?":** "Like Amateurs," and "Ball in Two Cities," unidentified clips, from the Spalding Scrapbooks.

87   **"I can not tell you. . . ":** "The Chicago Fakirs."

88   **"Anson Made Happy":** Unidentified clips from Spalding Scrapbooks.

89   **"Johnny Ward":** David Stevens, *Baseball's Radical for All Seasons: A Biography of John Montgomery Ward* (Lanham, Md.: Scarecrow, 1998), 30.

89   **"I have never seen surpassed. . . ":** Palmer, *Athletic Sports*, 193.

89   **"finest base ball grounds. . . ":** "Out at Los Angeles," *Sporting News*, 24 November 1888.

92   **"It was a jolly good time":** Ryan Diary, 16 November 1888.

92   **"a serious complication":** Spalding, *America's National Game*, 255.

92 "guns, magnesium wire and a lamp": John Murray, *A Handbook for Travellers in Lower and Upper Egypt* (London: John Murray, 1891).

93 "To-morrow we bid a fond adieu": Unidentified clip from Spalding Scrapbooks.

Chapter Five

95 "Neat and trim looking": Palmer, *Athletic Sports*, 199.

96 "God's earth. . . ": Quoted in Daniel J. Boorstin, *The Americans: The Democratic Experience* (1973; reprint, London: Phoenix, 2000), 519. See also Foster Rhea Dulles, *Americans Abroad: Two Centuries of European Travel* (Ann Arbor: Michigan, 1964); Dean MacCannell, *The Tourist: A New Theory of the Leisure Class* (1976; reprint Berkeley: California, 1999); and James Buzard, *The Beaten Track: European Tourism, Literature, and the Ways to "Culture," 1800–1918* (New York: Oxford, 1993).

97 "Twenty-five to one. . . ": Palmer, *Athletic Sports*, 203.

97 "Everyone seemed to want. . . ": John Ward, "Ball Tossers at Sea," *Chicago Tribune*, n.d., Spalding Scrapbooks; Adrian Anson, "Diary of Cap'n Anson," unidentified clip, Spalding Scrapbooks. Ryan Diary, 21 November 1888; George Bayly, *A Life on the Ocean Wave* (reprint; Victoria, Australia: Miegunyah Press, 1998).

98 "The sun shone down. . . ": Palmer, *Athletic Sports*, 203.

98 possibility of extending the trip: "What Is Ward's Scheme?" unidentified clip, Spalding Scrapbooks. On Thomas Stevens, See Thomas Pauly, introduction to *Around the World on a Bicycle*, by Thomas Stevens (1887; reprint, Mechanicsburg, Pa.: Stackpole Books, 2000).

99 racing against the clock: Just six months after Spalding and his men completed their circumnavigation, the pioneering journalist Nellie Bly set off from Hoboken, New Jersey, on a mission to beat Fogg's eighty-day record. She did, completing her voyage in seventy-two days, six hours, and eleven minutes.

99 "dead to rights": "All Dead to Rights," *Sporting News*, 2 February 1889.

100 **"I want to state emphatically. . . ":** Simon Goodfriend, "Story of the Trip," and Newton MacMillan, "Some Advertising Methods," unidentified clips, Spalding Scrapbooks.

101 **Tener was "instrumental":** John Tener, letter of 29 November 1888, Tener Family Papers, Historical Society of Western Pennsylvania, Pittsburgh.

101 **Brush Classification Plan:** See Seymour, *Early Years*, 129.

101 **"Won't Ward and the others. . . ":** Quoted in Voigt, *American Baseball*, 159.

102 **"Cannibal Islands":** Anson, *Ball Player's Career*, 170.

102 **"Our friends at home. . . ":** Newton MacMillan, "Like Sacrificial Heiffers [*sic*]," unidentified clip, Spalding Scrapbooks.

104 **"taken from the parent branch. . . ":** Palmer, *Athletic Sports*, 210.

104 **"buttonholed and pulled off. . . ":** "Received by a King," unidentified clip, Spalding Scrapbooks.

105 **"windows and doors. . . ":** Newton MacMillan, "The Alameda at Honolulu," unidentified clip, Spalding Scrapbooks.

105 **the Iolani Palace:** On the palace, and Hawaiian history generally, see Gavan Daws, *Shoal of Time: History of the Hawaiian Islands* (Honolulu: Hawaii, 1974). Palmer, *Athletic Sports*, 214; Simon Goodfriend, unidentified clip, Spalding Scrapbooks.

106 **"This is Mr. Spalding. . . ":** Harriet Spalding, *Reminiscences*, 100; Palmer, *Athletic Sports*, 222

106 **"He was courteous. . . ":** John Ward, "Arrival at Honolulu," unidentified clip, Spalding Scrapbooks; Anson, "Diary of Cap'n Anson."

107 **Alexander Cartwright:** It is possible that his move to Hawaii was for health purposes.

107 **invaders' own favorite pastime:** On baseball in Hawaii and the politics of the Spalding visit, see Frank Ardolino, "Missionaries, Cartwright, and Spalding: The Development of Baseball in Nineteenth Century Hawaii," *Nine* 10, no. 2 (2002): 27–45.

107 **"To A. G. Spaulding, Esq.":** Letter in Spalding Scrapbooks.

108 **"I was importuned. . . ":** Spalding, *America's National Game*, 256.

108 **"What Al Spalding does not know. . . ":** Ward, "Arrival at Honolulu."

108 **field in "splendid condition":** Palmer, *Athletic Sports*, 216–21.

109 **Archibald Cleghorn:** See Don Hibbard, *The View from Diamond Head* (Honolulu: Editions, 1986).

109 **"A perfect fairyland":** Harriet Spalding, *Reminiscences*, 101; Palmer, *Athletic Sports*, 221.

110 **"All of us knew. . . ":** Newton MacMillan, "Hawaiian Luau and Poi," unidentified clip, Spalding Scrapbooks.

110 **King Kalakaua, "merry monarch":** On Kalakaua, see Daws, *Shoal of Time.*

111 **"Mother, you speak. . . ":** Harriet Spalding, *Reminiscences*, 101.

111 **"barbaric plenty. . . ":** MacMillan, "Hawaiian Luau and Poi."

111 **"This he deftly inserted. . . ":** Ibid.; John Ward, "Ward's Pacific Letter," unidentified clip, Spalding Scrapbooks; Harriet Spalding, *Reminiscences*, 102.

113 **"The lithe forms. . . ":** Ward, "Ward's Pacific Letter"; Anson, "Diary of Cap'n Anson."

113 **"Fair Honolulu, City of the Sea. . . ":** Palmer, *Athletic Sports*, 228.

Chapter Six

115 *Gunner Jingo*: T. Bland Strange, *Gunner Jingo's Jubilee* (London: Remington, 1893).

116 **"If we are to maintain. . . ":** Ibid., 545.

116 **Sepoy Mutiny:** See Barbara Daly Metcalf and Thomas R. Metcalf, *A Concise History of India* (New York: Cambridge, 2002).

117 **conditions at sea:** Anson, *Ball Player's Career*, 186; Palmer, "Story of the Trip," unidentified clip, Spalding Scrapbooks; Palmer, *Athletic Sports*, 229.

118 **the situation in Samoa:** See Daws, *Shoal of Time*, 237–40.

120 **"it was a common sight. . . ":** Ryan Diary, 9 December 1888; unidentified clip, Spalding Scrapbooks.

120 **"They know how to live in New Zealand. . . ":** Palmer, *Athletic Sports*, 236.

120 **"The treat promised. . . ":** Clips from the *New Zealand Herald* and *Auckland Star*; clip in the Spalding Scrapbooks.

123 **"They seemed disposed. . . "**: "Auckland, N.Z.," unidentified clip, Spalding Scrapbooks.

125 **"It was glorious!"**: Palmer, *Athletic Sports*, 240–41; John Ward, "Ward's Base-Ball Gossip," unidentified clip, Spalding Scrapbooks.

125 **Australian prehistory**: On the colonization of Australia, see Stuart Macintyre, *A Concise History of Australia* (New York: Cambridge, 1999).

126 **"a self-conscious mixture. . . "**: Morton Herman, *The Architecture of Victorian Sydney* (Sydney: Angus & Robertson, 1956), 5.

126 **"No wonder Spalding. . . "**: "Baseball: A Hearty Welcome to Australia," unidentified clip, Spalding Scrapbooks.

126 **Jimmy Williamson**: See Phillip Parsons, ed., *Companion to Theatre in Australia* (Sydney: Currency, 1995).

127 **"Australia for Australians"**: On the *Afghan* incident, see C. M. H. Clark, *The People Make Laws, 1888–1915*, vol. 5 of *A History of Australia* (Melbourne: Melbourne, 1981), 16.

128 **as "level as a floor"**: Palmer, *Athletic Sports*, 246.

129 **"The game itself. . . "**: Ward, "Base-Ball Gossip"; "The American Game of Baseball and How to Play It" appeared in both the *Melbourne Leader* and the *Age of Melbourne* on 22 December 1888; Senex, "Baseball as She Is Played," *Sydney Herald*, n.d.

130 **"give a proper and hearty welcome. . . "**: "All-America vs. Chicago," unidentified clip, Spalding Scrapbooks.

131 **"Not a few of us. . . "**: Palmer, *Athletic Sports*, 247.

132 **"very speedy"**: Ibid., 250.

133 **"every delicacy"**: Ibid., 251.

133 **"The people of Sydney gave us. . . "**: Newton MacMillan, "Baseball Players Abroad," *Chicago Herald*, n.d., Spalding Scrapbooks; "Our Note-Book: The Baseballers," unidentified clip, Spalding Scrapbooks; MacMillan, "Baseball Players Abroad."

134 **"a dingy, old-fashioned affair"**: MacMillan, "Baseball Players Abroad."

135 **Samuel Perkins Lord**: On the subject of baseball's history in Australia, and on the Spalding tour in particular, see Clark, *History of Australian Baseball: Time and Again* (Lincoln: University of Nebraska Press, 2003).

135 "I believe that no city. . . ": Trollope quoted in W. H. Newham, *Melbourne: Biography of a City* (Melbourne: Hill of Content, 1956), 30; MacMillan, "Baseball Players Abroad."

137 **Among the featured displays:** *Official Record of the Centennial International Exhibition, Melbourne, 1888–9* (Melbourne: Sands & McDougall, 1890), catalogue of U.S. exhibits. Trading cards featuring athletes and other prominent figures were first enticements aimed at converting tobacco consumers to a new product: cigarettes.

138 **"Our professional debut in Victoria. . . ":** Palmer, *Athletic Sports*, 259; "Baseball: The American Baseball Players," *Melbourne Evening Herald*, 22 December 1888, Spalding Scrapbooks.

138 **"The sphere must have smiled. . . ":** "The Baseball Boom," *Melbourne Sportsman*, 24 December 1888, Spalding Scrapbooks.

139 **"An excellent game and. . . ":** *Melbourne Punch*, 20 December 1888, Spalding Scrapbooks; *Melbourne Argus*, 24 December 1888, Spalding Scrapbooks; Palmer, *Athletic Sports*, 259.

140 **would be "going to strange countries. . . ":** Palmer, *Athletic Sports*, 262.

140 **William D'Alton Mann:** See Andy Logan, *The Man Who Robbed the Robber Barrons* (1965; reprint, Pleasantville, N.Y.: Akadine, 2001).

141 **"It is certain that the banqueting. . . ":** Harry Palmer, "Baseball Takes Hold," *Chicago Herald*, Spalding Scrapbooks.

142 **positively "Mephisophelian":** "Bartholomew's Balloon: A Sensational Flight," *South Australian Register*, 28 December 1888, Spalding Scrapbooks.

143 **"Professor Bartholomew appears. . . "** Ibid.

143 **"Holidays are frequent in Australia. . . ":** Simon Goodfriend, n.d., *Sun*, Spalding Scrapbooks.

144 **"There seems little doubt but that. . . ":** "Baseball in Australia," *New York Times*, 27 February 1889.

144 **"If we could have shot. . . ":** Anson, *Ball Player's Career*, 214.

146 **the professor's instruction of "Let go!":** "The Parachute Leap," *Ballarat Star*, 31 December 1888.

146 **"The air in Australia offers. . . ":** Unidentified clip, Spalding Scrapbooks.

146 **"Our boys realized we could. . . ":** Palmer, *Athletic Sports*, 274.

147 **"The degree of skill attained. . . ":** Ibid., 275.

148   "The enterprising spirit. . . ": Unidentified clip, Spalding Scrapbooks; Palmer "Base Ball Takes Hold," *Chicago Herald*, n.d., Spalding Scrapbooks.

148   "Let football find its votaries. . . ": "From the Baseballers Arrival," *Melbourne Herald*, 19 December 1888.

149   "Baseball Takes Hold. . . ": Palmer.

Chapter Seven

151   "There is but one word. . . ": Henry James quoted in Dulles, *Americans Abroad*, 111.

151   "pleasure excursion": Twain, *Innocents Abroad*.

152   "reflect credit on the country. . . ": Spalding, *America's National Game*, 252.

152   "In the midst of an interesting description. . . ": Ibid., 284–85.

152   "My chief regret was that. . . ": Ibid., 285.

153   "Think of it!": Ibid.

153   "There were days. . . ": John Ward, "Tour of the Ball Teams," *Chicago Tribune*, n.d., Spalding Scrapbooks.

154   "Saturday, January 19th": Ryan Diary, 19–21 January 1889.

154   "There is no denying. . . ": Ward, "Tour of the Ball Teams"; Tener, letter of January 1889, Tener Family Papers.

155   "a shark of the man-eating variety": Ward, "Tour of the Ball Teams."

155   "His queer antics. . . ": Simon Goodfriend, "On the Indian Ocean," unidentified clip, Spalding Scrapbooks.

156   "vheat ghakes": Newton MacMillan, "Spalding's Ball Players," *New York Sun*, n.d., Spalding Scrapbooks.

157   "It was indeed interesting. . . ": Palmer, *Athletic Sports*, 282–83.

158   "coffee colored" Tamil children: MacMillan, "Spalding's Ball Players."

158   Calcutta–Bombay route: See *Bradshaw's Through Route Overland Guide to India* (London: W. J. Adams, 1884).

159   "People who have been at sea. . . ": Ryan Diary, 25 January 1889.

159   "I don't know what it means": Harriet Spalding, *Reminiscences*, 102–3.

159   "There is something heartless. . . ": Henry James, quoted in Buzard, *Beaten Track*, 155; MacMillan, "Spalding's Ball Players"; Ward, "Tour of the Ball Players"; Simon Goodfriend, unidentified clip, Spalding Scrapbooks.

160   "The dusky inhabitants. . . ": Palmer, *Athletic Sports*, 295, 301.

161   "It may interest those. . . ": MacMillan, "Spalding's Ball Players."

161   "The mode of charming is to squat. . . ": Ryan Diary, 26 January 1889.

161   "Ryan and I took good care. . . ": Palmer, *Athletic Sports*, 302.

162   "Such a scene as the road. . . ": Ibid., 303.

162   "It is a slugging game. . . ": "The American Baseballers in Colombo," *Ceylon Independent*, 28 January 1889, Spalding Scrapbooks; MacMillan, "Spalding's Ball Players."

163   "Pirates, boys, pirates!": Palmer, *Athletic Sports*, 307–10.

163   "The Arabs and Africans dress. . . ": Ryan Diary, 2 February 1889.

164   "Everything about reminds us. . . ": MacMillan, "Spalding's Ball Players."

164   "Hardly had we set our feet. . . ": Anson, *Ball Player's Career*, 231.

165   "Of all the tumble-down. . . ": Palmer, *Athletic Sports*, 312–13. On Suez, see Karl Baedeker, ed., *Egypt: Handbook for Travellers* (Leipzig: Baedeker, 1884), 172–74.

165   "more comfortable or modern dwellings": Palmer, *Athletic Sports*, 313.

165   "Great fields of grain. . . ": Ibid., 314.

166   "Clarence sprang through. . . ": Ibid., 316.

167   "Step on their trotters. . . ": Ibid., 317.

169   "It can be readily imagined. . . ": Simon Goodfriend, "Arrival at Cairo," *New York Sun*, n.d., Spalding Scrapbooks.

169   "There are no two persons. . . ": John Ward, "On the Mediterranean," unidentified clip, Spalding Scrapbooks.

169   "In its original form, the system": On the reserve rule, see Seymour, *Early Years*, 104–15.

169   had become "a chattel": Ward in Sullivan, *Early Innings*, 165.

170   "Base ball depends for results. . . ": Spalding, *America's National Game*, 270.

171   John T. Brush: See Ivor-Campbell, *First Stars*, 14.

171   "One of those thin. . . ": Spalding, *America's National Game*, 436; On Brush, see Ivor-Campbell, *First Stars*, 14 (entry by Rich Eldred.)

171   club manager who couldn't "handle salary. . . ": Seymour, *Early Years*, 130.

172   "Will they ever have done. . . ": Ward, "On the Mediterranean."

172   "*Tâlib min Allâh hakk lukme' êsh*": Baedeker, *Egypt*, xxii.

173   "Paris on the Nile": On Ismail's Cairo, see James Aldridge, *Cairo: Biography of a City* (Boston: Little, Brown, 1969).

173   "One can sit at the Eldorado Café. . . ": Palmer, *Athletic Sports*, 317.

174   "There is no circus here. . . ": Incident recalled in Anson, *Ball Player's Career*, 236–37.

174   "Baseball at the pyramids": Palmer, *Athletic Sports*, 323.

175   "Donkeys brayed, camels trumpeted. . . ": Ibid., 323–24.

176   camels, "lurching along. . . ": Anson, *Ball Player's Career*, 238.

177   "out for blood": Palmer, *Athletic Sports*, 333; John Ward, "And the Sphinx Looked On," unidentified clip, Spalding Scrapbooks; Newton MacMillan, "And the Sphinx Wept," unidentified clip, Spalding Scrapbooks.

178   "A triumph. . . ": MacMillan, "And the Sphinx Wept."

179   "he had no opportunity. . . ": Ward, "And the Sphinx Looked On."

180   "Every step meant a spasmodle. . . ": Ibid; Twain, *Innocents Abroad*, 466.

180   "There is perhaps no other. . . ": Baedeker, *Egypt*, 118.

180   "Rats!": Ward, "And the Sphinx Looked On"; Ryan Diary, 9 February 1889.

181   "There is that in the overshadowing majesty. . . ": Twain, *Innocents Abroad*, 472.

181   "One could easily spend. . . ": Palmer, *Athletic Sports*, 337–38.

181   "A better opportunity for seeing. . . ": Ibid., 343.

182   "The manners and customs. . . ": Anson, *Ball Player's Career*, 240.

Chapter Eight

183   "neat, feminine hand": John Ward, "Ward on Classification," *The World*, n.d., Spalding Scrapbooks.

184 traveling "like emigrants": "Just Like Emigrants," *Sporting News*, 9 March 1889.

185 "The equanimity of the traveler's own temper. . . ": Karl Baedeker, *Southern Italy and Sicily*, vol. 3 of *Italy: Handbook for Travellers* (Leipzig: Baedeker, 1883), xv.

185 "Perhaps, the loveliest spot. . . ": *Cook's Tourist's Handbook for Southern Italy, Rome, and Sicily* (London: Thomas Cook, 1892), 193.

186 "*Vedi Napoli e poi mori*": Ward, "Ward on Classification"; Baedeker, *Southern Italy*, vol. 1, 31.

186 "evil odours are. . . ": Quoted in *Cook's Southern Italy*, 195.

186 a program of slum clearance: On Naples, see Terry Kirk, *The Challenge of Tradition, 1750–1900*, vol. 1 of *The Architecture of Modern Italy* (New York: Princeton Architectural Press, 2005), 196–99.

187 "seemingly uncontrollable burst. . . ": Palmer, *Athletic Sports*, 358.

187 "The cast of a dog. . . ": Ibid., 352.

187 "Those who visit the ruins. . . ": Baedeker, *Southern Italy*, 125–26.

189 "burning liquids of the interior. . . ": Ibid., 122.

189 "I could not have stirred. . . ": Palmer, *Athletic Sports*, 355–56.

191 "*In di a tros!*": Ibid., 356.

191 "What is there for me to see. . . ": Twain, *Innocents Abroad*, 196–97.

192 "I have never been interested. . . ": Palmer, *Athletic Sports*, 364. Stallo's exact words are lost, but this was their essential meaning. On America's early diplomatic program, see Jane C. Loeffler, *The Architecture of Diplomacy* (New York: Princeton Architectural Press, 1998), 13–19.

193 "We are fond of baseball. . . ": Ibid., 371.

193 "It is an immense pile. . . ": *A Handbook of Rome and Its Environs*, 14th ed. (London: John Murray, 1888), 272; Karl Baedeker, *Central Italy and Rome*, vol. 2 of *Italy: Handbook for Travellers*, 285; Twain, *Innocents Abroad*, 201.

194 "Trojan" Forum: Ryan Diary, 21 February 1889.

194 "As one stands upon. . . ": Palmer, *Athletic Sports*, 366.

195 "the mighty athletes. . . ": Anson, *Ball Player's Career*, 247.

196 "a picturesque glade. . . ": Palmer, *Athletic Sports*, 372.

197 "unanimously voted by those. . . ": Ibid., 377.

197 ornamentation as too "American": On the Duomo façade and its "American" vulgarity, see Kirk, *Architecture of Modern Italy*, vol. 1, 210.

197 "dash and spirit. . . ": Newton MacMillan, "From Italy to France: The American Base Ball Teams," unidentified clip, Spalding Scrapbooks.

199 "a delightful succession. . . ": Karl Baedeker, *Northern Italy*, vol. 1 of *Italy: Handbook for Travellers*, 90; Palmer, *Athletic Sports*, 381–82.

200 "Here are twenty. . . ": "No Baseball in Nice," *Paris Herald*, n.d., Spalding Scrapbooks.

200 "Duchess and courtesan. . . ": Palmer, *Athletic Sports*, 386.

201 "Those who have gold. . . ": Ibid.

201 "more for weight and efficacy. . . ": "Pelted the Prince," unidentified clip, Spalding Scrapbooks; Palmer, *Athletic Sports*, 391.

202 "somewhat formal and monotonous. . . ": Karl Baedeker, *Paris and Environs*, 9th ed. (Leipzig: Baedeker, 1888), 156; Palmer, *Athletic Sports*, 395–96. On the development of Paris in the nineteenth century, see Barry Bergdoll, *European Architecture: 1750–1900* (New York: Oxford, 2000).

203 "Although we remained in Paris. . . ": Palmer, *Athletic Sports*, 400.

203 "You may not doubt. . . ": Barry Bergdoll, introduction to *The Eiffel Tower* (New York: Princeton Architectural Press, 2003), 9–10; Anson, *Ball Player's Career*, 256.

204 evinced little enthusiasm: On Eiffel, see Bergdoll, *Eiffel Tower*.

205 "The company is not the most select. . . ": Quoted in T. J. Clark, *The Painting of Modern Life: Paris in the Art of Manet and His Followers* (New York: Knopf, 1985), 212; *Cook's Guide to Paris* (London: Thomas Cook, 1893), 21.

205 *café-chantant*: See Clark, *Painting of Modern Life*, 205–58.

205 "a week of late hours. . . ": Anson, *Ball Player's Career*, 255.

206 "programme of wickedness": Palmer, *Athletic Sports*, 397; Twain, *Innocents Abroad*, 103.

206 "just enough to make. . . ": Palmer, *Athletic Sports*, 398.

207 "Sir—A newspaper paragraph. . . ": "On the Indian Ocean," Spalding Scrapbooks.

208 "The Frenchman cares little. . . ": "French National Sports," *Washington Post*, 8 January 1888.

208 "La Ligue Nationale de l'Éducation Physique": See Pierre-Alban Lebecq, *Pachal Grousset et la Ligue Nationale de l'Education Physique* (Paris: L'Harmattan, 1997). I am indebted to Kate Cambor for her ideas on the political implications of sport in France in the late nineteenth century.

209 he sent a letter of regret: Palmer, *Athletic Sports*, 400–401. Translation based on its original French in "Baseball in Paris," *New York Herald*, 8 March 1889, Spalding Scrapbooks.

210 "Coubertin was a passionate advocate. . . ": On Coubertin, see Stephan Wassong, "Pierre de Coubertin's American Studies and Their Importance for the Analysis of His Early Educational Campaign," translated by Neil King. Originally published in German as *Pierre de Coubertins US-amerikanische Studien: Analyse seiner frühen Erziehungskampagne* (Würzburg: Ergon, 2002). On Spalding, Sullivan, and the Olympics, see Levine, *Spalding*, 88, 137–38.

211 "An almost faultless game": Newton MacMillan, "A Fine Game in Paris," *New York Sun*, n.d., Spalding Scrapbooks; "Les Sports Athlétiques: Grand Match de Base-Ball entre les Équipes Américaines," *Revue des Sports*, 9 March 1889, Spalding Scrapbooks. My translation.

211 "Base ball or *balle aux bases*. . . ": "Les Champions américaines à Paris," *Le Temps*, 5 March 1889, Spalding Scrapbooks. My translation.

212 relation of *thèque* to American baseball: See David Block, *Baseball Before We Knew It: A Search for the Roots of the Game* (Lincoln: Nebraska, 2005), 147–51.

212 Chadwick's assertion that it. . . : Ward, *Base-Ball*, 21.

212 "While authorities differ. . . ": Albert Spalding, "In the Field Papers: Base-Ball," *Cosmopolitan*, October 1889, 603.

Chapter Nine

213 "Are these for washing?": Palmer, *Athletic Sports*, 403.

213 "The night was pitch dark. . . ": Ryan Diary, 9 March 1889.

215 "In Mr. A. G. Spalding,. . . ": "Life in London," *The Licensed Victuallers' Mirror*, 19 March 1889, Spalding Scrapbooks.

216 "Look 'ere, Mister. . . ": "One Offer," *Punch*, n.d., Spalding Scrapbooks.

216 "It is often said. . . ": Twain quoted in Robert W. Rydell and Rob Kroes, *Buffalo Bill in Bologna: The Americanization of the World, 1869–1922*

(Chicago: Chicago, 2005), 113; on Barnum and Tom Thumb, see Harris, *Humbug*, 93–109.

217   **Charles W. Alcock:** See Keith Booth, *The Father of Modern Sport: The Life and Times of Charles W. Alcock* (Manchester: Parrs Wood, 2002).

217   **"Royal good fellows":** "Royalty at the Ball Match," unidentified clip, Spalding Scrapbooks.

218   **"living hedge":** "The American Baseball Players," *London Times*, 13 March 1889.

220   **"Why's he doing that?":** Episode recounted in Spalding, *America's National Game*, 261–64.

221   **Among its questions:** Responses, including Albert Edward's, in Palmer, *Athletic Sports*, 411–12.

221   **"HUMPH!. . . ":** "A Penny for Your Thoughts," *Daily Spectator*, n.d., Spalding Scrapbooks.

222   **"Our American cousins are here. . . ":** "American Baseball at Kennington Oval," unidentified clip, Spalding Scrapbooks.

222   **"The London tailor is. . . ":** Palmer, *Athletic Sports*, 406.

223   **"Mother says, 'Don't buy'. . . :** Episode recounted in Harriet Spalding, *Reminiscences*, 107.

223   **"swellest of the swell. . . ":** Harry Palmer, "At Lord's: His Grace of Buccleuch Welcomes the Ball Players on Behalf of the M.C.C.," *New York Herald*, n.d., Spalding Scrapbooks.

224   **"Ward knows that the Brotherhood. . . ":** Ibid.

224   **"From advices which I have received. . . ":** John Ward, "John Ward Is Coming Home," unidentified clip, Spalding Scrapbooks.

224   **"personal affairs":** Simon Goodfriend, "Baseball in Paris," *New York Sun*, n.d., Spalding Scrapbooks.

225   **the "other affair" in question:** On Dauvray and Ward's breakup, see Di Salvatore, *Clever Base-Ballist*, 244, 322–39.

225   **"I deeply regret it":** Spalding quoted in Palmer, "At Lord's."

225   **the Crystal Palace:** Karl Baedeker, *London and Its Environs* (Leipzig: Baedeker, 1889), 307.

226   **"velvety soft":** Palmer, *Athletic Sports*, 415.

226   **"one of the finest examples. . . ":** Ibid., 419.

227   "I tossed him some easy ones": Crane quoted in "Base Ball Heroes Home: The Returning Globe Trotters Given Welcome on New York Bay," unidentified clip, Spalding Scrapbooks; Grace quoted in the *Bath Argus*, unidentified clip, Spalding Scrapbooks.

228   "the like of which had not. . . ": Palmer, *Athletic Sports*, 421–22.

228   "He experienced a relapse yesterday. . . ": "Williamson's Hurt Serious," *New York Herald*, n.d., Spalding Scrapbooks.

229   "The most interesting and brilliant. . . ": Harry Palmer, "At 'Orchid Joe's' Home," *New York Herald*, n.d., Spalding Scrapbooks.

229   "One of the grandest throws. . . ": Ibid.

230   "smoke-begrimed": Karl Baedeker, *Great Britain: England, Wales, and Scotland—Handbook for Travellers* (Leipzig: Baedeker, 1887), 366; Harry Palmer, "The Ball Players in Sheffield," *New York Herald*, n.d., Spalding Scrapbooks.

230   "Perhaps no fairer or more harmonious. . . ": Baedeker, *Great Britain*, 471.

230   "Had our train borne. . . ": Palmer, *Athletic Sports*, 424.

231   "Undoubtedly the most beautiful. . . ": Harry Palmer, "Baseball at Cottonopolis," *New York Herald*, n.d., Spalding Scrapbooks.

231   "Just where or what. . . ": Palmer, *Athletic Sports*, 426.

233   "unmistakably fashionable": Palmer, *Athletic Sports*, 430.

234   "Arf pawst foive. . . ": Ibid., 431.

234   "Our party was unanimous. . . ": Ibid., 435.

234   "Everything in Callan. . . ": Ibid., 432.

236   "Are yez goin' back. . . ": Ibid., 440.

Chapter Ten

238   "I'm crying boys. . . ": "Base Ball Heroes Home: The Returning Globe Trotters Given Welcome on New York Bay," unidentified clip, Spalding Scrapbooks.

238   "I had been led. . . ": "Home Again!" *Evening Sun*, n.d., Spalding Scrapbooks.

238   "I've had some good. . . ": "Around the World: The American Base Ball Teams Home Again," unidentified clip, Spalding Scrapbooks.

239 Well, I'm glad it's over": Ibid.

239 "We've had a splendid time. . . ": "Welcoming Home the Tourists," *New York Clipper*, 13 April 1889.

239 "It was when we stood. . . ": Palmer, *Athletic Sports*, 442.

239 A general sense of patriotic satisfaction: Anson, Crane, and Duval quoted in "Home Again!"

240 every city on the National League circuit: For the 1869 season, Henlon's Detroit club was dropped from the league and replaced with the Cleveland Spiders.

241 "Our twenty American athletes who roamed. . . ": "Welcoming Home the Tourists."

241 "One of the greatest affairs. . . ": Ryan Diary, 8 April 1889; "Welcoming Home the Tourists."

243 "rather uninteresting exhibition": Palmer, *Athletic Sports*, 449.

243 "The man who conceived. . . ": Ibid., 453.

244 "RESOLVED:. . . ": Ibid., 454.

244 "You have been a credit. . . ": Ibid., 455.

244 "the biggest venture. . . ": "Anson Was Downed," *Boston Globe*, 14 April 1889.

245 "I used to go to the games. . . ": Palmer, *Athletic Sports*, 456.

245 "about as warm as an icicle": Anson, *Ball Player's Career*, 283.

245 "I have no reason whatever. . . ": "A Statement from Mr. Spalding," unidentified clip, Spalding Scrapbooks.

245 "A Baseball Burlesque": *Washington Post*, 16 April 1889, Spalding Scrapbooks.

246 "Every kid on the South Side. . . ": "Chicago Caps the Climax," *Chicago Inter Ocean*, 20 April 1889, Spalding Scrapbooks.

247 "great blaze of light": Ibid.

247 "The great crowd that filled. . . ": Palmer, *Athletic Sports*, 457.

247 "Every one seemed. . . ": "Return of the Players," *Chicago Tribune*, 20 April 1889.

248   "I never realized. . . ": "Chicago Caps the Climax."

250   "To day we have completed. . . ": Ryan Diary, 20 April 1889.

Chapter Eleven

251   "There is no doubt. . . ": Spalding, "In the Field Papers," 609–10.

252   "There is no period. . . ": Palmer, *Athletic Sports*, 452.

253   Ward re-signed with New York: On Ward's troubled return, see Di Salvatore, *Clever Base-Ballist*, 244–56.

255   "take definite action. . . ": "Ball Players' Salaries," *New York Times*, 18 June 1889.

255   with a "sore arm": Pearson, *Baseball in 1889*, 53.

255   "under advisement": "The League vs. the Brotherhood," *Chicago Tribune*, 25 June 1889.

255   "the crowning point. . . ": Pearson, *Baseball in 1889*, 92.

255   "The League will not classify. . . ": Seymour, *Early Years*, 225.

256   "This man Spalding. . . ": "Classification of Players," *New York Times*, 14 July 1889.

256   The Brotherhood's plan for a new league: *Chicago Tribune*, 8 September 1889; *Chicago Tribune*, 22 September 1889; *New York Times*, 23 September 1889.

257   "The time for conference and. . . ": "The Brotherhood's Position," *Chicago Tribune*, 29 September 1889.

258   "There was a time. . . ": Reprinted in Spalding, *America's National Game*, 272–73.

259   "The National League of Base Ball Clubs. . . ": Ibid., 273–77.

259   "It was announced. . . ": Ibid., 285.

260   "Don't you see?": Ibid., 287–88.

261   "Stupidity, avarice, and treachery. . . ": John Ward, quoted in Di Salvatore, *Clever Base-Ballist*, 317. For my understanding of the history of the Players

League I am indebted to Seymour, *Baseball: The Early Years*; Di Salvatore, *Clever Base-Ballist*; and Pearson, *Baseball in 1889*.

262 **"The League is dead. . . ":** Ibid., 321.

Epilogue

263 **a reunion that was free of acrimony:** "Tourist Ball-Tossers Invited," *Chicago Tribune*, 26 February 1893; "Dinner to the Base Tourists," Ibid., 9 March 1893; "Base Ball Dramatized," *Sporting News*, 4 March 1893.

263 *Ninety Days:* "Ninety Days" file, New York Public Library for the Performing Arts.

265 **"Get on the bar, man. . . ":** "Fell from the Clouds," *Chicago Tribune*, 30 August 1891.

265 **Duval. . . treated as an honored guest:** "Notes of the Game," *Chicago Tribune*, 15 September 1898.

265 **too late for Jim Fogarty:** "Sporting News: Fogarty Dead," *Philadelphia Public Ledger*, 21 May 1891; photocopy in the James Fogarty file, National Baseball Hall of Fame Library, Cooperstown, New York.

266 **Ned Williamson:** See Edward Williamson file, National Baseball Hall of Fame Library.

266 **single-season home-run record:** On the home run record, see "A Short History of the Single-Season Home Run Record," online exhibition, National Baseball Hall of Fame website, http://www.baseballhalloffame.org/.

266 **"Just when we wanted his services. . . ":** Talcott, quoted in unidentified clipping, Ned Crane File, National Baseball Hall of Fame Library.

267 **"Until then, he never drank. . . ":** "Ned Crane Is Dead," *Sporting Life*, 26 September 1896, Ned Crane File, National Baseball Hall of Fame Library.

267 **"No, gentlemen, I once shut out. . . ":** Richard C. Saylor, "Major League Governor John Kinley Tener," *Pennsylvania Heritage*, September 2005, 6–13.

267 **Fred Pfeffer:** Fred Pfeffer file, National Baseball Hall of Fame Library.

268 **"Ned Hanlon is the great grandfather. . . ":** Bill James, *The Bill James Guide to Baseball Managers: From 1870 to Today* (New York: Scribner, 1997), 33–39.

268 "I go back to the stage. . . ": "Ward and His Wife," *Sporting Life*, 19 April 1890, John Ward file, National Baseball Hall of Fame Library; see also Di Salvatore, *Clever Base-Ballist*, 322–39.

269 he would forever resent: On Anson's financial losses, see *Ball Player's Career*, 284–85.

270 a bunch of loafing drunkards: See James, *Baseball Book 1990*, 255.

270 he had taken to the stage: On Anson's acting career, see the Adrian Anson files at the New York Public Library for the Performing Arts and the National Baseball Hall of Fame Library. See also, James, *Baseball Book 1990*, 256; and Robert H. Schaefer, "Anson on Broadway," *National Pastime* 25 (2005): 74–81.

271 "The secret of Anson's greatness. . . ": Grantland Rice, "Baseball Loses [missing]," unidentified clip, Adrian Anson file, National Baseball Hall of Fame Library.

272 the merger of the two circuits: Technically, the combined league was the National League and American Association of Professional Base Ball Clubs.

272 satisfying fall of Spalding's old nemesis: On the fall of Von der Ahe, see Seymour, *Early Years*, 300–301; Robert Tiemann and Mark Rucker, eds., *Nineteenth Century Stars* (Cleveland: Society of American Baseball Research, 1989), 130 (entry by Jim Rygelski); and David Nemec, *The Great Encyclopedia of 19th Century Major League Baseball* (New York: Fine, 1997).

273 the American Bicycle Company: On the ABC, see Levine, *Spalding*, 93–94.

273 "Think of a trust in baseball. . . ": Ibid., 67.

273 "syndicate" plan": On the rise and fall of "syndicalism," see Seymour, *Early Years*, 317–21.

274 "I am satisfied that baseball. . . ": Spalding, "In the Field Papers: Base-Ball," 603.

274 one Abner Graves: On Graves, see Block, *Baseball Before We Knew It*, 32–66.

274 "Spalding must realize. . . ": Chadwick to "Friend Crane," undated letter, private collection. As recently as 2005, a *Wall Street Journal* story (Joseph Pereira, "Old, Old Ball Game," *Wall Street Journal*, 22 October) stated,

"Abner Doubleday is believed by some to have invented the game, but a number of history buffs put that contention in the realm of mythology."

275   **Baseball was not invented by Abner Doubleday:** On baseball's origins, see Block, *Baseball Before We Knew It*.

276   **Abner Doubleday:** On Doubleday's Theosophism, and for a more conspiratorial interpretation of the role of Theosophy in Spalding's endorsement of the Doubleday myth, see ibid., 32–49 (chapter written by Philip Block).

277   **"I'm sure that I am. . . ":** "Spalding Likes Tingley Creed," *Chicago Tribune*, 30 March 1903.

278   **Lomaland's Raja-Yoga Academy:** On this incident, see Levine, *Spalding*, 126–29.

278   *America's National Game:* See Levine, *Spalding*, 115–16.

278   **Eventually Spalding appropriated the project:** Spalding also took possession of Chadwick's extensive baseball library, for which he built a fireproof vault at his Lomaland estate. The collection was donated, along with Spalding's own baseball library, to the New York Public Library in 1921 by Spalding's widow, Elizabeth.

278   **"I received the book. . . ":** Letter from John Ward to A. G. Spaulding [*sic*], 20 November 1911, Spalding Scrapbooks.

278   **"father of baseball":** "Spalding One of Baseball's Leaders," *New York Times*, 11 September 1915.

279   **"Mortals could ask no more. . . ":** *Sporting News* obituary, excerpted in Levine, *Spalding*, 144–45.

279   **"I want you. . . ":** Quoted in Emmett Greenwalt, *California Utopia: Point Loma, 1897–1942* (San Diego: Point Loma, 1978), 183.

280   **transforming themselves in America's image:** See Ernest R. May, *Imperial Democracy: The Emergence of America as a Great Power* (New York: Harcourt, Brace & World, 1961); Viscount James Bryce, *The American Commonwealth* (New York: Macmillan, 1888).

282   **the presumptive international sport:** The global dissemination of sport is a complex phenomenon shaped by historical accident, economics, nationalism, and the inherent characteristics of the game in question; every nation has its own unique sporting history. Baseball's spread to Latin

America came in the late nineteenth century, a result of physical proximity and cultural ties to the United States. The game also spread to East Asia in that period, brought there by American expatriates. See Stefan Szymanski and Andrew Zimbalist, *National Pastime: How Americans Play Baseball and the Rest of the World Plays Soccer* (Washington: Brookings, 2005).

BIBLIOGRAPHY

This book is, of necessity, a composite reconstruction from multiple, occasionally conflicting, sources. Every effort has been made to shape this material into a faithful and accurate representation of the tour as it happened. This narrative relies both on the firsthand accounts of the participants and on the news coverage generated by the tourists as they traveled—stories written by the traveling correspondents and also local news coverage that often presented somewhat different facts in an altogether different light. A great deal of this material is found in the Albert Spalding Scrapbooks, now at the New York Public Library. Unfortunately, much of the specific publication information from these items is lost. In addition to the articles in the Spalding Scrapbooks, countless other publications were consulted, in particular the following:

Chicago Tribune
Chicago Inter Ocean
London Times
National Police Gazette
New York Clipper
New York Times
Sporting Life
Sporting Times
Sporting News
Washington Post

The following bibliography represents the primary sources consulted on the history of baseball and the conditions of travel and international cultural and political exchange in the late nineteenth century. Not included in this list, for the sake of brevity, are the many tourist guides produced at the time of the tour—especially the Baedeker guides—which provide insight into the logistics of travel in the 1880s, as well as specific details about cities and sights the tourists experienced. For detailed information on the places visited by the tour, consult the chapter notes.

Special Collections

Player and world tour files. National Baseball Hall of Fame Library, Cooperstown, New York.

Spalding Collection. Manuscript and Archives Division, New York Public Library, New York.

Performer and show files. New York Public Library for the Performing Arts, New York.

Chicago Baseball Club Files. Chicago Historical Society.

Books and Journals

Anson, Adrian C. *A Ball Player's Career: Personal Experiences and Reminiscences.* Chicago: Era, 1900.

Barnum, Phineas T. *The Life of P. T. Barnum: Written by Himself.* 1855; reprint, Chicago: University of Illinois Press, 2000.

Bartlett, Arthur. *Baseball and Mr. Spalding.* New York: Farrar Straus & Young, 1951.

Baseball as America. Washington, D.C.: National Geographic, 2002.

Block, David. *Baseball Before We Knew It: A Search for the Roots of the Game.* Lincoln: University of Nebraska Press, 2005.

Boorstin, Daniel. *The Americans: The Democratic Experience.* 1973; reprint, London: Phoenix, 2000.

_____. *The Image: or, What Happened to the American Dream.* New York: Atheneum, 1962.

Buzard, James. *The Beaten Track: European Tourism, Literature, and the Ways to "Culture," 1800–1913.* Oxford, England: Oxford University Press, 1993.

Chadwick, Henry. *The Game of Base Ball.* New York: Munro, 1868.

Clark, Joe. *A History of Australian Baseball: Time and Game.* Lincoln: University of Nebraska Press, 2003.

Di Salvatore, Bryan. *A Clever Base-Ballist: The Life and Times of John Montgomery Ward.* New York: Pantheon, 1999.

Dulles, Foster Rhea. *Americans Abroad: Two Centuries of European Travel.* Ann Arbor: University of Michigan Press, 1964.

Elfers, James E. *The Tour to End All Tours: The Story of Major League Baseball's 1913–1914 World Tour*. Lincoln: University of Nebraska Press, 2003.

Foer, Franklin. *How Soccer Explains the World: An Unlikely Theory of Globalization*. New York: HarperCollins, 2004.

Frankfurt, Harry G. *On Bullshit*. Princeton: Princeton University Press, 2005.

Greenwalt, Emmett A. *California Utopia: Point Loma, 1897–1942*. San Diego: Point Loma, 1978.

Harris, Neil. *Humbug: The Art of P. T. Barnum*. Boston: Little, Brown, 1973.

———, ed. *Land of Contrasts, 1880–1901*. New York: Braziller, 1970.

Henderson, Robert W. *Ball, Bat and Bishop: The Origin of Ball Games*. New York: Rockport, 1947.

Ivor-Campbell, Frederick, et al. *Baseball's First Stars*. Cleveland: Society for American Baseball Research, 1996.

James, Bill. *The Baseball Book 1990*. New York: Villard, 1990.

———. *The Bill James Guide to Baseball Managers from 1870 to Today*. New York: Scribner's, 1997.

Koppett, Leonard. *Koppett's Concise History of Major League Baseball*. Philadelphia: Temple University Press, 1998.

Levine, Peter. *A. G. Spalding and the Rise of Baseball: The Promise of American Sport*. New York: Oxford University Press, 1985.

Lowenfish, Lee, and Tony Lupien. *The Imperfect Diamond: The Story of Baseball's Reserve System and the Men Who Fought to Change It*. New York: Stein & Day, 1980.

Lowry, Philip J. *Green Cathedrals*. New York: Addison-Wesley, 1992.

MacCannell, Dean. *The Tourist: A New Theory of the Leisure Class*. Berkeley: University of California Press, 1976.

May, Ernest R. *Imperial Democracy: The Emergence of America as a Great Power*. New York: Harcourt, Brace & World, 1961.

Moore, Glenn. "The Great Baseball Tour of 1888–89: A Tale of Image Making, Intrigue, and Labour Relations in the Gilded Age." *International Journal for the History of Sport* 11, no. 3 (December 1994): 431–56.

Morris, Peter. *Baseball Fever: Early Baseball in Michigan*. Ann Arbor: University of Michigan Press, 2003.

Nasaw, David. *Going Out: The Rise and Fall of Public Amusements*. Cambridge: Harvard Univerity Press, 1993.

Nemec, David. *The Beer and Whiskey League*. New York: Lyons & Burford, 1994.

———. *The Great Encyclopedia of Nineteenth Century Major League Baseball*. New York: Fine, 1997.

Orem, Preston. *Baseball: From the Newspaper Accounts*. Altadena, Calif.: self-published, 1961.

Palmer, Harry, et al. *Athletic Sports in America, England and Australia*. Philadelphia: Hubbard, 1889.

_____. *Sights Around the World with the Base-Ball Boys*. Philadephia: Edgewood, 1892.

_____. *Stories of the Base Ball Field*. New York: Rand McNally, 1890.

Pearson, Daniel M. *Baseball in 1889: Players vs. Owners*. Bowling Green: Bowling Green University Press, 1993.

Peterson, Harold. *The Man Who Invented Baseball*. New York: Scribner's, 1969.

Pfeffer, N. Fred. *Scientific Ball*. Chicago: Pfeffer, 1889.

Richter, Francis C. *Richter's History and Records of Base Ball*. Philadelphia: Francis C. Richter, 1914.

Riess, Steven A. *Touching Base: Professional Baseball and American Culture in the Progressive Era*. Chicago: University of Illinois Press, 1993.

Rosenberg, Howard A. *Cap Anson 1: When Captaining a Team Meant Something: Leadership in Baseball's Early Years*. Tile Books, 2003.

Rucker, Mark, and John Freyer. *19th Century Baseball in Chicago*. Charleston, S.C.: Arcadia, 2003.

Rydell, Robert W., and Rob Kroes. *Buffalo Bill in Bologna: The Americanization of the World*. Chicago: University of Chicago Press, 2005.

Said, Edward W. *Culture and Imperialism*. New York: Knopf, 1993.

_____. *Orientalism*. New York: Vintage, 1979.

Schivelbusch, Wolfgang. *The Railway Journey: The Industrialization of Space and Time in the 19th Century*. Berkeley: University of California Press, 1986.

Seymour, Harold. *Baseball: The Early Years*. New York: Oxford University Press, 1960.

Spalding, Albert (nephew of Albert Spalding). *Rise to Follow: An Autobiography*. New York: Henry Holt, 1943.

Spalding, Albert G. *America's National Game*. 1911. Reprint, Lincoln: University of Nebraska Press, 1992.

_____. "In the Field Papers: Base-Ball." *Cosmopolitan*, October 1889, pp. 603–10.

Spalding, Harriet I. *Reminiscences of Harriet Spalding*. East Orange, N.J.: n.p., 1910.

Spalding's Base Ball Guide and Official League Book for 1889. Chicago: Albert Spalding, 1889.

Stevens, David. *Baseball's Radical for All Seasons: A Biography of John Montgomery Ward*. Lanham, Md.: Scarecrow, 1998.

Sullivan, Dean, ed. *Early Innings: A Documentary History of Baseball, 1825–1908*. Lincoln: University of Nebraska Press, 1995.

Sullivan, Ted. *History of World's Tour: Chicago White Sox, New York Giants*. Chicago: Donohue, 1914.

Szymanski, Stefan, and Andrew Zimbalist. *National Pastime: How Americans Play Baseball and the Rest of the World Plays Soccer*. Washington: Brookings Institution Press, 2005.

Thorn, John, et al. *Total Baseball*. 6th ed. New York: Total Sports, 1999.

Tiemann, Robert L., and Mark Rucker, eds. *Nineteenth Century Stars*. Cleveland: Society for American Baseball Research, 1989.

Twain, Mark. *The Innocents Abroad: or the New Pilgrim's Progress*. 1869; reprint, New York: Signet, 1980.

Voigt, David Quentin. *American Baseball: From Gentleman's Sport to the Commissioner System*. Norman: University of Oklahoma Press, 1966.

———. *The League That Failed*. Lanham, Md.: Scarecrow, 1998.

Ward, John Montgomery. *Base-Ball: How to Become a Player*. 1888. Reprint, Cleveland: Society for American Baseball Research, 1993.

Ziff, Larzer. *Return Passages: Great American Travel Writing, 1780–1910*. New Haven: Yale University Press, 2000.

☙ ACKNOWLEDGMENTS ❧

All books are collaborative efforts, and this one more than most. I am, in particular, grateful for the encouragement, guidance, and sharp editorial eye of Peter Levine, whose ideas about Albert Spalding and his times have shaped mine. John Thorn, too, has been a generous advisor and sounding board. Tom Shieber's interest in the Spalding tour matches my own; I thank him for sharing his enthusiasm and encyclopedic knowledge, and for saving me from countless errors. John Molyneaux, Jeff Mann, and William Sear were generous of their time and thoughts on Spalding and his adventures. Pat Kelly, for whom no thanks is too great, helped procure the images used herein, as did Robert Lifson and Jeffrey Marren. More broadly, I am indebted to the devoted community of historians that is the Society for American Baseball Research, and especially to the members of its nineteenth-century committee, led by Paul Wendt, many of whom contributed their expertise to this project.

Much of this book was written in the Allen Room at the New York Public Library. I thank Wayne Furman for allowing me the great privilege of working in its handsome carrels, and all of the librarians, especially in the Archives and Manuscripts Division, who provided so much generous assistance. When it looked like this project might be forever stalled, Richard Brody and Harriet Washington offered sage advice to help me get it rolling. Kate Cambor lent her expertise on nineteenth-century France, but more than anything has been a good friend.

I thank my extended family at Princeton Architectural Press, a home away from home for more than a decade, for their support, in particular publisher Kevin Lippert. Among the many friends who have reviewed proposals and manuscripts, answered questions, and otherwise suffered my disquisitions on nineteenth-century baseball, I am grateful to Michael Morse, Philip Nobel, Andrew Bernheimer, Peter Hall, and Iylon Woo.

Matty Goldberg, publishing savant, introduced me to PublicAffairs. Clive Priddle, an Englishman, had the Spalding-esque temerity to acquire a book about American baseballists traipsing about his native land. Peter Osnos believed in this book from the start, and Susan Weinberg has been a most generous supporter. Nina D'Amario, Mark Melnick, Jeff Williams, Anita Karl, and Jim Kemp pimped its ride. Melissa Raymond kept things flowing through thick and thin. Laura Stine and Kate Scott were aggressive advocates with my best interests at heart. The tireless Jaime Leifer has ensured my tree hasn't fallen in deafening silence. Above all, I am grateful to David Patterson, steady hand at the till, whose confidence that this book could and would get done inspired my own, and whose editing has made it better on every page.

Sarah Burnes is a blessing for which I am grateful every day. Advisor, champion, confidant, editor, friend—she has been all of these things, and with unfailing patience, intelligence, and optimism. My debt to her is unpayable. I also thank Chris Lamb, a true southern gentleman, for his incisive editing, and everyone else at the Gernert Company for not hanging up the phone when I call.

Members of my family have given of themselves beyond any reasonable expectation through the long process of researching, writing, and editing this book. Mark and Valerie Kuchment provided shelter and quiet when it was needed most. My parents, Hal and Jane Lamster, have given a lifetime of support and encouragement for which I will be forever grateful.

Finally I thank my wife, Anna Kuchment, who has supported and improved this project and its author in every conceivable way. This book is dedicated to her, and to the memory of my grandfather, Brandon "Buddy" Stone, who introduced me to the joys of the national pastime with a bouncy pink ball called a Spaldeen.

❧ INDEX ❧